CARMEL IN NORTH AMERICA
The Early Founders and Foundations
of the Carmelite Province of the
Most Pure Heart of Mary

(1864-1900)

Myron M. Judy, O. Carm.

CARMELITE MEDIA

This book was originally published as an article in *The Sword* (1964) under the title "Carmel Came."

Edited by William J. Harry, O. Carm.
Layout and Cover design by William J. Harry, O. Carm. and Ken Pino

© 2015 by Carmelite Media
Printed in the United States of America
All rights reserved

No part of this book may be reproduced, stored in a retrieval system, or transmitted in any form, or by any means, electronic, mechanical, photocopying, or otherwise, without the prior written permission of the publisher, except by a reviewer, who may quote brief passages in a review.

Carmelite Media
8501 Bailey Road
Darien, Illinois 60561

Phone: 1-630-971-0724
Email: publications@carmelnet.org
Website: carmelites.info/publications

Printed Book: ISBN: 978-1-936742-11-0

TABLE OF CONTENTS

2014 Preface i

A Brief Postscript v

1964 Preface vii

Chapter 1: Transit and Transition 1

> 19th Century Europe and the Suppression of Religious Orders | Carmel Straubing Begins to Revivify | Cyril Knoll: Early History in Carmel | Early Ventures for Expanding the Order | Plans for an American Foundation

Chapter 2: First Foundations 31

> From Kentucky to Kansas | Expanding to Cumberland, Maryland | Beyond Cumberland: A Need for New Ministry Sites

Chapter 3: Separatists Movements 71

> Kansas Foundations Under Albert Heimann | New Foundations: Upper Marlboro Missions | Carmelite Life in Cumberland | New Foundations in Pennsylvania | Return to Kentucky: Foundations in Louisville and Western Kentucky

Chapter 4: Unifying Foundations 93

> Departing from Cumberland - Arriving in Pittsburgh | Carmelites in the Niagara Frontier | Toward Reunification of the Western Carmelite Communities | The Separate Foundations Come to an End | Foundations in New Jersey Join a Reunified American Commissariat

Chapter 5: Province and Prospect 139

> Commissary General Anastasius Smits | *Karmeliten Geist* | Commissary General Pius Mayer | From Commissary to Province | New Developments in the 1890s | 1900: The Beginning of a New Era

Appendices:

> Abbreviations Used in the Notes 175
>
> Endnotes 177
>
> List of Foundations and Ministries of the Province 217
>
> Residences of the Provincial and/or Offices 224
>
> Provincial Leadership 225
>
> Author's Biography 227
>
> Recommended Carmelite Websites 229

Index 231

2014 PREFACE

The year 2014 celebrates the 150th anniversary of the arrival in the United States of America of two German friars committed to establishing the Carmelite Order of Ancient Observance in America. *Carmel in North America: A History of The Early Founders and Foundations* details their success.

Following the near total extinction of the Order in Germany and throughout many parts of Europe in the early part of the 19th century, the Vicar Prior General of the Order, Angelus Savini, readily sought approval from the Vatican for the new mission that Frs. Cyril Knoll and Xavier Huber had conceived. Spreading the Catholic faith in new lands was also part of the evangelization vision of Pope Pius IX, who was a longtime personal friend of the Carmelite Vicar Prior General.

Evaluating the success of Knoll and Huber requires revisiting the unique landscape of post-Civil War America. The famous American author, Mark Twain, dubbed that period "The Gilded Age" – a time of great wealth and of great poverty and also a time of significant immigration, industrial development, the growth of cities, along with settlement of vast frontier areas. While leaders of industries such as railroads, oil and banking prospered, ordinary laborers, farmers and small businesses struggled. In 1900, nearly 20% of the country was deemed to be living below the poverty level and there was no so-called major governmental safety net.

Despite the impoverishment which touched most of the people who were the recipients of Carmel's ministries, churches and convents and other needed buildings for celebrating the Faith were somehow erected, wherever Carmelite friars were serving. Those early Carmelites obviously were a positive conduit for the energizing graces of the Holy Spirit which caused so many to be so generous with their limited monies, time and talent.

Knoll and Huber came to America, encouraged by the Ursuline Sisters of Louisville, Kentucky, whom they had worked with in Germany, expecting to minister with the burgeoning German community in the United States. The second half of the 19th century was a time of large scale immigration to the United States. Approximately 14 million immigrants arrived in the United States between 1865 through 1900. Two of the most prominent groups were the Germans and the Irish, both of whom had significantly diverse views on the role of the laity, assimilation/acculturation and on many other issues, such as the adequacy of services being provided to them by the Catholic Church. Initially the Carmelites did work primarily with German Catholics, many of whom were recent immigrants themselves. However, because the Carmelite Vicar Prior General Savini was able to send over many English speaking Carmelites, the Carmelites as they moved East were able to accept assignments among the Irish and other non-German immigrants. The friar who succeeded Knoll in 1881 as commissary general of America, Anastasius Smits, was of Dutch origin. He had come to the United State in 1868 and spoke English well.

Two major concerns that faced the Catholic Church in the United States after 1865 were the needs of the four million recently emancipated black persons and a renewed anti-Catholic bigotry, evident in the public school system where some teachers and texts appeared hostile to Catholicism. Addressing the first concern, the Second Plenary Council of Baltimore (1866) urged dioceses to establish programs that would address the needs of the former slaves. Unfortunately, because there was no central, comprehensive plan, the needs for the most part went unaddressed. However, just five years after coming to the United States, several Carmelites undertook staffing parishes and mission stations just outside of the District of Columbia, primarily focusing on the large recently freed black population in Maryland. While available data about this ministry is somewhat limited, from the reports that exist, the Carmelites attended to the spiritual and educational and social needs very well.

The Third Plenary Council of Baltimore (1884) addressed the bigotry issue in the public schools by decreeing that every parish in the United States was required to have a Catholic elementary school. However, by 1900, only 37% of the nation's parishes had been able to comply. The early Carmelites did have schools at all of their parishes and in many instances had made the creation of such a priority before the Council decree. Typical of the response to the concern for the welfare of Catholic children was the promise of the first Carmelite pastor in Our Lady of Mt. Carmel Parish in Tenafly, New Jersey, Theodore McDonald, who pledged that his parish would have a Catholic school even if it meant that he would have to sell his only coat to help with the funding.

Catholic religiosity in post-Civil War America, as evidenced by the prayer books of the times, pictured God as Judge. The revolutionary spirituality that Carmelite St. Therese of Lisieux introduced portraying God as Love would not be known until the 20th century. Because Mass was not conducted in the vernacular, devotions to a variety of saints in native tongues became an important alternative resource for a lively piety. At all of the early Carmelite foundations, there was an obvious concern for enhancing the faith. The interior of churches were often upgraded, devotions to a variety of saints including Our Lady of Mount Carmel were conducted and festivals highlighting the celebration of liturgical feasts and Church milestones, such as anniversaries of the pope, regularly occurred. Especially popular were week long or longer parish missions with their focus on many religious talks for men and women and children of all ages along with benediction and confession. Despite their limited numbers, the Carmelites were able to create a formal mission band whose sermons, focused on rekindling the faith, received many accolades. These talks, of course, reflected the known means of the day for interpreting the scriptures, such as the use of insights, often allegorical, from the Fathers of the Church.

Frs. Knoll and Huber had initially planned on beginning the Carmelite Order in Louisville, Kentucky. Circumstances, however, soon brought them to the frontiers of Kansas where their first foundations were initiated. From there, they would move to wherever ministry needs beckoned and wherever there seemed opportunities for further establishing the Order in the East, Midwest, South and even Canada. By 1890, their numbers and resources enabled them to move from the status of a commissariat to a province of the Order. By 1900, when Cyril Knoll died, what had started as the dream of two pioneering Carmelites to found the Order in America had become the lived vision of 35 priests, 21 brothers, 20 clerics, 2 novices and 10 scholastics.

The proverbial journey of a thousand miles from the Old World to the New World and then many more across the terrains of an exciting North America and eventually the landscapes of Central and South America parallels similar stories of many religious orders. But, much like each Order, the story of the early Carmelites had its unique characterization, reflective of the basic and historic Carmelite spirituality which colored and shaped the successes and setbacks of the journey they undertook. Those early Carmelites could be very proud of the contribution they made to the Church in the New World; their collective work confirmed and helped realize the vision of the Carmelite vicar prior general and Pope Pius IX.

Hopefully, the initial modest publication of their story and this re-publication on the occasion of the sesquicentennial celebration of their venture clearly confirms what was accomplished in their response to Jesus' command to "Go Forth and Bring the Good News to All People."

Myron M. Judy, O. Carm.
Casa del Carmen
Philadelphia, Pennsylvania
Feast of Our Lady of the Rosary, 2014

A BRIEF POSTSCRIPT

Carmel in North America: A History of the Early Founders and Foundations of the Carmelite Province of the Most Pure Heart of Mary (1864-1900) is essentially a reprint of "Carmel Came," a lengthy article that was published in the 1964 edition of the *Sword*, a publication of the Carmelite Province of the Most Pure Heart of Mary (PCM), to celebrate the centennial of the arrival of the German Carmelites in America.

The article reflected research that had been done by Myron M. Judy, O. Carm. as part of his work towards achieving a Master's Degree in American History at the University of Notre Dame. Because of his other obligations as a student of theology, his original research was confined, for the most part, to the limited archives at that time of the PCM Province. The author recognizes that the format of a Master's thesis differs from the format of a popular history.

So to guide the reader through the maze of events recounted, this reprint now carries subheadings and highlighted sections along with a few emendations and some new data that have been added. The author welcomes more extensive research of this period of the early foundations of Carmel in America and hopes that others will carry the magnificent story of the early Carmelites past 1900 to the present time.

The author especially hopes that his fellow Carmelites might follow in the footsteps of St. Thérèse by leaving the story of their souls. As he wrote this history, he wished that archives had held more such autobiographies of the men in these pages. Where men were stationed and how they ministered provide good history about the externals of Catholicism or the Order in any period. However, a more comprehensive and evangelizing portrayal of a period comes about when we learn about their experience of God as they lived out their religious lives.

Finally, the author is most grateful to a host of Carmelites who helped him in so many different ways publish the first version of this story and now this reprint.

1964 PREFACE

In the spring of 1864, two Bavarian Carmelites crossed the Atlantic to win souls for Christ. One hundred years later, the work they began had grown into a great service of salvation for nearly 500 Carmelites in the Canadian-American Province of the Most Pure Heart of Mary. From a simple beginning in Leavenworth, Kansas, this province counts 43 priories with men engaged in a variety of apostolates embracing high school education, parochial endeavors, seminary formation, specialized pursuits, retreat and mission band activities, communication projects, and foreign missionary assignments. The centennial history of the Carmelite Province of the Most Pure Heart of Mary, however, cannot be realized from just the real estate the province now possesses. That history lies in church records, newspaper files, and most of all in the memory of each priest, brother and cleric listed in the necrology of the province. This essay attempts to reveal those records and refresh that memory.

Carmel Came [the title used in the 1964 publication of this history] is the story of the pioneer years in the Carmelite Province of the Most Pure Heart of Mary. It is the history of the resurrection of a Carmel in Germany that faced imminent extinction through civil suppression. It is the history of a search for viable foundations to maintain a monastery at Straubing in Bavaria. Fr. Cyril Knoll sought several solutions; eventually, he came to America. His purpose was simple; its achievement nigh impossible. The hardships endured because of lack of personnel, physical equipment and finance were minor compared to the strained relations within his community that such a pioneer type of religious life triggered. The dissident elements in his commissariat soon separated and formed four distinct groupings beyond the jurisdiction of Knoll. If there is one lesson the history of those pioneer years tells the American Carmel of today, it is that small separate commissariats could not thrive. United once again in 1881, these Carmelites worked to weld together the Province of the Most Pure Heart of Mary that was established in 1890. This unification brought a growth in personnel, physical equipment and finances along with adequate provision for the essentials considered basic to a well-ordered religious life. Fr. Cyril Knoll had come to establish the Carmelite Order in the United States. By the time of his death, in 1900/ just nine days before the turn of the century, the status of Carmel in America showed his purpose had been attained.

Writing in 1937, the year of this author's birth, Rev. Bonaventure Gilmore, O. Carm., proposed the composition of the history of the Province of the Most Pure Heart of Mary. A new provincial quarterly magazine, *The Sword*, had just been published. In its first issue Fr. Bonaventure wrote: "One important purpose of *The Sword* is to encourage the organization of a complete and accurate history of our province. . . .What is needed now is to gather complete accounts of all our houses, including if possible those which have been discontinued, to add to these and check them with the memoirs of the older priests, to have these accounts preserved in a permanent provincial repository, and finally on the basis of these accounts to write the story of the province." Fortunately, in the past, several sketches and brief histories had been composed. These narratives contained at least a chronicle of facts that awaited a more precise historical method to verify their authenticity and enlarge their contents. While offering a small outline history of the province, in 1956, Rev. Norman Werling, O. Carm., once again petitioned for a provincial history: "Our province is approaching its centenary (1964) and such an event in the history of the American Church deserves to be proclaimed in grand style."

In the summer of 1961, I began work on the campus of Notre Dame University toward a Master of Arts degree in American history. As part of my pursuit of that degree, I proposed to Rev. Thomas J. Engleton, C.S.C., administrative head of the department, a treatise concerned with the pioneer years of the province. I wanted to write that history for the centenary as a small token of my appreciation for all the opportunities the Carmelite community has offered me. Yet, unless such a treatise could also be submitted to meet requirements for the history program at Notre Dame, the press of theological studies would not allow me to take up the pen. Fr. Engleton, however, was most encouraging and with the help of one of the American Catholic Church's leading historians, Rev. Thomas McAvoy, C.S.C., my topic was approved. V. Rev. Joachim Smet, O. Carm., an outstanding Carmelite historian, then directed me to the available sources for such a study.

Within the past year there has been the private publication of the history of the Baltimore Province of the Redemptorist Fathers entitled, *The Provincial Story*, The author, Michael J. Curley, C.S.S.R., had already written

1964 Preface

several reputable works, among them, *Venerable John Neumann, C.S.S.R.,* In preparation for his current piece, he was granted leave by his superiors to visit many well-ordered archives in Europe and America. I relate these facts not out of any sense of disappointment that such opportunities were not extended to me, but merely to point out to the readers the limitations of this study. My historical judgments have not been sharpened by many years of careful study and writing. This thesis represents the first historical work of any proportion I have undertaken. I have spent a great deal of effort gathering materials for this study, but the time allotted to this project has been curtailed by my theological studies. Perhaps the greatest disappointment has been the discovery of so little data. Limited materials have been saved and with little attention given to their preservation. The wear of decades has made these few pieces almost, illegible. A tremendous amount of time had to be devoted to the problem of deciphering and editing manuscripts.

In the past, I have been somewhat surprised to open a standard American Catholic history and find no reference to Carmelite activity. One might expect such excellent local studies as *Our Catholic Heritage in Texas* to offer a few lines about the Carmelite apostolate in that area. Yet, it is the rare work that does mention such data. Catholic historians can hardly be blamed for this negligence when they have no published source of Carmelite history to consult. I had hoped originally to bridge this gap by printing a history spanning 100 years. I have not abandoned this plan, but for the present *Carmel Came* will not consider the history of the province since 1900. Many friends, far wiser than I, have advised against the immediate publication of facts past this date. There are many reasons for this decision. A definite era in American Carmelite history closed with the turn of the century. Furthermore, material since 1900 in the Carmelite Archives in Rome is currently unavailable for consultation. Deprived of the resources of this primary deposit, I could not hope to compose a completely accurate historical record of events since 1900. Moreover there is another reason for withholding publication of those years. While the facts may be known and the policies pointed out, the effect of these policies cannot be accurately studied until some time has elapsed.

Some of the topics herein considered necessarily involve history that occurred past 1900, such as the opening of the hospice at Niagara Falls. Readers somewhat familiar with the chronicle of this project will be surprised to discover there is no mention of its income and activity when it was in competition with the Clifton House or the Windsor House, and other exclusive hotels on the Niagara frontier. Although the erection of the hospice is a topic for concern in chapter five, the use of the facilities of the hospice and the ensuing financial crisis this use provoked is a topic closely bound to the Carmelite history of the first decades of this century.

Some of the members of the province may find few facts they did not already know from oral traditions. Yet, I do hope this essay will furnish many missing details and especially reflect the causal relationships hitherto unknown between these facts. Finally, let me apologize for the style of this essay. Necessarily I have been curtailed to a somewhat formal approach since this essay shall also serve as a thesis. Yet, I have tried to keep the non-technical reader in mind in presenting the material in a palatable fashion.

One of the most pleasant tasks which confronts a writer is to make due acknowledgement of the many generous collaborators who have assisted him in his work. I am indebted to our present provincial, V. Rev. Brendan Gilmore, O. Carm., who has encouraged me to write the history and has followed every step of its progress with his kindly interest and constant support. To Rev. Leander Troy, O. Carm., my prior, and Rev. Malachy Smith, O. Carm., Carmelite Regent of Studies, a debt of gratitude is owed for the part they played in making this work possible. Special recognition must be paid to Rev. Canisius [Peter] Hinde, O. Carm., who as master of clerics at Whitefriars Hall has supported this endeavor in untold ways. I am particularly happy to express my thanks to Rev. Thomas McAvoy, C.S.C., of the University of Notre Dame and to the V. Rev. Joachim Smet, O. Carm., assistant general, for their many helpful suggestions. As my professor of church history at Catholic University, Msgr. John Tracy Ellis helped me understand and appreciate 19th century American Catholicism.

The former Carmelite provincial archivist, Rev. Kenneth Moore O. Carm., opened many doors for me and guided me in my initial use of the archives. He also called attention to numerous documents I might have missed. Among those who have helped most in gathering materials for this study, I must include Revs. Norman Werling, O. Carm., and Franz Lickteig, O. Carm. I owe a deep debt of gratitude to those who put at my disposal their expert knowledge of languages, especially Rev. Bernhard Baurele, O. Carm., and Mr. and Mrs. A. Lickteig. There have been many others, such as the current provincial archivist, Rev. Romaeus O'Brien, O. Carm., who have been instrumental in helping to bring this work to its conclusion. Would that I could name them all.

When it came to the tedious and time consuming task of typing the final draft of this essay, I was extremely fortunate to be able to call upon my capable friend, Fr. Donald Buggert, O. Carm. Graciously and willingly he took this exacting work off my hands, typing from a copy that to many others would have been illegible. There are numerous other friends who encouraged me to complete the manuscript at times when I felt like abandoning the entire project. To all these, this small expression of gratitude must be inadequate.

As I write these lines, there is a lurking fear that my memory may have missed someone who has cooperated in the production of this work. If I have overlooked anyone, I should like, in the words of Cardinal Newman which appear in the closing paragraphs of the *Apologia* to express my appreciation of those "who have been so sensitive of my needs; who have been so indulgent of my failings; who have grudged no sacrifice if I asked for it; who have done so many good works and let me have the credit of them."

Myron M. Judy, O. Carm.
Whitefriars Hall
Feast of the Most Pure Heart of Mary, 1964

1
Chapter One: TRANSIT AND TRANSITION

Early 19th century Europe witnessed the demise of many religious orders because of the confiscation and closure of their properties. In the whole of Western Europe, only two Carmelite monasteries of the Ancient Observance barely remained in existence– Straubing, Germany and Boxmeer, Netherlands. In 1842, several events caused the Bavarian government to allow for replenishment and rebuilding. Another series of events propelled Cyril Knoll, a priest of the Diocese of Regensburg, to apply for admission to the Straubing Carmel. Shortly thereafter, Knoll was made prior and began to implement his vision of resurrecting and sustaining Carmel through expansion of the Order beyond Straubing, including expansion to North America.

19TH CENTURY EUROPE AND THE SUPPRESSION OF RELIGIOUS ORDERS

OCTOBER 18, 1813! The events of that day were as auspicious in the history of Carmel as they were disastrous for the fortunes of Napoleon. Leipzig and Schellenberg—two gathering spots in the German lands—were the center of action. At Leipzig, the decline and fall of the First Empire was sealed. The Grand Army of Napoleon, more than decimated in the land of the Tsar, fought the Austrian, Prussian and Russian armies for nine hours. In the heat of the fray, the Saxon and Wurttemberg corps went over to the Allies and Napoleon had only to retreat, eventually to Elba. On that same day when the French sun was setting, John Knoll, destined to bring the Carmelite Order to America, was born in the small town of Schellenberg, near Perasdorf in Bavaria.[1] There was an important connection between the French emperor and the German peasant: it was October 18, 1813.

The enlightened despots had already attempted to make the Church subject to the state before the French Revolution. They had usurped power over all the externals of the life of the Church. The French Revolution and Napoleon continued and extended this work by nationalizing all Church property and suppressing all religious orders. The efforts of this policy profoundly altered the map of Germany and in doing so wrought what was little short of a revolution in the structure and temper of the Roman Catholic Church in that land. The great ecclesiastical states with their prince bishops and many a smaller ecclesiastical state either disappeared or were badly weakened. Mitre after mitre tumbled into the Rhine. Napoleon's successful campaign against Austria and her allies resulted in the deeding of the whole of the west bank of the Rhine to France in 1801.

In 1803 the Imperial Diet decreed the outrageous *Reichsdesputationshauptschluss* which abolished the suzerainty of the ecclesiastical princes of the entire Holy Roman Empire and ordered that the lands of the Church throughout Germany were to be handed over to the secular princes. Abbeys and monasteries were placed at the disposal of the civil rulers. In 1806 Napoleon drew together several German states into the Confederation of the Rhine, distributing among its members the territories of a number of counts and knights of the Holy Roman Empire.

That year the Holy Roman Empire ceased to exist. These decrees meant that the monasteries on the east bank of the Rhine were suppressed soon after those on the west.

In the German territories outside those annexed to France the acquisition of ecclesiastical possessions by several states was followed by great changes. The clergy were given their support by the state. Most of the Catholic universities were discontinued: only three, Freiburg, Munster, and Wurzburg remained. The clergy in effect were reduced to a civil bureaucracy. A large proportion of German Roman Catholics were now ruled by Protestant princes.

The defeat of Napoleon signaled at Leipzig profoundly altered but did not completely change the course of events. The Congress of Vienna erased the Napoleonic division of Germany and redrew the German Confederation. The Age of Metternich above all sought the end of hostilities. Some of the restrictions on religion evaporated. There was a tempering of policy for the sake of peace, even religious peace. This slight thaw allowed the Church just enough of a transitory foothold to revive and establish itself firmly enough against the coming *Kulturkampf*.[2] It was into this transition role that John Knoll was called to step as the Carmelites gained their foothold.

In Bavaria, the Carmelite Order had especially fallen upon evil days. King Maximilian IV, in accord with the spirit of Luheville, began the wholesale confiscation of Church property. Most of the Carmelite houses of the Lower German Province were situated west of the Rhine. The Carmelite houses of the Upper German Province fell victims during the provincialate of Fr. Franzishus de Paula. The friars were given a small pension; in some cases they were allowed to continue to live in the monasteries as private individuals. Under the hypocritical guise of freeing the buildings of religious orders for educational purposes, the enlightened sought to legislate religious life out of existence. Bamberg, the main house of the Upper German Province, was suppressed in 1802. Over the next two years the possessions of the monastery were gradually auctioned off, the valuable library being transferred to the State.[3] A community of 21 priests and nine lay-brothers were poorly pensioned off, limited gradually more and more in its freedom and work and finally turned out altogether.[4] The same doom descended on the other houses of the Province: Neustadt an der Saale, a house of 12 priests, 5 brothers;[5] Ravensburg with 19 priests, 6 brothers;[6] Rottenburg am Necker, with 6 religious;[7] Wurzburg, with 14 priests, 8 brothers.[8] At the same time Abensberg,[9] Dinkelsbuhl,[10] and Heilbronn were suppressed.[11]

For those who wished to continue their religious life, a central monastery, the *Aussterbekloster*, was provided, one for each order. For the Carmelites, their house at Straubing in Bavaria received this dubious award. In the whole of western Europe after the storm of revolution had passed, only two Carmelite monasteries remained in existence: Straubing and Boxmeer, and these had no hope of survival as the admission of novices was forbidden. By 1830, only three Carmelites were left at Straubing, and by 1840 Boxmeer in Belgium was reduced to the same number.[12]

In Southern and Eastern Europe the aftermath of the French Revolution followed a similar pattern. In this fashion the ruin of the greater part of Carmelite learning was accomplished by the destruction, confiscation, or sale of libraries and of the monastic houses. But a number of the archives and manuscripts found their way into various government and municipal collections and have been preserved there. Against heavy odds, the priors general of the Order did what they could to save what remained and to bring about a revival of Carmel. Attempts to convoke a general chapter would be made in 1832 but the difficult conditions and the few surviving monasteries resulted in a decision to elect a superior general by postal vote. Sixteen provinces were still in existence at the time but five significantly gave no sign of life. Of the other eleven, eight were in Italy. The most thriving province, centered in Rome, did not have 100 members until 1849.

It would not be until 1838 that for the first time in 50 years a general chapter would be able to meet. Only representatives from nine provinces or rather what was left of nine provinces could be present. For all practical purposes, the only non-Italian province present, Portugal, was nonexistent. The Provinces of Ireland, Poland, Gallo-Belgium are named as absent from the chapter. Since to gain new members was the most vital need pressing Carmelites in the nineteenth century, it is significant that this chapter concerned itself mainly with the reorganization of the houses of studies and the novitiates. The saintly and energetic Fr. Joseph Catalda was elected prior general and he was very active in bringing about a revival of study and learning in the Order. Among his successors, Fr. Joseph Lobina, who governed from 1849-1854, was distinguished by his efforts to restore and reorganize the Italian provinces. A second general chapter was able to meet in 1856. The list of representatives, however, shows that, apart from the Italian provinces, only Ireland and Galicia still survived. No further general chapters would be held until the year 1889.[13]

Straubing thus became a graveyard for German Carmelites, where the priests and brothers might stay, on a small pension, until all were dead and the buildings could be taken over entirely by the State. At the start of secularization, when the dispossessed Carmelites from Abensberg were moved to Straubing, the community totaled 63 members. The most galling restrictions were put on their freedom of work and of movement. It was forbidden to preach or to hear confessions in any church except their own. Their financial allowance barely covered the strictest necessities. Even the right of being buried in the crypt in their own church was denied them. Many used the papal permission to leave the monastery and go into sacerdotal work as secular priests. They consoled themselves with the hope of returning again if the monastery should ever be allowed to accept novices once more. Others sought different outlets; for example, Fr. Wendelin Zink left Straubing at the prior general's command to do mission work in the north of Germany at Stralsund with Fr. Sylvester Bayerlein from Bamberg. The Straubing school board took possession of part of the monastery for the town gymnasium, replacing that destroyed in the fire of 1780. It began to function in 1806 and remained there until 1909 when a new gymnasium was built on Carmelite property in another part of the town. The school authorities were so anxious to seize more space that they barely waited until a Carmelite died before they made over his cell into a classroom. There was a real danger that the last of the Carmelites would be turned out.[1]

The Straubing monastery and the German Province owe their salvation principally to one man, Fr. Peter Heitzer (1777-1847). A born Straubinger, he was a fellow novice of Wendelin Zink. They were the last to make their solemn profession in Straubing in 1799 and were ordained in 1801. Peter Heitzer was unanimously elected prior in 1815 although then the youngest of the priests. He was well chosen; through the poverty stricken years, as the community dwindled, he kept his courage.

Carmel Straubing Begins to Revivify

A new king, Ludwig I, came to the throne in 1825, succeeding Maximilian IV and his anti-Catholic minister, Count von Mongelas. In the name of the four priests and two brothers at Straubing, Fr. Heitzer appealed for permission to reopen the novitiate. The townspeople of Straubing, concerned for the education of its children and dissatisfied with the makeshift gymnasium taught by lay teachers, also appealed to the king in 1830. They urged that the Carmelites be permitted to receive new novices so that they could train priest-teachers for the gymnasium and also provide assistance in the care of souls. The permission to reopen the novitiate had already been given to the Benedictines at Metten.[15] But these appeals failed on the ground that the Carmelites themselves lacked the means to finance the reopening and the State could not assume the cost.

Unexpectedly help finally came in 1840. A neighboring pastor, Joseph Angermueller, wished to found a Capuchin monastery in Straubing. This proved impossible. Bishop Franz Xavier von Schwabel of Regensburg suggested that he give the money instead for the reopening of the Carmelite house. Fr. Angermueller did so. Fr. Heitzer, now almost alone, renewed his plea to the government, emphasizing the new source of financial help. On July 4, 1841, the long hoped for permission came. At the same time the monastery brewery and garden were returned to Carmelite hands.

Fr. Wendelin Zink, who had kept in close touch with Fr. Heitzer for four decades, had died in 1840. But the Carmelite, Fr. Edmund Withinger, who had gone into parish work in 1802, resigned his pastorate and returned to Straubing as soon as he heard the news. Thus, the last survivors of the German Carmel, two elderly priests, took charge of the restoration. On July 20, 1842, Bishop Valentin von Riedel of Regensburg presided at the solemn reopening of the monastery and renewal of vows by the two priests. Once the novitiate was opened again, a number of priests and lay brothers made application to enter Carmel. Fr. Wirthinger died at the age of 79 in November 1846. Four months later Peter Heitzer, on February 15, 1847, followed him to the grave after five agonizing days of intestinal gangrine.[16]

Bishop Riedel provisionally appointed Fr. Albert Weiss as prior of the Carmelite community which them numbered four priests—Albert Weiss, Eliseus Primbs, Louis Fritz, and Xavier Huber—as well as three brothers—Valentine Poppel, Brocard Bauer and Berthold Wartner.[17] Carmel in Germany had survived the period of secularization. The past was to be left behind. A period of transition between the old order and the new now started. A new horizon lay ahead, outwardly manifested by the fact that the Straubing community would see on the feast of Our Lady of Mt. Carmel of that year one of its own, Xavier Huber, raised to the ranks of the priesthood.[18] Yet, though the darker clouds had passed, the atmosphere was still ominous for religious observance and life had suffered much during the troublesome period.

The house *horarium* gave every sign of earnestness in restoring the austere framework that was the foundation of religious life. The morning bell was sounded at 4:30 a.m. At 5 a.m. the little hours of prime and terce were recited in choir, followed by a half hour of meditation and community Mass. Spiritual reading and study along with pastoral chores were to occupy the morning until 10:30 when the office hours of sext and none were recited. At 11 a.m. lunch was served and the typical European rest period was enjoyed. The early hours of the afternoon were to be spent in study or with parochial tasks, especially the visitation of the sick. Vespers and compline were recited at 3 p.m. The evening hours witnessed another period of meditation and recital of matins and lauds for the following day.

Yet, the scarcity of hands clearly noted in the monastery records and *tabella,* coupled with the momentous tasks of the day, made more burdensome by the fact that parochial chores had been nearly abandoned for 40 years, demanded that house discipline be somewhat relaxed. Meditation periods, thus, were freely dispensed with and the novitiate year was more a pastoral year involved with the vigorous routine of care of souls.[19] Religious life, therefore, was not something to be learned and reflected upon in the peace of a novitiate year. Rather it was something one imbibed over a period of time by living in the confines of a busy religious house. Yet, despite the imperfection such a system offered, the monastery records attest to the fact that a good number of candidates sought admission to such a way of life. One such candidate was John Knoll.

CYRIL KNOLL: EARLY HISTORY IN CARMEL

It was not surprising that Knoll should have been attracted to the Carmel at Straubing, for his family home was less than 20 miles from the monastery. Furthermore, he had been ordained for the diocese of Regensburg on July 31, 1838,[20] and for his first assignment he was named to the staff of a preparatory school for boys at Straubing. He was also appointed chaplain of the Ursuline Sisters on Burggasse Street, quite near the Carmelite enclosure.[21] The son of an artisan, a member of the building trade,[22] he stood only five feet tall. His features were not impressive and were somewhat marred by a high forehead, beetling eyebrows, a Roman nose, pointed chin and facial lines that highlighted a weak mouth.[23] The first indications of his vocation to Carmel are contained in the formal permission to enter the monastery given as standard procedure by the Chamber of the Interior in the name of the King of Bavaria. At the time of his entrance, he was assisting at the mission at Neubau.[24] Knoll entered the Straubing monastery on November 12, 1846.[25] For some unknown reason, his stay was quite brief. The monastery register lists his departure on January 7, 1847.[26]

In a letter addressed by the vicar general of the diocese to the prior of Straubing and dated November 14, 1848, there are indications that Knoll had made contact once again with the Carmelites and wished to re-enter the Order.[27] Once more the Chamber of the Interior gave its permission.[28] The Bishop's office at Regensburg was quite willing to allow him re-entry provided that Knoll wait until at least April 30 of the following year. Due to the shortage of priests, no one could be exempted until after the Easter confessions were finished on April 29. As an assistant priest at Dingelfing, Knoll's services were needed.[29] Fr. Knoll re-entered Carmel, therefore, on June 7, 1849. At the time of his entrance, the prior, Weiss, described him to the prior general as a candidate with great love for the Order and a well-founded reputation for zeal for the welfare of the city's souls.[30] It was during his postulancy and novitiate days that a very important appointment came, one which was eventually to bear weight in his decision to come to America. The vicar general of the diocese notified the Carmelites that the mother superior of the Ursuline convent had requested that the bishop name Knoll as ordinary confessor to the community. His bond with the Ursulines was again given recognition. The appointment was made on June 4, 1850,[31] just five days before Knoll made his solemn profession and stepped forward as Fr. Cyril Knoll into the full ranks of Carmel.[32]

The correspondence of the Straubing house at this time reveals much about its daily life. On the death of the prior, Albert Weiss, May 22, 1850, just a few days before the solemn profession of Knoll, the bishop of Regensburg appointed Fr. Louis Fritz as provisional prior of the Carmelites.[33] Although Fritz, the son of a farmer, had only been professed since September 30, 1847,[34] the choice seemed a wise one. Fritz was not only a representative figure of the new group and spirit that entered Carmel since its restoration; he was also a man of excelling religious example. As a gifted orator and a man who edited many volumes of homilies on the mysteries of the rosary and the Little Office, he brought the name of the Carmelites before the people.[35]

Fritz apparently took the burden of his appointment to heart. His correspondence reveals a true concern for the community. For example, in a letter dated February 2, 1851, Fritz wrote to Joseph Lobina, the new prior general of the Order appointed by Pope Pius IX, requesting that the ruling on age be lifted for electing a novice master and the law restricting voting in the community to members who had been professed at least five years be suspended. Furthermore, although the constitutions stated that the novice master was to be appointed either by the definitors or provincial, provision should be made in the future to allow the local prior to designate as master any man he saw fit, despite his age or the number of professed years in Carmel.[36] True, these practical innovations could only tend to take away certain safeguards built into religious life to insure its soundness, yet, the problems of the day dictated such innovations. A novice master who by reason of his own recent profession could hardly be called steeped in Carmelite tradition still offered more promise for the formation of novices than an older man for whom, harnessed by other duties, the task of novice master could be but a part time concern.

But despite this seemingly practical and realistic view of communal obligations, the rigors of Fritz' administration had appeared and caused obvious unrest among his brethren. The bishop of Regensburg explained the difficulties, as he saw them, to the prior general. Not being able to hold a canonical election on the death of Weiss because Knoll could not fulfill the requirements prescribed to receive active or passive voice, the bishop reported that he had chosen Fritz as a temporary prior—an appointment which greatly pleased the local civil authorities. Though he never aspired to the job, once appointed Fritz pledged himself to religious discipline. Before he had entered the monastery he was known as a pious priest and a worthy pastor of souls. Yet, his rule had been too exacting and the discipline he had tried to enforce had given way to chaos and murmuring.

Therefore, on March 4, 1850, the bishop appointed Knoll as vicar prior of Straubing. But, on March 11, Fr. Cyril, acting in his new capacity, received a communiqué from the prior general, unsuspecting of the bishop's new appointment, stating that he as prior general approved Fr. Fritz as prior for another three years. At the time Fritz was in the country visiting a sick priest. The bishop of Regensburg called a hurried conference with Fritz explaining the situation before the brethren of the house would hear of the new re-appointment. Bishop von Riedel felt that the

Chapter One: Transit and Transition 11

clemency of Knoll would go further in restoring order.[37] Fritz realized the situation and in a letter to the prior general dated June 28, 1851, begged to have his appointment rescinded, stating that "he was unequal for such work."[38]

In his first letter to the prior general as official prior, Knoll exhibited an enviable balance, a sense of need for religious discipline yet also a realization of the practical limitations of his surroundings. On the one hand he sought the necessary dispensation needed for electing a novice master and recommended either Fritz or Joseph Maier for that position.[39] His initial years also revealed a balance of mercy and justice. He knew the power he had and he knew when not to use it. He refused, for example, to extend any leniency toward Br. Brocard Bauer.[40] This member of the community had rejected the ordinary demands of discipline on the grounds that his profession was invalid since to avoid being refused admission, he never admitted a defect caused by a hernia. Given to drink and general carousing, he dissipated the meager communal funds he could find and in general brought scandal to the house by his actions. Knoll's method of handling this case eventually forced this subject to apostatize in May 1851.[41] In the rigorous mind of Cyril, there had been no loss.[42]

On the other hand, he exhibited mercy and patience to one of the most temperamental, though gifted, members of the community. As a result of a June visitation in 1853 of the community by the procurator general of the Order, Fr. Jerome Priori, one of the resolutions recommended by the visitator took the form of a condemnation of too great a desire for financial gain on the part of some of the community. Joseph Maier apparently felt this statement was directed to him and asked Knoll to remove it from the visitation decrees once the procurator general left.[43] Knoll rightly refused. Bitter that his objection had been overruled, Maier next wrote a small booklet to the reverend bishop of Regensburg and his cathedral chapter explaining the many "abuses" of community life at Straubing. He asked that his complaints be forwarded to Rome. The bishop saw the source of the sketch and sent the booklet back to the prior. As Knoll rightly noted, the scandal this incident stirred deserved that the full rigor of the constitutions be applied and that the culprit be inflicted with excommunication from the prior general. But, Knoll asked that he be excused because "he is sorry now and asks that the book be burned. All things that happen can only be attributed to human frailty."[44]

Following the June 1853 visitation of Jerome Priori, Knoll laid plans to put his community on a more stable footing. He had already centered his concentration on receiving priests as postulants rather than younger candidates because they could immediately bring stipends into the house and at the same time bring the name of Carmel more noticeably before the public. A mere six days before Christmas 1853, Knoll spoke of the scarcity of food and money and of his determination to solve these administrative problems through expansion. The bishop of Regensburg had promised him a new foundation at Sossau near Straubing but since it had not been granted, Knoll made pointed appeals to the city of Abensberg where the Carmelites had been from 1389 until 1802. Immediate response from the town indicated that three of the Fathers could be expected to make a new foundation there before the end of the year.

Yet, the latest word on this affair was not Christmas cheer. The bishop of Regensburg for some unknown reason had discouraged a delegation from Abensberg in their efforts to secure the Carmelites. So hard pressed was the Carmelite community that Knoll penned a request to the cardinal archbishop, Joseph Seitowski, primate of Hungary, pleading for a foundation.[45] Indeed, he was faced with a difficult problem. To insure a suitable caliber of religious life new candidates should be kept close to the hearth for a longer and more substantial training in Carmelite life. On the other hand, the Carmelite traditions could not be carried on at all without the basic necessities of life. Fr. Knoll made his choice, a decision that was to guide most of his policies throughout the rest of his life. The external concerns received first attention; the internal life was given second place. There could not be Carmelites without Carmels, though admittedly there could hardly be Carmels without true Carmelites. For these years of formation, he chose to allow men to put on the habit and exist in surroundings that had the barest of Carmelite essentials. He did not like the agonies that such an arrangement would bring; nevertheless, it seemed the only practical solution.

EARLY VENTURES FOR EXPANDING THE ORDER

As a reward for his zeal, the curia of the Carmelite Order issued a decree the following July 2 creating him titular provincial of Scotland and thus granting him a seat in the second general chapter of the century to be held in 1856.[46] Knoll was most appreciative of this gesture and vowed to walk to Rome if necessary to attend.[47] The year 1854 also brought an explanation of why the bishop of Regensburg had turned down the delegation from Abensberg; the bishop himself had decided to entrust the mission sanctuary at Sossau, about two and one-quarter miles from Straubing, to the care of the Carmelites. The last vicar of Sossau, a Fr. Nothaas, had been transferred to Reibensdorf.[48] With the offer of Sossau, Knoll could say: "The spiritual and temporal things of this house are gradually looking better with the favor of God."[49] The Thursday night conferences given by Fr. Fritz in thanksgiving for blessings during this Holy Year of 1854 took on additional meaning.[50]

During the early months of the following year, the bishop of Regensburg made final arrangements for the Carmelites' new administrative charge. The shrine of Sossau[51] itself was to remain incorporated with the city parish in Straubing although its caretakers would be the Carmelites. Furthermore, the Carmelites were forced to promise to abide by a series of regulations geared to avoid any prejudicial action against the parish of St. James.[52] The permission of the bishop had been won through a Fr. Amberges, closely associated with the cathedral, and through Mother Xaveria, the long time friend of Knoll's at the Ursulines.[53] Knoll planned to transfer the novitiate to Sossau because of over crowding at Straubing and also because he felt circumstances there would be more amenable to a novitiate atmosphere. On May 30, Fritz, the prospective novice master, and Frs. Anselm Hoffmann and Gerhard Wieselhuber along with Br. Elias Kirschner left to open the new house. The townsfolk seemed delighted; some of the secular clergy, however, seemed a bit offended at this advance of the religious.[54]

Yet, Sossau did not immediately prove to be a blessing. The scarcity of manpower coupled with the task of renovating and remodeling an old foundation discouraged many of the candidates that entered the novitiate. Furthermore, the initial expenses and outlay that the new apostolate forced upon the Carmelites created an oppressive burden at a time when the bank accounts of the community was already bone dry. Receipts were first sidelined for food bills and then only used for furnishing the shrine. The sacristan's books at the end of 1855 showed that 5,435 florens had been accepted by the community over a long period of years for 10,870 Masses which had gone unsaid. The money had already been spent on necessary expenses and Fr. Knoll was forced to write to the Holy See for a condonation from the treasury of the Church.[55] A letter addressed to the King of Bavaria at this time dramatizes their plight:

> The monastery of the Calced Carmelites in Straubing founded in 1362 by the Dukes of Bavaria, Albert I and Albert II, secularized in the year 1802, was in the year 1842 declared to be restored by the highest decree of Your Majesty, to the joy of all good people. Fourteen years have passed since then and during this time the monastery itself, in spite of hostile elements, was brought up to a condition not unworthy of the number of monasteries in the kingdom. Twelve priests and seven lay brothers, all Bavarian sub-

jects by birth, live here. It fulfills the purpose of its restoration; the work and business circle in which it moves speak for it; the labors of the cloister-community in the field of education and care of the souls vouch for it; the city and vicinity prove this. The monastery community would be happy if it were not for our sad economic conditions.

Like the sick man, who does not want to die, often tries to hide the danger of his sickness to himself, so we too tried to hide the danger of our situation, always in expectation and hope of a lucky event, which would bring about a change for the better of our economic situation. Alas, so far nothing of the sort has happened and we are at this moment on the point from which we can see the abyss which threatens to engulf our existence as a monastery.

When we ask ourselves for the basic causes from which this great burden of our debt grew, we find foremost among them the fact of unsatisfactory endowments of lands and other sources of stipend; the purchase of a brewery house with outside money and the mismanaging of the brewery by outside help; the augmentation of convent members by accepting poor novices; the increase in price of the victuals.

Your Majesty! If our existence as a monastery community shall not cease, then we must pay at least a part of our debt. But how? We know no other way, the way to You, Your Majesty, to the fatherly heart of our great, reverend and exalted King Ludwig. Well known, Your Majesty, is Your compassion for the poor and needy; well known Your great sacrifices for purposes of our holy religion. This encourages us to dare to present with confidence this most humble plea: that Your Majesty might be moved to declare graciously a money-subsidy to our Monastery for part-payment of our debt. The present community of the Calced Carmelites in Straubing has in the past always honored in the person of Your Majesty the magnanimous creator of our monastery and expressed our feelings of gratitude through our daily prayers to the King of Kings for Your Majesty's well-being—as on occasion of Your Majesty's sickness and in celebrating solemn Masses for the speedy recovery in our monastery church—although the public press kept silence about it. So also in the future our community shall always honor in the exalted person of Your Majesty the preserver of our monastery and pour out our prayers before God with highest feeling of thanks.[56]

Although this first experiment at Sossau failed to bring superlative results, Knoll still believed that expansion was the only solution for solving their long-term difficulties. In December of 1856 a very welcome Christmas gift came in the form of over 28,000 square feet of

Chapter One: Transit and Transition

property. Baron Karl von Frauenhofen donated his mountain castle-retreat at Poxau, about ten hours ride on horseback from Straubing, to the Carmelite community. With the house was a chapel dedicated to St. Charles Borromeo. Under the main altar were the remains of the Virgin Juliana. The property was surrounded by prosperous fruit groves. To this house Cyril dispatched Frs. Thomas Handl, 36 years of age, who was professed on March 15, 1852, and ordained 12 days later, as vicar and novice master,[57] Xavier Huber and Br. Elias Kerschner, an excellent cook.[58] Once again the local secular clergy complained of an infraction of their rights. The people of the countryside, however, sent a petition to the bishop to issue the Carmelite installation. Knoll's sole comment evoked poison satire. "*O jura parochialia*!" "O Parochial Rights!"[59]

The end of the year brought more good news. On December 30, Cardinal Seitowski wrote Knoll to inform him that he was willing to give him and the Bavarian Carmelites permission to begin a foundation on the Danube. He gave Knoll three years to accept or reject this offer. Cyril hoped to send two or three priests with a lay brother to begin this new foundation.[60] As soon as the Danube became passable, Knoll laid plans to journey to Pesth, Hungary (now part of Budapest, Hungary) to arrange for the opening of the house.[61] There were many who did not seemingly agree with Knoll's policy of expansion in Straubing. With the announcement of a settlement outside the borders of the Fatherland, this element grew louder. Never had an official appointment been sent approving Knoll as prior, though the prior general certainly had ratified the bishop's appointment. Still, on the occasion of the proposed expansion into Hungary the dissident element in the community questioned the need for obedience on the grounds that Knoll was not a legal prior.[62] Knoll's reaction was bitter: "Some of the brethren would rather see the Order fold."[63] Yet, not all looked with the same disdain on his efforts. The Dutch Province made numerous requests that he join with them in helping them expand and escape their less fortunate plight.[64]

The last days of April saw the passing of the winter thaw. Knoll prepared to inspect his new foundation. So optimistic were his first impressions that he was determined to send four priests: Joseph Maier, Anselm Hoffmann, Gerhard Wieselhuber and Peter Koehler along with the lay brother, Simon Edenhoefer, to open the new house. Maier and Koehler, however, were among the dissenters who refused to go. Their decision left Knoll with an unhappy choice. Either he must leave Straubing and accompany the group to assist in the work, thus leaving a large group of dissenters at home to murmur in the absence of the prior and cause division in the community, or send Fr. Fritz, who though willing to go anywhere, was a certain risk because of his poor health.[65] Perhaps there was a third solution. Fritz had already been rejected by the brethren as prior. Perhaps his appointment as prior once again might have good effects. For those who could not respect him as prior, the opening at Pesth might prove a happy outlet to which they would be willing to give their energies.

The Carmelites were called to staff the chapel in Resurrection cemetery. Their work, therefore, primarily was to center about saying funeral Masses and conducting interment services. It was understood, of course, that they could be of assistance throughout the rest of the city for other parochial duties. Their chapel was a rather small structure measuring no more than 26 feet long and 13 feet wide. A five-room house with a kitchen, wine cellar and refectory was standing on the property facing out on a fine garden orchard. The climate was salubrious both physically and financially. There was a generous donation of Mass stipends and the burial offerings would be a welcome increment to community funds. Knoll claimed there were ten to twelve funerals a day. And what is more, the Cardinal Primate promised to pay for the trip from Straubing and to help renovate the house according to the friars' desires.[66] Realizing his exuberance was showing forth, Knoll captioned his report to the prior general in Rome with the words: "I suppose you can read my heart, that I am very happy. In a short time, our Order will gain a great increment from Hungary."[67]

The pilgrimage began on October 1857 with Knoll at its head.[68] Unwilling to risk sending any of the disapproving Fathers who might provide grounds for irritation in the new house, Knoll was forced to go himself along with Frs. Huber, Anselm Hoffmann and Br. Simon Edenhoefer. Arriving on October 11, the Fathers were pleasantly surprised to find a fairly large gathering of town counselors waiting to greet them.[69]

But there was still the problem of Straubing. Who was to reside as vicar in Knoll's absence? Fr. Joseph Maier was certainly competent to administer the Straubing house. But, since he was opposed to the prior's policies, he could hardly be expected to carry on as Knoll wished. There was the possibility of moving Fritz, a hard worker and a man proven in his religious observance, from Sossau to Straubing and sending Maier as vicar of Sossau. Knoll even mused that the best plan was to close Straubing completely. The living conditions certainly appeared to be better in Pesth. To the prior general he wrote:

> Please, I ask that you let me live and die in Pesth. The only attachment in Straubing that would stop me from leaving it entirely is the Ursuline convent. And if they could find a good confessor, which

I am sure they could were Fritz stationed at Straubing, I would be less anxious for them."[70]

The settlement at Pesth was quite revealing for it showed up several traits of Knoll's character that were to plague him for the rest of his career. He had obviously let his desire for expansion get a bit out of hand so that he was ready to claim each new stepping-stone as paradise regained. Concomitant policies, hence, demanded a shift of the best and numerous manpower to each new oasis. The same vigor exhibited by this leader was not shared by his compatriots. This fact in itself did not auger well for a harmonious future. But even worse was the fact that Knoll would brook no opposition to his schemes. For those who opposed the new move, the new expansion, there could be no compromise. If they did not care to follow, they could apply for a dispensation and leave. Such an attitude naturally created tension in the ranks. Disobedience soon turned into religious rebellion, with the result that separatist factions arose, operation in spite of, instead of because of, their prior. These same tendencies were to surround his policy decisions in his foundations in the United States. The question ultimately could be resolved to a problem of personality, to whether one was an opportunist or a long-range planner. Fr. Knoll was among the former.

During the first months at Pesth there is mention of bustling activity. Lenten devotions were conducted and missions held in the neighboring countryside by the Carmelites. A scapular confraternity was also begun.[71] The cardinal also made frequent visits during these days and expressed his high regard for the Carmelites.[72] Yet, the trials associated with any missionary adventure were certainly present. Above all, that sense of alienation from the Fatherland remained strong. In fact Knoll feared that should Fritz be moved from Straubing and a new man installed as prior, the brethren at Pesth might find the atmosphere in the homeland more cordial and pack their bags for departure.[73] For the present, however, that was not likely to happen, for the home fires were burning.

The events that lead up to the conflagration, the sparks that touched off the explosion are not known. It seems that Fritz sent Maier a letter on Septuagint Sunday in 1858 instructing him to function in the parochial church of Alburg near Straubing where the parish priest had called for assistance. Maier missed his promised ride into the country and made no efforts to go to the church by other means or to notify Fritz or the pastor that he was not coming. On Friday of the same week, he managed, however, to saddle up for the ten-hour ride into Straubing from Sossau to hear confessions of the members of the Third Order of St. Francis of which he was the spiritual director. Fritz was angered by his appearance and learning of his failure to go to Alburg refused him permission to use the Straubing church for the confessions. Whereupon Maier proceeded to lead the tertiaries to a downtown secular parish. There he readily received permission from the pastor to shrive his penitents.

Since the death of the bishop of Regensburg the previous November, this pastor was anxiously waiting on the sidelines to have the sanctuary of Sossau placed under his own care. He now saw an opportunity to cause a rift in the Straubing community. The pious females had their confessions heard there for several weeks. Fritz was able to counter this move by having the provincial of the Capuchins replace Maier as director of the group. Thereupon, Maier threatened to leave the Carmelites and seek entrance with the Redemptorists. In the interim the souls who worshipped at the sanctuary at Sossau were the innocent victims whose needs went practically unattended.[74]

There was much to be done in Pesth if the foundation was to be profitable. The size of the chapel did not satisfy the dreams of the Carmelite community. In late December of the very first year in Pesth, a campaign was begun to secure resources to improve the building. The initial collection produced the meager sum of 700 florins and 30,000 bricks. According to Knoll, the Carmelites needed a minimum of 10,000 florins. Knoll addressed his plight to the Hapsburg king, Franz Joseph:

> Most gracious, great, Mightest Emperor and Lord!
>
> With your Imperial, royal, apostolic Majesty's permission, His Eminence the Most Reverend Cardinal Archbishop Seitowski has given the Order of the Calceated Carmelites a little house and chapel at Pesth in Hungary. On October 11, 1857, we [the Carmelites] took possession of this through three priests of the Order from Straubing in Bavaria. Since its transplanting from the orient to the west, the Calced Carmelite Order has always combined the contemplative life with the active life. Since its readmission into Bavaria, its special work and obligation has been the care of the souls in pastoral labor. As long as we here in Pesth have only a small chapel—twenty-six feet long and thirteen feet wide, we are unable to measure up to our work and obligations as we would wish and as is necessary, partly because we come in contact with only a few of the faithful, partly because it is difficult to increase the number of priests for the lack of a larger convent and church.
>
> With this in mind, we have on December 15 of last year petitioned for permission to be allowed to make a collection for the purpose of enlarging the present chapel into a more fitting church in the district of Pesth. This alms collection was graciously permitted us by the decree of the City Vicar on the 21st of December. The col-

Chapter One: Transit and Transition

lection by one of our Order priests is now completed. The result is 700 florins and 30,000 pieces of masonry tiles. Therefore, we find ourselves with the sad alternative either of abandoning altogether the planned building of a church, or leave the building to an insecure future; for at least a sum of 10,000 florins would be required. In this desperate situation dare we to approach in deepest reverence the steps of the Throne of Your Imperial, Royal Apostolic Majesty with the most humble, obedient plea: That Your Imperial, Royal, Apostolic Majesty may deign to cause to remit to the Convent of the Calced Carmelites at Pesth a money subsidy most graciously for the aforesaid purpose, benefitting the Order and the faithful. May the Lord pour down his heavenly blessing in fullest measure upon the reigning house of Austria. This favor we incessantly beg of God in our prayers.[75]

The answer from the regal treasury was a flat rejection of the plea on the grounds that the chapel did not need to be enlarged![76]

Nevertheless, the campaign to solicit funds continued and must have proven successful enough by mid-1859. In May of that year, the magistrate of the city granted a permit for one year to allow the desired additions and construction. The permit set down the most minute details including specifications on thickness of walls, arrangement of stairwells, and layout of the sewage system.[77] The following year on March 16 when application was made for a renewal of the permit,[78] the city officials took a different tack. Approval was given for the employment of the contractor Laurent Lofehl, but the magistrate pointed out that a permit to erect a building did not include a permit to use the land upon which that building was to be built. It seems that the cemetery grounds were owned by the city which leased the land to the Church on which the ecclesiastical buildings stood.[79] Knoll returned a polite reply within a fortnight. In the first place the prior indicated that he had not suspected that besides a permit to build one might need a permit to use the land upon which the building was erected. In the second place, he argued that such a permit seemed unnecessary, for the enlarged church would merely occupy the area where the former chapel and also the enclosed garden stood.[80]

Work had obviously begun on the new project even though the current hassle regarding the permit was not resolved. Extant receipts give clear testimony of bi-monthly installment payments made to carpenters, masons and plasterers as well as painters.[81] By July 4, 1860 a complete estimate of final costs was available:

```
Masons' and apprentices' wages  ................................. 4,006.90
Masonry material  ..................................................... 6,001.50
```

Plumbing and iron work and materials	355.20
Painters' work and material	174.72
Roofing tiles and roofers' wages	462.94
Tinsmith's work and material	360.00
Glasswork and material	142.30
Stonecutter's work and material	1,690.53
Carpenters' work and lumber	1,700.16
Cabinet maker's costs and materials	935.00

Total: 16,829.25 fl.[82]

The work advanced with good speed, although there was a great deal to be done. Wood paneling decorated the main part of the chapel, the ceiling of which was stucco-plastered and calcimined. Nor was the interior furnishing neglected.[83] Three new altars were placed in the enlarged chapel and Mass was celebrated on the main altar dedicated to Our Lady, Refuge of Sinners, for the first time on the First Sunday of Advent in 1860.[84] The increased tempo of building only angered the city authorities. On May 9, 1860, the Office of the Magistrate demanded that an explanation be given as to why building had begun without necessary permits.[85] Knoll again explained his position in a polite but explicit way, this time asserting that he had been given to understand that the grounds actually belonged to the Carmelites.[86]

The forces that opposed the Carmelite expansion seemed evident to Knoll. In a letter to the Prior General Priori in May, Knoll reported that the magistrates of the city were beginning to reflect the prejudices of the religions they represented—Jewish, Calvinistic and Lutheran. The religious leaders of these segments detested the growth of Catholicism.[87] But by the feast of the Holy Name of Mary in 1860, Knoll even felt the Catholic leaders opposed his presence. The chief objection he heard voiced on the part of the secular clergy was the charge that the Carmelites were far too concerned with the last will and testaments of the people soon to be buried. There was also the usual complaint that the religious had relied for support too heavily on their privilege as mendicants to beg throughout the city, thus receiving alms that otherwise would have been donated to diocesan funds.[88]

Besides these prejudices that Knoll believed were at work, undermining the Carmelite foundation, there was obviously the force of nationalism to be reckoned with. In the wake of the revolutionary days of 1848 and the subsequent defeat of the ambitions of Louis Kossuth, the Hungarian Regent-President, the Hapsburg Empire was ruled from Vienna by bureaucratic methods. A concerted effort was made to undermine the national movements by a policy of vigorous Germanization.

Hungary lost its historic identity and was divided into five administrative districts ruled by German officials and by gendarmerie directed from Vienna. This system of despotism came to be known as the Bach System after Baron Bach, the Austrian minister of the interior. The Magyars of Hungary during these years nourished a bitter hatred against the Germans and Austrian overlords.[89] An American tourist, Charles Loring Brace, reflects this bitterness in a scene recorded in Pesth at this time:

> I went by accident into a saddler's shop, and the moment he found I was no Austrian, he burst out with his feelings over the change in his country. "It was so pleasant a land! And we had our own freedom, as they have now in America, and Pesth was so lively. The gentry used to come here to the shop and buy so much for their hunts and races, and talk politics here! And everything was so cheap! Wine was only two kreutzeurs (1 1/2 cents) a bottle. But now we have to pay all the Austrian taxes; and the gentry are all gone; and we are all just like slaves! If I can only sell my stock I shall go over at once to America!"[90]

The ill constructed Empire sustained repeated shocks. The Crimean War isolated her in Europe and cost her the friendship of Russia; the Italian War in 1859 had shown her military weakness; the headship of Germany was passing to Prussia. By 1859, Vienna was forced to extend some concessions to the Hungarians to avoid revolt. In 1859, it was decreed that German no longer need be the sole language taught in the higher schools. The October Diploma of 1860 offered the shadow of local autonomy; the embittered Hungarians rejected it, awaiting the day when they could seize complete independence. And that day must not have seemed too far distant. For Kossuth was abroad in 1860, plotting revolution. On May 6 a Hungarian National *Directorium* was established at Paris and in that same month a Hungarian Legion was organized.[91]

There is no doubt that the pressures of nationalism hampered the Carmelite activity in Pesth. To what extent the German Carmelites were despised for their national origin is unknown. In 1859, the only additional Carmelite added to the community was Fr. Angelus Traidner.[92] But when a thirty year old novice entered for a few weeks in the winter of 1859, Knoll extolled the event beyond due proportion. John Barnas, who took the religious name of Alber, had been a member of the Franciscan Order. He was well versed in theology and since his home was in Upper Hungary, he was able to speak the Polish, Slavik and Hungarian tongues. That Knoll was anxious to identify the community with the nationality of the surrounding countryside is obvious from the comments made to the prior general, hailing the event as singular and an example to all youth of

Hungary to enter the confines of Carmel.⁹³

The anger of nationalism certainly played a strong role in forcing the departure of the Carmelites from Hungary. On October 31, the chancery issued an emergency decree that showed the temper of the times:

> In view of the turbulent times, I feel obliged to request your Reverence in all earnestness, in order to avoid all possible demonstrations from the uneducated class of the people, to say all your sermons and prayers on the following holy days of All Souls and All Saints day only in the Hungarian language; in no way to conduct devotions in German and, in case no member of your convent can speak Hungarian, to omit all such devotions otherwise usually said in German.⁹⁴

Pius Mayer, whose brief history of the American Carmelites based on original sources has proven most accurate, states that the Carmelites were forced to leave Hungary for a seeming triviality: the Carmelites said requiem masses with vestments trimmed in yellow borders, the colors of Austria, as opposed to those usually used in Hungary, silver and gold.⁹⁵ Such an incident now seems quite implausible as the motive which finally forced the Carmelites to leave. In itself such a mistake seems too small to demand expulsion, but when viewed against the political times, the magistrates of the city may well have used such a club of nationalism. There was no expression of thanks for services rendered to the community. The Carmelites were not to enjoy the new improvements they had labored to attain. The notice from the city hall was quite clear; its stipulations spelled expulsion:

> February 16, 1861
>
> The undersigned city attorney was empowered by the general meeting of the City of Pesth on 8 February 1861, to serve notice to the Carmelite institution, situated on the general cemetery on Kerepest Street, being established there—without the consent of the city authority—and on the right side of the Kerepest Street Cemetery—all those parts of property of the city—occupied by them.
>
> In consequence of this order I announce to the Carmelite Cloister a warning of dispossession of said premises and places on St. George's Day, 1861. They shall vacate all buildings on the Kerepest Cemetery occupied by them, with all parts belonging to it by St. George's Day, 1861.
>
> Notifying herewith the Rev. P. Cyril Knoll and through him all other convent priests by delivering by hand a copy of my notice of vacating; a second copy of it shall be returned to the city authority

with signature of receipt of such papers.

Respectfully,
Paul Neuhoffer
First assistant at the office of the City of Pesth.[96]

The final resolution of the Hungarian experiment is unknown, as no historical records have come to light to disclose what transpired. By October 1, 1861, Xavier Huber was carrying out his duties as chaplain at the shrine of Sossau.[97] The last extent letter penned by Knoll in conjunction with this foundation was written in Vienna on October 2, 1861. It is a plea to the emperor for a donation. No indication is given as to what work the Carmelites undertook once "the ill times" forced them out of Pesth. There is only mention of the possibility of purchasing a new monastery at Waldhausen on the Ens, which for some time had been used as a private residence.[98]

Plans for an American Foundation

The abandonment of what had promised to be the principal support and means of growth for the Straubing house sounded again the knell to search for a new foundation if expansion was to be the order of the day. Back in Straubing[99] Knoll now unfolded a plan to come to America. He had first conceived of this major immigration while he was still in Hungary, when it became clear the foundation in Pesth would have to be abandoned. It was in the summer after Knoll set out for Pesth that the cloistered Ursulines of Straubing had been enticed to the Kentucky frontier.[100]

On the afternoon of August 24, 1858, Fr. Leander Streber,[101] a Franciscan priest from Louisville trudged along narrow Burggasse Street to the Ursuline domicile. He had been sent back to Europe by the bishop of Louisville to secure some nuns to staff his school at St. Martin's parish in that city. Louisville numbered approximately 50,000 souls with a number of Catholic churches, but only three of the edifices opened their doors particularly to the great German immigrant influx. Three days after his visit, a letter from the then residing bishop of Regensburg, Ignatius von Senestry, further encouraged the sisters to answer the call. With the permission of their Straubing superior, Mother Josepha, Mother Salesia Reitmeier, with her companions Mother Pia Schonhofer and Sr. Maximillian Zwingler, sailed for America on the Cunard Line's *Ariel* on September 28.

They arrived on October 20, 1858, in Louisville. The pioneer community established itself in a frame cottage on Campbell Street between

Kellar and Chestnut. In spite of numerous reverses and trials, the community continued to flourish. In 1860, they built their first motherhouse on Chestnut and Shelby Streets. In a short time, there were 20 boarders and 40 day students in the girls' academy with over 200 girls in the grammar school. To care for this expanded apostolate, postulants were recruited from the neighborhood. By 1864, with the arrival of more nuns from Straubing, the community numbered 15 professed sisters.[102]

The Carmelite house at Straubing obviously made little effort to answer Streber's plea for German priests to immigrate to Louisville. For one thing there were barely enough priests at Straubing to handle the Carmelite obligations in the neighborhood. Sossau and Poxau were new foundations taxing the strength of a community whose members were for the most part opposed to any rigorous expansion. At the same time, the two most talented figures of the community, Maier and Fritz, were in open rift, unable to agree on any policy. What there was of an expansionist element in the community had already set out for the new foundation in Hungary.

Nevertheless, the close ties that had existed on a personal basis between Knoll and the Ursulines[103] enabled Knoll to keep in close contact with the developments of their community in America. The mails brought a steady flow of information and on one occasion as a rejoinder to his own somewhat hesitant group in Pesth, he held up the courage and success of the Ursulines in America in undertaking their new establishment.[104] Back in Straubing, after the Pesth foundation collapsed, Knoll wrote to Fr. Leander Streber who had sought priests five years earlier for the mission fields of America. Knoll asked that the Carmelites be recommended to some bishop to whom they could be of service.[105] When the Ursulines at Louisville heard that Knoll was planning to initiate a foundation in America, they begged him to come to Louisville and become their confessor and catechist.[108] Fr. Streber also promised sufficient work at the parish, for he was much in need of an assistant.[107]

In writing to the prior general to receive his benediction and permission, which was needed before a religious could obtain a passport, Knoll explained the simple motive that promoted all his travels; "I am, have been, and will be wherever I am a Carmelite and I shall labor that our Order increase wherever I am."[108] Statements of this nature were needed to offset any impression that Knoll was merely looking for an easy solution to an unhappy situation. The Straubing community once again was in turmoil with his announced plans of expansion. The dissident element balked at any thought of a new foundation until they understood that

Knoll himself would go. Their sulking turned to joy with the prospect that this whirlwind character would be swept from their midst.[109] Since there were now a total of eleven priests and six brothers, Knoll could leave with some feeling of security that Straubing was a solid foundation.[110]

The response of the prior general to this new request reflected very clearly the superior general's own policies. His response was quick and affirmative:

> Hoping to provide for the needs of Catholics in these lands and the increase of the Order and its diffusion everywhere, gladly do we concede to you permission for setting out from Straubing to America and for transferring you there as commissary through our authority, with the power of establishing a convent there.[111]

Knoll issued no proclamation as to his purposes or goals in transplanting the Order to the United States. Just a few years before in 1845, Fr. Boniface Wimmer bore a similar task as Knoll—that of transplanting the Benedictine Order to America to care for the German colonists; he published his manifesto in that same year. The aims and methods it embodied propose the piece as the charter of the American Benedictines:

> What religious Order is most adapted for the American missions ... to provide for the spiritual necessities of German immigrants? In my opinion (the Benedictines) are the most competent to relieve the great want of priests in America ... History abundantly proves: that we owe the conversion of England, Germany, Denmark, Sweden, Norway, Hungary, and Poland almost exclusively to the Benedictines, and that in the remaining parts of Europe, Christendom is deeply indebted to them ...
>
> That this feature must be ascribed to the fact that the Benedictines are men of stability; they acquire lands and bring them under cultivation and become thoroughly affiliated to the country and people to which they belong ... That the Benedictine Order is so constituted that it can very readily adapt itself to all times and circumstances. ... The conditions in America today are like those of Europe one thousand years ago, when the Benedictine Order attained its fullest development and effectiveness by its wonderful adaptability and stability.[112]

This manifesto also adduced numerous schemes for promotion of higher education, the liturgy and a host of practical parochial objectives. The purpose of the Straubing Carmelites in coming to the German communities in the United States was admittedly not so well defined or planned. When Knoll wrote to the prior general, as quoted earlier, that "I am, have been, and will be wherever I am a Carmelite and I shall labor that our Order increases wherever I am," he proclaimed his simple manifesto. He was ready to undertake any apostolate to expand the Order and to that apostolate he would bring the traditions of Carmel.

The Carmelite Order takes its name from Mount Carmel, a mountain range in northwestern Palestine. Following the famous battle of Hattin in 1187, where a large Crusader army was defeated by the Saracen forces of Salidan, individuals displaced by the advances of the Sultan moved westward. Some of them were hermits who ended up at the Wadi 'ain-es Shiah on Mount Carmel.

Desiring to live as an eremitical religious community, they asked the Latin Patriarch of Jerusalem, Albert of Avogadro, sometime between 1206 and 1214 to write for them a Way of Life. The opening paragraph of Albert's *Formula Vitae* tells us that these hermits were gathered in cells near what has been known as the Fountain of Elijah, suggesting how the prophet was an inspiration and model for contemplative zeal for God from the earliest beginnings of the Carmelite Order.

Amidst their cells, these early Carmelites also constructed an oratory, dedicated to Mary. Recalling her continous podering of God's will which led her to selfless action for others, Mary has been viewed by Carmelites as a model for the active and contemplative dimensions of Carmelite life and as their Sister and Patroness. As a result, these religious men became known as the Brothers of the Blessed Virgin Mary of Mount Carmel by the time the Order had spread to Europe. There, the brown scapular became a popular symbol of Carmelite devotion to Mary.

As the eremitical life proved impractical in the West, the external organization of the Order was modified after the pattern of medieval friars, while its internal goals remained. By the fifteenth century, the Order had 37 provinces and hundreds of illustrious members, known for their sanctity, learning, and apostolic zeal. Carmel in England, France, Italy, Spain and the Low Countries, in particular, had areas where the Order was truly flourishing.[113]

It was these traditions and charisms, rooted in the history of the Order, which Knoll was preparing to bring to the New World.

In the midst of these preparations, Fr. Xavier Huber, who had accompanied Knoll on the ill-fated Hungarian expedition came under a severe ecclesiastical attack while acting as chaplain at Sossau. Joseph

Chapter One: Transit and Transition 27

Huber, the son of a carpenter, was born on July 23, 1819 at Kirchenreuth in Upper Bavaria. He entered the Straubing Carmel on February 24, 1844, with the express purpose of becoming a brother and serving the community's needs as a cobbler.[114] A report from his elementary school teacher, Joseph Obermuller at Riedenn, is typical of his excellent character references: "It is herein attested that Joseph Huber ... has attended the local elementary school and Sunday school for six years and very diligently with great industry and talent shown good progress. His moral deportment was always praiseworthy."[115] The same note of excellence sounded in the reports of the pastor of Altöttling, the seminary director, Bernard Hogl at Metelen, the parish priest at Rieden, where Huber had worked as sexton and janitor.[116]

He was professed in the Straubing Carmel on September 16, 1845, and received the religious name of Francis Xavier. Because of his talents, he was promoted to the priesthood on July 16, 1847.[117]

The official charge brought against Huber in 1863 was made by the bishop. Supposedly Huber had been encouraging the residents near Sossau to petition the bishop to allow them to separate from the city parish and establish Sossau as a distinct parochial unit.[118] There also was some idle gossip about undue time spent in the spiritual direction of women.[119] Though he was blameless, Fr. Peter Koehler, the prior, was forced to remove him since his apostolic endeavors were greatly hampered by this ill-begotten reputation.

A change of atmosphere would be good. As a result, Huber made a hasty decision to go with Knoll to America if the prior general would grant the permission. The prior general agreed provided Knoll was willing to have him as a companion. Knoll had been away at Munich visiting the offices of the Ludwig Missionsverein to obtain money for his trip to America, so as not to overburden the Straubing house with the new adventure. When he returned at the end of March 1864, he gladly agreed to take Huber with him to America.[120]

To cover the expenses of the trip for both, the Ludwig Missionsverein sent 600 florins on April 28, 1864.[121] The venture had been planned for the 23rd of April, but since the money for passage did not arrive by that date, the trip had to be delayed until May 2.[122] Accompanying the Fathers were three Ursulines, Mother Aloysia Schorner, Sister Wendelina Leipold, Sister Marina Greineder and two postulants, Mary Wenninger, later professed as Sister Antonia, and Mary Steinberger, the future Sister Georgianna.[123] The Cunard Line vessel left from Bremen on the 7th of May.[124] In their diary notations, the Ursulines described the trip as a voyage imperiled by continuous storms to such a degree that for a good part of the journey waves towered over the sides of the boat.[125] While they were on the high seas, the Carmelite prior general, Savini, went to the Congregation of Bishops and Regulars at the Holy See, where he was granted an audience on May 13. He presented the plan of the missionaries to the secretary of the Congregation for approval, so that when the two Carmelites arrived in the New World, they would have the full weight of authority behind their undertaking:

> Father Angelus Savini requests the Holy Father's permission that Father John Knoll of Straubing, a religious of proved virtue, unusual learning, about 45 years of age, be allowed to go to Luisvil [sic] in North America to found a religious house of the Order, assisted by Father Xavier Huber, his fellow religious, and to live outside the cloister until regular observance can be established.

To the prior general's petition came an affirmative answer.[126] The day of American disembarkation dawned on Trinity Sunday, May 22, 1864. Knoll recorded his first impressions:

> Not fully free of the sentiments which move the heart of an immigrant by leaving his fatherland, I landed at New York. I would gladly have remained here a few days in order to see one or the other of the two hundred and forty-nine churches of the Catholics here in the United States; however, pecuniary considerations forced me to speedy departure, since the immediate goal of our journey, Louisville on the Ohio River, was still so very far.[127] Thereto we travelled by way of Newark, St. Vincent's and Cincinnati. On June 8, 10 o'clock a.m., I was hail and sound at my destination.[128]

The stop at St. Vincent's Benedictine Abbey in Beatty, Pennsylvania, was to consult with the Archabbot Wimmer, who himself was somewhat of an authority on the German immigrants and their needs in the United States. He had been in Kansas in April of that year and could have informed them of the German needs there. For so long a time the attention of Wimmer had been attracted to the West. He felt the apostolate of the Benedictines to the German Catholics could be accomplished only if they had a foundation in the western states or territories, because these areas were attracting the great majority of German immigrants. "The West ought really to become our center of activity because it has the most Germans and the least priests; because these affairs are still developing, the Church ought not be without its influence there. The Bishop of Kansas is also continually urging me to send help. . . ."[129] Any encouragement Wimmer might have given them for settling in the West was undoubtedly strengthened by Kilian Guenther, whom they met on their trip. Guenther, a student at St. Vincent's, was attached to the Vicar Apostolic, Miege, whose headquarters were in Leavenworth, Kansas.[130]

At long last, they had completed their transit and were about to make a new foundation and beginning!

2
Chapter Two: FIRST FOUNDATIONS

Arriving in the United States to work with the Ursuline sisters from Straubing and the fast growing Catholic population in Louisville, Kentucky, Cyril Knoll and Xavier Huber found America burgeoning with new immigrants and many other possibilities for their ministry. While the earliest years of Carmel in North America saw the establishment of several foundations, those years also presented challenges for personnel, finances, formation of new members to the Order, and advancement of the faith among the laity.

From Kentucky to Kansas

THOUGH Sherman had yet to march to the sea and many months were yet to take their toll before Appomattox, the threat of war engulfing Louisville had long since passed. Louisville had been aroused in the early Fall of 1862 when Bragg and Kirby Smith carried the Confederate banner across Kentucky lines. Seldom did the Confederates ever find an opportunity so enticing. Kentuckians, despondent with the Union cause so recently embraced,[1] stood by as Smith occupied Central Kentucky and threatened Cincinnati. Bragg meanwhile was leisurely proceeding to Louisville, only to let Buell beat him there. On October 8, the bloodiest battle ever fought on Kentucky soil took place at Perryville.[2] Although the Confederates were driven from the state, the guerillas became a menace to river traffic as they sought their individual plunder. John Morgan so completely disorganized the traffic on the Ohio in the summer of 1863 that General Burnside forbade steamers to ply between Cincinnati and Louisville without permission and ample protection.[3] The river business was never completely freed from restrictions until the war ended.

Yet, by the summer of 1864, Louisville with a population just under 100,000 was reaping prosperity from the river trade.[4] Before the war, when traffic glutted the canal around the falls at Louisville, there were packet steamers running on regular schedule between Louisville and Liverpool.[5] A cavalcade of stage celebrities like the Barnum-sponsored Jenny Lind made their entrances and exits on the city's stages.[6] It was these forces of culture and commerce that made Louisville a rival of

Cincinnati, the Queen City of the West.[7] A new era, however, was beginning which would gradually shift commerce to the railroads and make of the glory of the river a tale that was told.

The Catholic community in Louisville emerged from the war none the worse. In 1848 when Martin J. Spalding was made co-adjutor bishop to Benedict Flaget, the whole Catholic population of the state of Kentucky was probably 30,000. Sixteen years passed and within that period Eastern Kentucky had been formed into a separate diocese with a see at Covington.[8] Names like Quinn and Long and Murphy and Riordan had been added to the list of "martyrs" who fell on that "Bloody August Monday" when religious prejudice dominated a gubernatorial election. But that was long past now. As sectional interests came to the fore, the short and typical career of the Know-Nothing party, which had avoided sectional issues, came to a close.[9] In 1864, the Catholic population of the diocese of Louisville alone was 70,000. In 1848 there were but 43 Catholic churches in the State; in 1864 there were 85 in the diocese of Louisville alone.[10]

Knoll and Huber found warm hospitality at St. Martin's rectory in the East end of the city where Fr. Leander Streber was pastor.[11] Three days after their arrival, Bishop Spalding received the papal rescript which named him archbishop of Baltimore.[12] The see of Baltimore was not only the oldest in the United States, but it was also the first in point of dignity. Its latest occupant, Archbishop Kenrick, whom Spalding had called "the greatest, best and most learned of our prelates,"[13] died on July 8 of the preceding year. Knoll and Huber were somewhat disappointed with the news of Spalding's appointment, for they were hoping the bishop would assign them a foundation. Now his concern could certainly not be with any new undertakings in Louisville. Spalding's brother, Rev. Benedict J. Spalding, was named as administrator of the diocese until a new bishop could be named.[14] The two Carmelites hoped this appointment would be soon.

In the interim period, Knoll and Huber were forced to seek work immediately, for their finances were limited. At the same time, St. Martin's offered few tasks for them to do as it was well staffed by Streber and his two assistants, Fr. John Nayhurst and Fr. B. Keller. Across the Ohio, some thirteen miles to the north of Louisville, lay St. Joseph's Hill in Clark County, Indiana. In 1853, the Catholics dedicated a small mission church there to St. Joseph where Mass was said by priests from Assumption parish at New Albany. The first resident pastor, Fr. Michael, built a brick rectory at a cost of $2000 in 1864 only to find himself transferred on April

Chapter Two: First Foundations

16 of that year to the Union Camp at Jeffersonville.[15] Bishop Maurice de Saint-Palais, then enjoying the fifteenth year of this episcopal reign at Vincennes,[16] was happy to entrust the parish to the Carmelites. The situation appeared ideal to Knoll who wrote: "Two priests and a lay brother could be stationed here. It seems to me this would be a good novitiate house —but where are the novices?"[17] The first recorded parochial activity by Knoll was the baptism of Regina Zeitvogel on June 26.[18] Two baptisms were performed by Knoll in June and from mid-July to mid-January of the following year the parish register shows seventeen baptisms by Fr. Huber.[19]

In mid-July Knoll was back in Louisville, oppressed by the heat and the burden of learning a new tongue which "while he was in Europe he always abhorred." He was assisting at St. Martin's and at the same time making arrangements for other assignments which he was sure he could obtain in Louisville or Leavenworth.[20] It was not many days, however, before Knoll gave up any hope of receiving a parish in Louisville. The third bishop of Louisville, Peter J. Lavialle, was not consecrated until Sunday, September 24, 1865.[21] This would have been too long a wait for as restless a spirit as Knoll's. On August 23, 1864, the Bavarian Carmelite followed Guenther's suggestion, supported no doubt by Archabbot Wimmer's account of Kansas, and wrote to Bishop Miege for a foundation.[22] Miege, in need of priests for his far-flung territory, welcomed any assistance.[23] Both he and Huber departed to the Kansas frontier. Knoll explained his decision in a few brief words.

> Louisville, a flourishing; city in which, a most beautiful Catholic life is unfolding: I would have gladly chosen for my residence for the remaining' days of my life, but I could not and I dared not in consideration of the mission given me by the most Reverend General of the Order. Convinced of the impossibility to begin anything definite for the establishment of our Order here in Louisville, I turned to the Indian territory which is now the state of Kansas.[24]

Little account has been left of their actual trip. The provincial historian Jerome Reichwein notes that "on account of the Civil War it was rather dangerous to travel through the state of Missouri. Hence, they selected a more safe but much longer way through the state of Illinois and the northern districts of Missouri by stagecoach."[25] Undoubtedly, the danger stemmed from the Confederacy's attempt to recapture Missouri through the raids of "Pap" Price in September and October of 1864.[26] "At nine p.m. on October 7," writes Knoll, "I and my travelling companion, Fr. Xavier, entered the residence of the bishop where we found a most kind reception and hospitality which was a compensation for the troubles of the journey."²⁷

Possessing as Bishop Miege did the happy combination of Alpine virility, proper to the Savoyards, tempered by a French finesse of manner and an imposing yet difficult bearing, he was peculiarly fitted to be the first resident ecclesiastical superior of a virgin country called the Great Plains. In his career as vicar apostolic could be found all that was best in the characteristics of the pioneer, self-sacrifice, suffering, energy, initiative, ruggedness, fortitude, and versatility.

In laying the foundation for Catholicism in Kansas, he was doing the work of a pioneer, clearing the way, breaking the soil, and forming a solid if unpretentious groundwork on which his successors could and did build.²⁸ James McGonigle, a business associate and a parishioner, offered a vivid sketch.

> He had the rare gift of being able to adjust himself to humors and characters. But one of his finest characteristics was the depth of his sympathy, springing from a broad, warm, human heart. . . . He was a remarkable handsome man with a commanding appearance whose presence would attract attention. He possessed a fine mind and was one of the most lovable of men. The most humble of his parishioners could always get his attention and be treated with the utmost courtesy and kindness.²⁹

In mid-July 1850, when Pope Pius IX in compliance with the request of the Seventh Provincial Council of Baltimore, named John Baptist Miege as vicar apostolic, there were but two Catholic Indian missions in his territory east of the Rocky Mountains (excluding Arkansas, Missouri, and the territory of Minnesota).³⁰ Settlement of the area needed the stimulus of the Kansas-Nebraska Bill in 1854. On June 13 of that very year a group of prominent Missouri slave owners drew up articles of incorporation for the first community in the new territory, Leavenworth City. The sectional alignment of organizations for the conquest of Kansas which followed and the bloodshed to which this alignment led gave the territory national significance and hastened its settlement.³¹"

The rapid settlement of the country confronted Miege with several problems. Among the first to be attacked were the location of his residence, the establishment of mission stations, and securement of priests to attend the religious needs of the immigrants. When the bishop made Leavenworth the administrative center of his nascent Church in 1855, he had only six priests and all of them were engaged at the Indian missions.³² Only nine families attended the first episcopal Mass, but by January 1859 there were some 2,000 Catholics in the cathedral parish.³³ The growing

Chapter Two: First Foundations

Catholic population included many Germans, their number increasing from between twelve to sixteen families in 1856,[34] to about sixty families in 1860.[35] The original parish was divided in 1858, and St. Joseph's church was built by Fr. Casimir Seitz, O.S.B., and dedicated July 10, 1859.[36]

The land and church building, which was a practical affair measuring thirty by sixty feet with room for a school and pastor's quarters in the lower story, had cost $4100.[37] A large part of this sum was raised by the parishioners although most of them were laborers.[38] The altar in the upper story of the structure was made by a parishioner, Sebastian Wager.[39] The Ludwig Missionsverein aided the parish with grants of 400 gulden in 1857, 600 gulden in 1858 and 600 gulden in 1861; the last sum helping to extinguish the debt.[40]

When Kansas was admitted to the Union as a state on January 29, 1861, Leavenworth was the metropolis of the West with a population of 7,000 and a $5 million freight business.[41] The state was far removed from the main theatres of the war and suffered principally from the hands of border ruffians. Leavenworth was full of soldiers in 1862. This condition led to the only incident of any importance directly affecting the Church in Leavenworth during the Civil War. The Ninth Regiment of Wisconsin on its arrival was quartered in St. Joseph's church without the formality of unlocking the doors, and apparently on the sole authority of one of its officers. Fr. De Coen, S.J., writing to a friend in Milwaukee described the intrusion.

> I found a sentinel walking up and down along the Communion railing. I asked him by whose authority he was there and who had broken open the church door. He told me that he was ordered to do so by his officer. The officer said he was sent by the captain; the captain could not be found.

As the pastor of the church, Fr. William Fisch, was ill and the bishop was on retreat, De Coen threatened to see the commandant of the fort. This sufficed to assure the removal of the troops. The only damage was a broken lock, some splintered pews, a dirty floor and some missing firewood.[43]

Fr. Fisch, who had been pastor at St. Joseph's since 1859, made a trip to Germany in 1860 on account of his health. He was not enthusiastic about Kansas but felt it his duty to return and did so early in 1861.[44] His ill health, however, continued. In 1864 he was again in Europe on that account and seems not to have returned.[45] Until the bishop could find a replacement, he named Fr. Anton Kuhls as the temporary pastor.[46] In such circumstances, Miege was more than pleased to gain the services of the two German Carmelites. On October 9, 1864 he formally transferred the care of St. Joseph's parish in Leavenworth to them.[47] A letter to the Carmelite prior general, Angelus Savini, two months later revealed Knoll's first impressions.

> Most of the buildings and homes of the city are entirely of wood as is also the house in which we dwell and our church both of which are under the same roof. The congregation is composed of about a hundred families who speak the German tongue. The entire number of inhabitants of all creeds may approach twenty thousand. There are sixteen churches of which two are Catholic, namely, the cathedral and our church. All things are going well. A small convent is being built, for already two priests of the diocese have asked to be clothed in the habit of our Order at the end of the present month of December.
>
> One of them is Joseph Heymam [sic] the other Kilian Guenther [sic], Joseph Heimann was born in 1815 and so stands in need of dispensation because of age; Kilian also needs a dispensation for having worn another religious habit. After wearing the habit of the Jesuits for seven months, he left them; for what reasons I did not inquire. Both priests are of great and exceptional merit whom the vicar apostolic honors with fond esteem, and whom he allows to take the habit only out of condescension to our Order . . . Both speak the English language which is so necessary and they are well known to the townspeople and enjoy their favor, a tie from which great advantages can accrue to our Order. Moreover, Fr. Heimann owns 160 acres of farmlands which he has already handed over to our Order. I humbly ask, therefore, that a dispensation be granted from these impediments and that the time of their novitiate be shortened so that they can be more readily sent forth to perform priestly duties both in the city and out in the country as the scarcity of priests demands be done. The Reverend Apostolic will also give us 80 acres adjoining those (lands) already mentioned for the support of the convent. These we are trying to enlarge as farmlands for the plots are cheap just now. Next spring it will be necessary for Fr. Xavier to go to Europe to take up as many collections as possible in order to build a church worthy of God and God's Mother here [where] not only city folk but also country dwellers may assemble who will visit us from a distance of twenty miles and more.[50]

Fr. Xavier had returned to the other St. Joseph's Carmelite parish in Indiana. The parish record there shows that he performed baptisms at least until January 22, 1865, despite the fact that Fr. Herman Panzer had been named pastor in early January.[51] In the meanwhile, when Fr.

Chapter Two: First Foundations

Guenther entered the new Carmelite novitiate just after the New Year, his parish at Eudora had been left without a pastor. Fr. Aloysius Mayer was transferred to that parish and Scipio, where he had formerly resided, was put in charge of the Carmelites and the novice, Fr. Guenther, was sent to reside there.[52]

The now famous Osage Catholic mission, founded by Jesuits and Sisters of Loretto from Kentucky in 1847, became the launching pad for many Catholic missions throughout southeastern Kansas.[53] Among the more prominent of these missions was that of the Pottawatomie settlement, later to be known as Scipio. Following passage of the Kansas-Nebraska Bill, a group of German colonists from Cole County, Missouri, settled in the valley along the Pottawatomie Creek.[54] They were joined by settlers from Illinois, who included Frank Fennhaus, Henry Wuestemeir, Christopher Wittkop, Christopher Feuerborn and Otto Wisebrock the following year.

When the wives of Feuerborn and Wisebrock died in 1855, victims of a fever, there was no priest near to attend them. In 1857, a child was born into the Wolken family for whom there was no priest to administer the sacrament of Baptism. The visits of the Jesuit Fathers from the Osage Mission house could be but casual and brief. In conference with the Rev. Bishop Miege, John Wolken obtained the promise that a Jesuit would visit their community once a month.[55] When Fr. Ivo Schacht came from Nashville to be the first resident pastor at Pottawatomie in the fall of 1858, the settlers began to construct a church. On March 13, 1859, the small building which measured only sixteen feet wide and twenty-eight feet long was dedicated and placed under the patronage of St. Boniface.[56]

Like the Osage Mission, St. Boniface's parish had numerous mission stations attached to it. Making his home in the settlement, Fr. Schacht journeyed forth to attend the Catholics residing in Anderson, Coffy, Franklin and Johnson counties.[57] In 1859, when the little log church of the settlement was scarcely finished, the bishop transferred Fr. Schacht to Lawrence, a fast-growing town that had become more important than the small colony on the Pottawatomie.[58] Fr. Schacht took up his residence in Lawrence and from there attended to the needs of his former parishioners until the appointment in the fall of 1860 of Fr. Aloysius Mayer as resident pastor at St. Boniface's church.[59] Mayer attended all the missions established by Schacht and even extended his mission territory as far south as Eureka.

Not only was Knoll concerned with caring for the needs of his new parishioners at St. Joseph's and St. Boniface's parishes, but he was faced with all the trials accompanying the establishment of a religious community. The mere establishment of Carmelite communities would not be enough to ensure the foundation and expansion of the Carmelite Order in America. Though his immediate occupation necessarily was mainly with external problems, Knoll's correspondence shows he was at least aware of the need to foster within his community an interior life based on Carmelite ideals. "We need three or four missals," he wrote to the prior general, "and as many or even more breviaries, some copies of the constitutions and a martyrology. As regards a directory on Carmelite life, I don't know what to do. I don't know how to compose nor do those brethren who are with me and will be with me in the future."[60]

Despite these difficulties Knoll was optimistic that the Order would take root and spread. Its appeal lay mainly in its spirit, in its dedication to silence, solitude and the spirit of prayer. On the noisy frontier, a community which offered some resemblance of organized religious life could be attractive to many a priest who spent the day in the saddle.

Knoll expressed his optimism in writing:

> The significance and importance of an Order whose members combine the contemplative life with the active life of the care of souls is in the widest sense of the word inestimable. The establishment of such an order in one of the most forsaken parts of the United States of America is certainly the object of the most firm desire of every Catholic wherever he may live and dwell.[81]

Knoll seemed to have no doubt that many priests would join the Carmelites, for he asserted: "If we would have the necessary rooms and the necessary means of living, the secular priests of Kansas without exception would have joined up."[62]

To accommodate these envisioned crowds, Knoll hoped to convert the present two-story structure at St. Joseph's into a monastery and at the same time, of course, to build a separate church. He petitioned the Ludwig Missionsverein for which he had often preached many times in Bavaria to assist him in the erection of the new church which he thought would cost between $30,000 and $40,000. Using every convincing argument, he ended his appeal with a final plea. "My petition is the petition of a Bavarian priest, supported by the powerful voice of the Church militant, suffering, and triumphant." This first appeal brought a return of 1250 francs. Knoll also sent Huber to Europe to beg for funds.[63]

Begging in the United States was not easy, for the people were short of means. But there were other reasons that made the task a daunting one. Discussing the collection taken up for St. Joseph's church a few years before, Heimann commented:

> Naturally the necessary money for the building has to be collected, but no business is more troublesome and disagreeable for the priest as to collect money for churches here in America, especially among the Germans. On his laborious and humiliating visits from door to door, he quite frequently comes to people who although born and educated in our holy faith, do not want to hear anything about God and religion. With scolding and rough words, he is greeted at entrances and if he dares to speak his mission, he is accused of keeping his flock in ignorance so that he can press them for more money. Another (parishioner) may cry out, "I will gladly give money to tear down the church but for the building of a church, I have no money."[64]

Huber left for Europe on May 2, 1865.[65] A visit to the prior general of the Carmelite Order in early fall encouraged the major superior to issue a letter approving of Huber's quest for funds and suggesting that Huber continue his collection in America.[66] Huber had every reason to expect profitable returns. Just prior to Fr. Huber's visit in Rome, the prior of the Carmelite community at Straubing had informed the prior general that the Catholic people in the town around his monastery were becoming more wealthy and quite generous.[67] Huber arrived at the Carmelite parish in Straubing on October 7. One of the brothers from the monastery, Simon Stock Edenhoefer, planned to return to America with Fr. Xavier when he sailed on November 4.[68]

In the meanwhile, Cyril Knoll had time to make a more accurate survey of his surroundings in Kansas. Two other candidates, Norbert Bausch and Angelus Kempen, had entered the community and were studying theology.[89] The commissary had also made the crucial decision. "It is intended," Knoll reported, "that this shall be the birthplace and cradle of our Order in America. This is at least my intention and my wish, if it be the Lord's."[70] To the Ludwig Missionsverein he penned this important letter on the condition of the German-Catholic immigrant:

> It is true that the Catholic Church in America is in a flourishing condition, but in spite of this it is a fact that, as a Catholic newspaper expresses it, 100,000 Catholics are lost annually that, as a bishop maintains, the United States should count 10,000,000 Catholics Instead of 2,000,000 if everyone who was born and raised a Catholic would profess allegiance to the Church. According to this statement there are at least 8,000,000 fallen-away Catholics. I can understand that statistic from the conditions here in our St. Joseph's parish. It numbers six to seven hundred souls but would surely count fifteen hundred if the majority had not fallen away.

And the ones that have fallen away are at times, people out of very Christian homes in old Bavaria. Why this sad condition? The cases here are too many. One of those causes is ignorance of the Catholic religion .... One cannot be surprised at this if he considers that the real dogmas of the faith are very seldom preached from the best pulpits. Preachers do not consider this necessary.

They are satisfied with the usual moral sermons, especially since the people like them .... Of ignorance in religious matters is for thousands the reason of their falling away from the Church; the lack of priests is still more so a cause. Faith comes from hearing; the hearing has to come from the sermon on the word of Christ. Most of the immigrants are forced according to their circumstances and conditions to seek places in which sometimes no priest has been seen for years. Therefore it happens that for years they would not hear a sermon, attend Mass or receive the sacraments.

In the beginning, many of them make a trip of 100 and 200 miles in order to go to confession and communion at Easter time. But gradually this fervor becomes cold even among the best ones; a man gets used by and by to live without a sermon, without Mass, without sacraments, and he quiets his conscience with the thought: "Well, the Church law does not oblige in times of necessity." And the children of such Catholics grow up without religious instruction in ignorance even of the most necessary truths of faith. They enter in the state of marriage, become fathers and mothers without having been baptized themselves .... Finally, if one considers the efforts of Protestant agents and the snares of the Freemasons, he will not be surprised over the fact that so many Catholics in America have fallen away.[71]

Knoll's conclusions were hardly startling. On the contrary, since 1836 when Bishop England sent his famous letter[72] to the Society for the Propagation of the Faith with the unscientific guess that 1,200,000 Catholics had already been lost to the faith in the United States, few problems have been more widely discussed and controverted among Catholics themselves than that of the so-called "leakage."[73] But, the letter the commissary had written was timely, for the number of German immigrants was to vastly increase. Catholics made up an average of around 35% of the total German immigration to the United States during the years after the Civil War. They totaled around 700,000 in number from 1865 to 1900, and were to become the largest Catholic immigrant group arriving in the States.[74]

The primary cause for the increased immigration was the militaristic policies of Otto von Bismarck. Jealousy and antagonism between Prussia and Austria, the two leaders of the German Confederation established after the Congress of Vienna, came to a head in 1866 in the Seven Weeks' War from which Prussia emerged the victor. The Seven Weeks' War had been preceded in 1864 by the Schleswig-Holstein War between Denmark on the one side and Austria-Prussia on the other. Denmark was defeated, and the division of the spoils was one of the contributory causes of the Austro-Prussian War. This victory, together with the later split between Prussia and Austria, and the unification of northern Germany, had not, however, been accomplished without cost to the German people. The echoes of the revolutionary days of 1848 were yet reverberating when in 1862 the Prussian parliament, resenting the imperialistic, and militaristic policy of William I, refused to appropriate any funds for military purposes. Bismarck, thereupon, called to the post of prime minister, proceeded to ignore the wishes of the parliament. He reorganized the army by great expenditures and by a stricter system of military service. To Germans burdened with increasing taxes, the United States Homestead Act of 1862 offered cheap lands on the American frontier with the hope of a bright future.[75]

On January 19, 1866, Huber came back from Europe with the proceeds from his fund raising campaign. The returns were meagre.[76] The impatience which had characterized so much of his European undertakings once again prompted Knoll to look elsewhere for a Carmelite foundation.[77] If the Order was to expand in America, candidates were needed. New candidates needed to be housed and without funds a shelter could not be provided. It was true that Leavenworth was a city on the rise. It had secured a railroad connection with Weston, Missouri and the levee was handling tonnages similar to those seen on the docks of salt-water ports. Employment was on the rise in the wagon, shoe and stove factories.[78] The Kansas-Pacific Railway was also attracting foreign tourists to the frontier. It ran special round-trip excursions daily from Leavenworth to Lawrence for ten dollars to anyone who wanted to "bag a buffalo." Its posters showed herds of buffalo stopping its trains and its circulars boasted that "buffaloes are so numerous along the road that they are shot from the cars nearly every day."[79]

EXPANDING TO CUMBERLAND, MARYLAND

Despite these prognostications for an opulent future, Knoll felt he needed funds immediately. Before the end of the year, the two-story structure would be redone so as to accommodate five rooms within the cloister and two additional bedrooms outside. At the same time a separate school would be erected.[80] But even these enlarged quarters would not be able to hold the numbers Knoll believed would be willing to join the Carmelites had he the room to provide for them. Besides those American candidates whom he expected to volunteer, the General was sending Carmelites from Europe to the new foundation. Frater Alexis Lenarkiewicz and Fr. Evodius Baszez had received their obediences to go to the United States on January 25, 1866.[81] When Huber had been in Europe he was to return with Simon Edenhoefer, a brother from the monastery at Straubing. There was, however, some confusion in plans, for the Ludwig Missionsverein was petitioned for his passage money to sail with some Ursuline nuns and Benedictine Fathers on November 15.[82] At the time, the German aid society was unable to pay his passage,[83] but Knoll was aware that the brother might arrive in the United States at any time.

Miege, who had viewed the Carmelites as an answer to his manpower needs in the diocese, was more than disappointed to hear of a proposed move East that Knoll was supposedly contemplating.[84] The relationship between Bishop Miege and the Carmelite Order had promised to be a lasting one. On September 8, the date on which a Scapular Confraternity was erected at St. Joseph's;[85] Miege was granted the supreme honor of affiliation with the Order.[86] The commissary's decision to establish the main foundation of the Carmelites in the East met with loud disapproval from all of his mid-western novices. They argued that there were too many Orders well established in the eastern United States to "compete" with for vocations. A more serious objection centered around the complaint that they would be left without any Carmelite to guide them in the ideals and spirit of the Order to which they were about to make their profession of vows.[87] This was an uncontestable problem which deserved more attention than Knoll seemed to give to it.

Albert Heimann and Louis Guenther were professed on the feast of St. Joseph, 1866, in St. Joseph's church at Leavenworth.[88] Kempen was ordained on August 24, 1866, by Miege.[89] Their novitiate training in Carmelite life can only be described as inadequate. As soon as Kempen joined the Carmelites he spent his days teaching in the school for the Catholic boys of Leavenworth.[90] Heimann and Guenther also spent their novitiate teaching there and assisting at Scipio.[91] The mission stations connected with Scipio needed to be maintained which meant many hours in the saddle riding to such places as Greeley, Emerald, Ottawa, Westphalia, and Olathe. Catholics in Miami, Anderson, Franklin, Coffey, Washington, Republic, Cloud, Nemaha, and Marshall counties all received their care.[92] When Knoll moved East, Heimann returned to St.

Chapter Two: First Foundations

Joseph's in Leavenworth and Kempen was stationed at Scipio.[93]

The promise of a regular community life which the Carmelite Order held out never was able to materialize for these early novices. Knoll was necessarily more worried about collecting a community and obtaining foundations before he could be concerned with fostering religious life in the foundations. Undoubtedly, however, there was a close interplay between both elements and neglect of attention to the Carmelite life could not but weaken the Carmelite foundations. Heimann was an elderly priest set in his ways; the other members were too young to have been formed in any way. It was too much to expect that any of the newly professed members could imbibe the Carmelite spirit in such a short period or in such a haphazard manner. Heimann summed up their bitterness at such a disappointing training.

> From the beginning of the New Year (1865) to the end of July, Fr. Louis [Guenther] and I taught the children to help support us in the beginning and after that we attended the missions. It was a poor way of making a novitiate and consequently a very poor way of making a thorough religious, but considering circumstances as they were, we had to be satisfied. Yet, if Father Cyril had cared for our happiness in this life and in the life to come, he ought to have provided for us at least some instructions in the Rule and Constitutions of the Order. But, not even once for one quarter of an hour was this done. If money was brought in, everything else was all right. The rules could be easily dispensed with. That was our novitiate. After the novitiate, Fr. Louis returned to St. Boniface alone, eighty-five miles from Leavenworth. I went on a mission in the northwestern part of the state, one hundred to two hundred miles from Leavenworth, travelling on horseback, hunting up scattered Catholic families in the state. Certainly this was a very disagreeable way of living, but we looked forward to brighter days. [94]

By mid-1866, Knoll reported he was ready to move east to Cumberland, Maryland with the permission of the Bishop of Baltimore.[95]

The provincial of the Redemptorists, Fr Helmpraecht, had visited St. Joseph's before that decision and had persuaded Knoll to come East where a more rapid expansion for Carmel was assured.[96] But what made the suggestion even more enticing was the fact that the Redemptorist monastery at Cumberland which Helmpraecht offered to sell to Knoll was already designed for a novitiate. With this in mind, Knoll asked the prior general to send a priest from Straubing to act as a master of students for the novices and clerics who would soon seek admission. His preference was for either Joseph Maier or Fritz.[97] The new monastery at Cumberland could house fifty friars and its closeness to New York, fifteen hours by water, and other large urban areas offered a promise of more vocations.[98] Moreover, the provincial of the Redemptorists promised to recommend any candidates he might find to Knoll.[99] The price paid for possession of St. Peter and Paul monastery was $20,000; the sum was to be paid in regular cash installments or by saying Masses for which the Redemptorists Fathers had retained a stipend.[100] This was a staggering debt but the fact that it was paid in nine years indicates that the decision was not financially imprudent. Those who opposed the action were forced in similar circumstances to do the same thing.

As early as 1840, German Redemptorists had begun to visit Cumberland three or four times a year to attend the spiritual wants of Catholics. Leaving Baltimore on Friday, they drove in their own carriages along the National Pike, remaining in Cumberland over Sunday, and starting homeward again on Monday morning. Each trip consumed at least five or six days, and was necessarily expensive and fraught with many dangers. This inconvenient mode of travel was naturally abandoned after the Baltimore and Ohio was built and passenger trains were running on reasonably regular time.[101] St. John Neumann, as superior of the Redemptorists, visited Cumberland after Christmas 1847 and managed to purchase a plot of ground overlooking Wills Creek and the Potomac River. The deed was drawn in the name of the Archbishop of Baltimore and the German settlers there began the foundations of a new church.[102] On July 4, 1848, the cornerstone was laid by Archbishop Eccleston. The first resident pastor of Sts. Peter and Paul's church, as it was named, was Rev. Anthony Urbanszeck.

Almost as soon as a small monastery was completed, Redemptorist students began to make their appearance in Cumberland in April, 1851.[103]

Fr. Van de Braak, a veteran Wittem professor who served as lecturer in theology at the new seminary, held the pastorate of the parish from 1854 to 1857. He made an addition to the monastery at an expense of $20,000. The students had by this time increased to thirty-five in number. Theology and philosophy were both taught in the monastery and on all extraordinary occasions the students took part in the church ceremonies. The community at the close of Fr. Van de Braak's administration numbered seventy members. The spiritual condition of the parish also appeared excellent; the church records show an average of about 10,000 communions received yearly. The Reverends Francis Xavier Seelos and Michael Muller held pastorates at Sts. Peter and Paul's before the Carmelites arrived.[104] During the Civil War the Redemptorists Fathers

Chapter Two: First Foundations

experienced several disagreeable ordeals. On one occasion when the Indiana Zouaves were encamped around Cumberland, a captain stormed the building with armed men to search for Confederate weapons of war which were supposedly concealed in the monastery.[105] In June 1862, the student body was transferred to Annapolis and the novices who had been at Annapolis were sent to Cumberland.[106]

The Redemptorist historian Wuest states that there were two main reasons for selling the property to the Carmelites. In the first place, he notes that the high altitude of Cumberland and the rigors of the mountain winters had been injurious to the health of the Redemptorist students. Pulmonary consumption had carried a few to the grave. Wuest also states that the Redemptorist provincial who was then living in Baltimore desired to have the novitiate closer to his residence.[107] More recent research, however, reveals that both the superior general of the Redemptorists, Mauron, and the provincial of the Baltimore Province, Helmprecht, wanted to maintain primarily only mission houses without the care of souls. For the same reason, Helmprecht relinquished an established foundation at Detroit,[108] Fourteen Holy Martyrs parish in Baltimore,[109] and Holy Redeemer parish in Rochester.[110] These foundations did not fit into his concept of what a Redemptorist foundation in the United States should be. There was feeling that the care of souls in parishes was somewhat a betrayal of the ideal proposed by St. Alphonsus. He seems to have preferred to limit Redemptorist activity to only missions, talks, and spiritual exercises. But as the coming decades were to prove, this school of thought failed to note and accurately appraise the exigencies of the times forced on all religious orders as a result of the tremendous flow of immigration.[111]

On September 10, 1866,[112] Frs. Cyril Knoll and Louis Guenther left Leavenworth with Br. Simon Edenhofer for Cumberland. Edenhofer had received passage payment from the Ludwig-Missionsverein and sailed from Germany on May 15.[113] The details of their trip back East are not recorded. The Commissary did contact Fr. Huber at St. Charles, Missouri, where he was collecting alms at the prior general's instigation for the proposed monastery in Leavenworth.[114] Knoll and Edenhoefer reached Cumberland on October 3 and by the time the monastery was formally presented to the Carmelites on October 21, Fr. Guenther and Fr. Philip Vogg had also arrived.[115] Philip Vogg had been the first Benedictine to visit Marshall County in Kansas. He was ordained March 17, 1860 by Bishop Miege.[116] He was the first new recruit for the Cumberland monastery. Huber completed the new Carmelite community when he came to Cumberland on October 30.[117] Knoll made his first down payment of $2,000 to the Redemptorists upon his arrival.[118] That sum, unfortunately, represented the alms that Huber had collected for expanding facilities at Leavenworth and also stipends for Masses said by Knoll at Leavenworth.[119] The Carmelites that Knoll had left behind, to care as best they could for his Kansas houses, felt the money should have been invested in developing Carmelite foundations on the frontier instead of in the East. This point was to become a bone of contention for many years to come.

At the same time the monastery was given to the care of the Carmelites, Sts. Peter and Paul's parish was also handed over to their trust. The financial status of the parish was in good order. Three months previous to the transaction, the roof of the church had been covered with slate at a cost of $1,185.94. To meet this expense a sum of $1,049.50 had been realized by means of a raffle for a music box and by special collections. When the account ledger was given to the Carmelites on October 20, the cash assets of the parish showed $686.14.[120]

The primary reason for moving to Cumberland was outlined in a letter to the Ludwig Missionsverein:

> Because of the circumstance that Kansas is so very far from the landing places of the immigrating Europeans, I decided to move closer to the East and this was made possible for me through the friendly relations of the present provincial of the Redemptorist Fathers .... Since everything which belongs to a monastery according to the ideas I brought along from Germany is present in their house, I thought we might risk it ($20,000). I left (Kansas) with two priests of the Order and a lay-brother .... Our meager resources are thus split and divided between Leavenworth and Cumberland. But this fact does not cause any extra worry since I am now in a condition to receive candidates for the Order who until now had to be refused on account of lack of room. I am able to find them a cell, to introduce them into the rules of community life, which I have already begun at this time.[121]

There were secondary motives behind this move and these he explained to the Archbishop of Baltimore:

> If God will second my plans, I intend to establish here in our large house, after some time, a kind of an academy for boys, which may serve even as a preparatory school for the ecclesiastical state. If your Grace be pleased with such work and would lend me your kind assistance in accomplishing it, I would, indeed, be greatly encouraged in my undertakings. Besides this project, I see how abandoned the people on these different mission sta-

Chapter Two: First Foundations

tions are. Therefore, I have conceived another idea, which, if carried out, would be of great help to these poor mountaineers. In case I should get enough Fathers, I would like to have two priests at Westernport permanently who could attend to all the different mission stations around. And, if Frostburgh had a priest, the whole of Alleghany County would be more than satisfactorily supplied with priests. . . .[122]

The Archbishop initially seemed eager to have the Carmelites undertake the care of all the souls around Cumberland in the nearby mission stations which the Redemptorists had staffed.[123] The main missions the Carmelites were called to staff were at Westernport, Oakland, Lonaconing, and Barton.[124] Westernport was originally laid off in land grants, given as a bonus to the soldiers of the American Revolution at the confluence of the Georges Creek and the Potomac River. The grading of the Baltimore and Ohio Railroad in 1849 brought many Catholic young men to Westernport, the majority of whom were Irish. With the opening of coal mines in the Piedmont Valley, Fr. Slattery, at that time pastor of Frostburg, erected in 1857 St. Peter's church, the first Westernport church. A parochial school was begun under the Redemptorists by Fr. Eberhardt.[125] St. Peter's church at Oakland, on Oak Street between Fourth and Fifth Streets, was also relatively new. It was dedicated on June 29, 1852.[126] On Christmas, 1865 the Holy Sacrifice of the Mass was offered for the first time in St. Mary's church, Lonaconing.[127]

The settlement at Barton was a rather strange mixture of Scotch, English, Welsh and Irish immigrants. Fr. O'Reilly of Frostburg gave a cryptic description of Barton in 1860: "Work was plentiful, wages high, and whiskey about twenty-five cents a gallon." When the Carmelites took charge of the mission, the parishioners numbered nearly six hundred souls. The tasks of erecting a new church fell upon Fr. Philip Vogg. Though the people admired him for his priestly zeal, they were somewhat dismayed at his lack of administrative ability. The site he chose for the new church was in a marsh-ridden flatland, affording the most prosaic view for miles.[128]

A description of Sts. Peter and Paul's church in Cumberland at this time is best seen in Knoll's own words

> The church attached to the community is a parish church for the German community of two hundred and fifty families, some of whom have emigrated from the diocese of Regensburg. The divine services are really very solemn so that on Sunday and on feast days one would imagine himself to be in a city parish church in Bavaria. The religious life of the community has been promoted by the zeal

of the Redemptorist Fathers so that in the confessional and in the pulpit we have more to do than we really are able to do. The school has about two hundred children. Two ladies are doing the teaching. As soon as some of our vacant rooms have enough occupants, we shall open a kind of boy's seminary. I have good hopes for its success because of the encouragement extended to me not only on the part of the Catholics but also on the part of the Protestants.[129]

The immediate transfer of all these parochial assignments to the Carmelite's care placed an almost insurmountable burden on the three priests. Bishop Miege in Kansas was beseeching Knoll to send back the help he had promised for the beleaguered community in Kansas. Knoll had petitioned the General in Rome, Savini, to send some priests who spoke English to assist in the missions.[130] The Commissary could not detain Fr. Xavier in parochial work any longer. The Commissary in these early days was dependent on the alms Huber could collect by preaching as he made a circuit around the country.[131]

Beyond Cumberland: A Need for New Ministry Sites

A crisis was reached in mid-summer, 1867. Shortage of manpower and a plethora of assignments forced Knoll to consider abandoning either Cumberland or Leavenworth. The entire affair reflected once again his inability to bestir a spirit of buoyancy comparable to his drive for expansion. In a letter to the prior general, he weighed the pros and cons of surrendering either Leavenworth or Cumberland. Cumberland offered spacious quarters in comparison to the five rooms for religious in Leavenworth. Furthermore, the debt at Cumberland had already been reduced from $20,000 to $14,800. A large sum of money would be needed to build in Leavenworth and at St. Boniface's in Scipio. The proceeds from Cumberland amounted to nearly $1,400 yearly not including stipends, whereas in Leavenworth, the annual returns were only $700 and at St. Boniface's $200. In Cumberland there were many aspirants "pounding down the doors" whereas only a few elderly priests had tried to gain admission in Leavenworth. Yet there were bad points about Cumberland: The services rendered by the Carmelites were not vitally needed in the East. The parishes entrusted to them could be assigned to the secular clergy on a moment's notice. The Archbishop of Baltimore appeared disinterested in their affairs, whereas Bishop Miege was friendly and desired their return. And what was more, the land acquired in Kansas would always provide sustenance and eventually with enough hands might bring in extra funds. Furthermore, both Huber and Guenther were anxious to return to Kansas, unwilling to take on the burdens of Cumberland.[132]

Chapter Two: First Foundations

In the fall of 1867 two young Irish Carmelites, Fr. Peter Thomas Meagher (Maher) and Fr. Theodore McDonald, who had been promised earlier, arrived from Rome.[133] They had graduated from the famous Carmelite College of the Immaculate Conception at Knocktopher, among whose graduates (1852-1899) were over 400 priests, and then went to Rome to be at the general's disposal.[134] To have two English speaking priests was in Knoll's words "an acquisition for which I cannot thank God enough."[135] Their arrival was extremely timely for Huber had displeased Knoll with his unspecified "practice of medicine" and he banished him to Kansas on December 19.[136]

Knoll had followed closely a policy of encouraging only ordained priests who had spent several years in the ministry to join the Carmelites. Such personnel required little training in priestly duties. Knoll also supported this policy by asserting that "a young cleric can be conscripted for military action, even though he be a priest."[137] The elderly type priest, however, who was attracted to a religious order often had been troubled with a personal problem or a difficulty with some other religious order. A collection of this type of religious made for a trying and cantankerous community. This was the case at Cumberland.

The year 1868 was one of tribulation. Pius Mayer writing some years later placed the blame on the Fathers in Kansas who supposedly obtained a mandate from the prior general in Rome ordering the Cumberland Fathers to return to the Midwest.[138] The dismissal of Huber to Kansas persuaded Fr. Philip Vogg to leave since Fr. Xavier had been his closest friend at Cumberland.[139] In the wake of the confusion that followed Huber's reassignment, Angelus Kempen, who had come to Cumberland in December of 1867, interviewed the Archbishop in Baltimore with a view to secularization.[140] Hilarion Driessen, another candidate, apostatized.[141] When Huber arrived in Kansas, embittered by Knoll's action, he sent a sharp report to Savini in Rome:

> Fr. Knoll bought the monastery in Cumberland for $20,000 which we shall scarcely be able to pay off in twenty years. The house can hold seventy and when will we have that many? Maybe fifty years from now. The fear of the building falling apart and the fact that the area was hardly conducive to the pursuit of studies were the reasons why the Redemptorists sold it after six years. Fr. Cyril bought it at night without seeing it. There are many orders in the diocese—Passionists, Jesuits, Dominicans, Redemptorists. An independent prior should be appointed for Kansas. We have $6,000. So great is the immigration that three new churches are being built here. Many priests and laymen would enter our Order

but Cumberland the novitiate is 1500 miles away. The bishop and our neighbors will help erect a monastery. The distance and the expenses and dangers in travelling to Cumberland are great. Under Fr. Cyril's rule nothing has prospered neither in Hungary, nor in Bavaria, nor so far in America.[142]

The report was a ringing denunciation of Knoll's policies. The pressure to expand had already been felt by the Fathers in Kansas before Fr. Xavier returned. His report to them, tinged with bitterness, only assured them that Cumberland with its multiple mission stations and low income could never help materialize their dreams for progress. Knoll was upset at the turbulence expressed in the Kansas foundations and suggested that Bishop Miege had prompted the Carmelites in his territory to seek a separation from the Commissary's jurisdiction. Fr. Cyril did acknowledge that the distance between the several foundations argued for a separate superior for St. Joseph's and St. Boniface's priories, but he knew of no religious among his men competent to hold such a position.[143]

On July 15, 1868, two Carmelites, Fr. Anastasius Smits and Br. Berthold came to Cumberland from England.[144] Their unexpected arrival is shrouded in mystery. On March 2, the prior general had given permission to Fr. Smits to seek alms[145] necessary to build a Carmelite house at Merthys Tydvill, South Wales.[146] What sort of funds either of them expected to collect in a country that was dependent itself on the generosity of Europe is unknown. They had disembarked on April 16 and were collecting alms in New York when the prior general ordered them to report to Cumberland.[147] On the very day of their arrival, Knoll received word from the archbishop that he intended to place the mission stations surrounding Cumberland in the care of the diocesan clergy. Knoll's immediate response was to be expected in view of his past decisions. He declared he would abandon Cumberland and seek another foundation![148]

The archbishop's announcement was merely one in a series of causes which made Knoll reconsider his commitment to Cumberland. The truth of the matter was that Cumberland had neither prospered financially nor in terms of vocations. The income for 1867 was $3,834.52 against $3307.22 in debts.[149]

As regards vocations, Smits later wrote: "Fr. Helmprecht promised to send him candidates. The novices came. This was the unfortunate beginning in Maryland. Many of these prospective Carmelites, in fact a number were either of doubtful character or they were discharged novices of the Redemptorists."[150] Apparently, the only novice to complete his course as a Carmelite was Fr. Bernard Fink. Smits reports that the more serious minded members of the house were disturbed over such candidates whom Knoll had say Mass and preach.[151] Mayer and Smits[152] indicate that Smits was named prior and novice master of Cumberland at this time and that this appointment angered Knoll.[153]

For the next several months, the house was in turmoil. There were several problems connected with the candidates accepted by Fr. Knoll. There were national differences between the Germans, Irish and Dutch. There was great discord about whether the future development of Carmelites should be as parish priests, educators, or as home missionaries. Fr. Cyril's views on lineage had been tersely stated a month before: "A German is a German although he has shaken off the dust of his fatherland and everywhere a true German longs for a greater Germany. I am one of those who wants to remain a German."[154]

In November 1868, Frs. Anastasius Smits, Peter Thomas Meagher, Theodore McDonald, and Br. Berthold sought permission to leave and found a new house.[155] Simon Edenhoefer even attempted to return to Straubing. At the same time, Louis Guenther was sent back to Kansas. His report to the Fathers there only encouraged them to seriously consider joining the ranks of the secular clergy since Knoll had been unable to support them with manpower or money from Cumberland.[156]

In the first week of November there was a great flurry of letters to the prior general as each of the disputants presented his case.[157] Unfortunately, the prior general felt he was not able to support his delegate and never again was Fr. Cyril able to exert his full authority. Problems arising from personality differences were given as much credence as those trials that stemmed from administrative difficulties. Savini rushed letters of pacification to the Fathers in Kansas.[158]

At the end of the year, Knoll, as usual, had already set his sights on a new foundation. Writing to the Archbishop of Baltimore, he stated that he had counted on the missions attached to Cumberland to help contribute funds to pay off the debt he had accumulated at Cumberland. Although the Carmelites had no intention of leaving the diocese permanently, Frs. McDonald and Maher were being sent out to Bishop James Duggan in Chicago who had invited them to open a house there.[159]

But, it seems that the Fathers surrounding Knoll had other plans once they left Cumberland. "The three of us—Frs. Maher, McDonald, and myself," writes Smits "devised ways and means of getting away from that nest and obtaining a new place to make a clean start. It was resolved that I go to Chicago and obtain a place from Bishop Duggan, which he promised me cheerfully. On December 7, however, he wrote to the

Archbishop of Baltimore for our recommendation but that was against us, whereupon Bishop Duggan withdrew his promise."[160] Smits then turned to New York.

> We wrote to our Fr. General explaining the status quo at Cumberland, whereupon he ordered us to look for a new foundation in or about New York, where we three were to make a new start. I went to New York, but the Archbishop, afterwards Cardinal McCloskey, would not hear of the Carmelites coming into his diocese. He would not even let me say Mass in any church, but only in a private convent chapel. The cause I heard afterward was that our poor Father Xavier Huber had very imprudently been collecting money in New York to pay on the debt of the new church at Leavenworth. The Archbishop was very angry and indignant at us.[161]

Fr. Smits' next attempt was in New Jersey where some of his relatives lived. He recounted his experience there some years later.

> Bishop Bailey (sic) of Newark gave me Englewood and all of Bergen County under the condition that I bring with me Fathers Maher and McDonald. When these two on their way to me came through Baltimore, they called on the archbishop. On the plea of a friendly visit for a few days, he kept them until he got by wire an order from the Genl (sic) Savini for them to stay with him. Then he gave them little places in Prince George County where they had about 2,000 Negroes to attend to and a few Catholic planters. Bishop Bailey (sic) of Newark was very angry for their not coming forward. He advised me to become a secular priest and to stay with him. I said nothing but remained alone where I was at Englewood.[162]

Left to his own resources Fr. Smits and Br. Berthold had gone to Jersey City on February 1, 1869, when Smits was given charge of Fort Lee and several missions.[163]

Fr. Smits was very downhearted at being left alone, but the two Irishmen seemed pleased to have their own foundation away from Cumberland. Fr. Meagher wrote to Archbishop Spalding:

> Your very kind offer of Upper Marlboro and the annexed churches to us has been most gratefully received by all our Fathers here. We return our most sincere thanks and hope through the assistance of God and the Blessed Virgin Mary, our holy mother and patroness, that we will succeed in the faithful discharge of our duty towards that congregation, and secure for ourselves a permanent home. I have written to Mrs. Graham to know how soon those persons who reside in the parish house will be able to vacate it. When I get

her letter I can decide on the time to go down as I would have no business there until the house would be ready. When I get her note I will write your Grace.[164]

Knoll summed up what happened very tersely: "Just a few days ago eighteen people lived here; most are gone. Frs. Maher and McDonald left for Marlboro; they intend to remain joined with us. Where Fr. Smits and Br. Berthold have gone I don't know and I am not sorry."[165]

Thus began the seeds of two separatist movements that were to bring even greater discord and less results than had been witnessed under the sole regime of Cyril Knoll.

From the Archives

Facade and steeple of the Carmelite church in Straubing, Germany. Straubing is located on the Danube river in the southern or Bavarian region of the country. *(Photo Courtesy of William J. Harry, O. Carm.)*

Exterior of the *Karmelitenkloster*, the oldest Carmelite house with a continuous presence of Carmelites. The house was founded in 1368 by Carmelites from Regensburg. *(Photo Courtesy of William J. Harry, O. Carm.)*

View of the internal cloister courtyard of the Carmelite monastery in Straubing, Germany. *(Photo courtesy of William J. Harry, O. Carm.)*

From the Archives

Peter Heitzer (1777-1847), "the last German Carmelite," who saved the house in Straubing from closure by appealing to the government to reopen the novitiate. Permision was given on July 4, 1841. This portrait hangs in the refectory of the monastery. *(Photo courtesy of the William J. Harry, O. Carm.)*

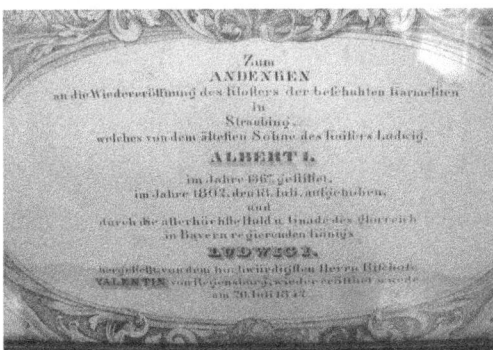

Plaque which reads "In memory of the reopening of the monastery of the calced Carmelites in Straubing, which was founded by the eldest son of Emperor Ludwig, Albert I in the year 1367, dissolved in the year 1807, on July 18th, and recreated by the sovereign grace and graciousness of the gloriously governing King in Bavaria Ludwig I, reestablished by Most Reverend Bishop Valentine of Regensburg, on July 20th, 1842"

King Ludwig I of Bavaria in Royal Robes, original by Joseph Stieler, copy by Langermaier, original date 1826. Saint Vincent Archabbey Art Collections, Latrobe, Pennsylvania.

From the Archives

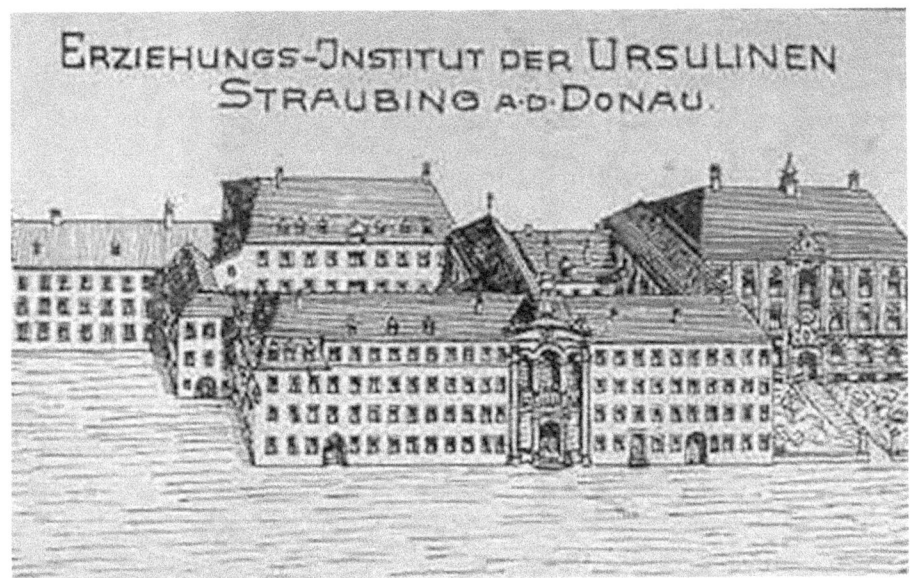

Engraving of the Ursuline convent and school in Straubing, Bavaria, before 1858. The building is located behind the Carmelite monastery. Cyril Knoll had been a chaplain to the sisters in Straubing and was invited to join them in Louisville. The Ursulines had already founded a school for girls and worked among the German immigrants there. *(Courtesy of the Archives of the Ursuline Sisters of Louisville, KY).*

Mother Salesia Reitmeier, the leader of the group of Ursuline sisters from Straubing who settled in Louisville, Kentucky, in 1858. By 1864 there were 15 professed sisters in the Louisville community. *(Courtesy of the Archives of the Ursuline Sisters of Louisville, KY.)*

From the Archives

(Above) **St. Joseph's Parish, St. Joseph Hill in Sellersburg, Indiana**, was the first Carmelite parish in the United States and was administered by the Carmelites from June to December of 1864. Pictured above is the parish as it looked during the pastorate of Franz Xavier Huber, O. Carm. *(Photo courtesy of the Archives of the PCM Province)*

(Left) **St. Joseph's Church, Leavenworth, Kansas,** the oldest foundation still served by the Carmelites in the United States. It was received by the Carmelites from Bishop Miege in 1864. This is a modern picture of the church and school building, built by Albert Heimann, O. Carm.

From the Archives

(Above) **Original church of St. Boniface, cemetery, and rectory** from a 1860 painting. Then known as the *St. Boniface Settlement*, it is now known as Scipio. These building were destroyed in a prairie fire and the church and monastery were rebuilt further up the hill. The location of the original church and rectory is today the parish cemetery. (Below) **The stone church of St. Boniface** that stands today. To the right is the building built as a college to educate the local youth. The college building no longer stands. An attached monastery was later added to the church building and exists today. *(Photos courtesy of the Archives of the PCM Province)*

From the Archives

(Above) **The college building in Scipio** with the steeple of St. Boniface Church in the backgound. Cyril Knoll, second from the left in the back row, was a member of the community when they and their dogs gathered for this photo. (Below) **A later Carmelite community in Scipio, Kansas** ... Back Row: Br. Baptist Goor, Br. Victor Heilmeyer, Br. Bonaventure Tenhaap, Br. Elias Maurer, Br. Augustine Maurer. Front Row: Fr. Joseph Walsh, Fr. Alphonsus Brandstaetter, Fr. Albert Wagner. *(Photos courtesy of the Archves of the PCM Province)*

From the Archives

(Above) **The Carmelite Monastery and Church in Cumberland, Maryland**, purchased by Cyril Knoll from the Redemptorist in 1866, because Kansas was so remote from the newly arriving German immigrants. However, the Redemptorist found the high altitude and the rigors of the mountain winters to be a bad combination for the health of their students. A few Redemptorists had died of pulmonary consumption. *(Photos courtesy of the Archves of the PCM Province),*

(Above) **Original Church of St. Cecilia in Englewood, New Jersey**. This parish was founded by Anastasius Smits who was given responsibility for Ft. Lee, New Jersey and several chapels in 1869. He soon relocated to Englewood from Ft. Lee.

3
Chapter Three: SEPARATIST MOVEMENTS

While moving east to Cumberland, Maryland, initially offered promise for a solid expansion of the Order, unforeseen events proved that was an untenable solution. These events would necessitate further moves to Upper Marlboro, Maryland, a return to Kentucky, this time Western Kentucky as well as Louisville and to several towns in Pennsylvania. Excellent ministry occured for a time in all these places, suggesting that such expansion and the division into smaller juridical entities would enhance the Order in North America. However because of their distance and disconnection from each other, there were not enough available priests and brothers to sustain some of them or to provide the staff necessary to properly form candidates in the essentials of Carmelite life.

Kansas Foundations under Albert Heimann

THE work Fr. Albert Heimann accomplished once Knoll left for the East throws a bright light on his loyalty to the Order of "our dear Lady of Mt. Carmel" as he was fond of calling it. Practically unaided he built the church of St. Joseph in Leavenworth that still serves the parish today. At Scipio he developed a farm, built a new church and monastery and attempted, though in this he was unsuccessful, to institute a college. For fifteen years he maintained monasteries at both Leavenworth and Scipio as Carmelite monasteries. He was, in years to come, able to obtain for the Order a foundation at Niagara Falls, and, through his vicar, Fr. Pius, established there the best-developed Carmelite seminary in America. All of this was done by a former diocesan priest who had known only two Carmelite priests, whose novitiate had been most inadequate, who was, indeed, practically abandoned by the rest of the Order and who, most of the time, had to endure the bleakest poverty and the most grinding hardships.

Though Fr. Cyril's decision to leave Kansas had been an unwelcome decision, Albert set to work with characteristic energy to promote the welfare of St. Joseph's parish. While Knoll traveled east, Heimann held a mission preached by the famous Fr. Wenninger, S.J. who encouraged the pastor and parishioners to begin the building of a much needed new church.[1] The parish had grown considerably, after the opening of the coal mines in Leavenworth which attracted a large colony of Catholic Poles.[2] The estimated cost of the new church was between $30,000 -

$40,000. Heimann, of course, could not expect to raise this sum from the newly landed immigrants. He pointed out in his request for funds to the Ludwig Missionsverein that these immigrants "were largely of the laboring class who did not have a home but live rather in rented places." As migratory workers they could not be expected to give. In requesting aid of the Ludwig Missionsverein, he argued that the new church edifice should be a moderately ambitious structure, since it was to be built in the see city of the diocese.[3] He had no intention, however, of relying solely on the mission society's alms for erecting his new church. When Huber was banished to Leavenworth by Knoll in late December, 1867, Heimann resolved to make good use of his ability to raise funds. The next year found Huber on a begging tour in the East once again. When Louis Guenther was sent back to Kansas by Knoll in 1868, Fr. Albert gave him charge of the parish while he himself sought alms on a trip through Illinois.[5]

The cornerstone of the present brick church was laid September 6, 1868 by Bishop Miege in the presence of many priests and parishioners. Frs. Wenninger and Garesche, both Jesuits, preached on the occasion.[6] The church was to be 132 feet long by 60 feet wide with a roof extending 66 feet high. The foundation cost $3,000— a sum collected from the members of the parish.[7] Fr. Albert received a few thousand dollars from the soldiers at the fort and some of the men who were working on the railroad.[8] In the years from 1866 to 1869 the Ludwig Missionsverein granted 2,500 gulden for the new church. Despite these contributions, work on the structure was halted several times because of the lack of funds.[9]

During these trying times the commissary general had no intention of entirely neglecting the Kansas Fathers, though he did concern himself primarily with the Cumberland foundation. In writing to the Ludwig Missionsverein for aid, Knoll pictured Leavenworth as "still suffering the travails of birth." At the same time he insisted that his main concern was the $12,000.00 debt from Cumberland due in 1872.[10] After the departure of the Fathers in late 1868 from Cumberland, Knoll brought the Carmelites in Kansas to the verge of communal apostasy. Faced with the large exodus from Cumberland, he directed Fr. Xavier to come to Cumberland. At the time, Huber was collecting donations so that the new church in Leavenworth could be completed.[11] His services were vital to both Heimann and Knoll. When Heimann heard of Knoll's order, he planned to remove his community from the Commissary's jurisdiction.

> I am now fully determined to leave the Order not gladly but with a sorrowful heart if our affairs cannot and will not he put in better

shape. Under no circumstances will I remain under Knoll. I am trying to make a statement to Fr. General from the very beginning in Kansas and then ask for my dimissorial letters unless God and the Blessed Virgin Mary change or turn our affairs into a better course. I am willing to do all I can to advance the interest of our holy Order in this country but I cannot go along any longer with Commissary Knoll.[12]

Throughout 1869 his attitude did not change.

> Had I known or had I the least suspicion that Father Cyril would leave Kansas, I would never have joined him at my advanced age of 50 years. Neither Father Guenther nor I have yet known the life of a religious; nay, we are even more in a worse condition than secular priests. I think my complaint is just. And as the Order has never taken any interest for my good, neither for time or eternity, I ask in all justice to be dispensed from its obligations. I will not and cannot remain any longer under Father Cyril, a man who has neither judgment nor Christian feeling. I loved my state; I have labored faithfully for the good of the Order. I have sighed and prayed for its prosperity but all in vain. And so I have finally concluded to return to the secular priests.[13]

Heimann sent his lengthy report to the prior general in December of 1869 ending: "Fr. Cyril is not the proper person to perform this great work. He has not the judgment, the ability or the prudence to advance the interests of our Order."[14]

A solution actually less drastic than complete abandonment of the Order was actually envisioned by Fr. Heimann. He laid this latter proposition before Fr. Meagher.

> In a year the bishop intends to build a church for the English speaking Catholics in the city. Now, if you and Father Theodore were here, how good that would be for us. We could have two congregations in the city and several in the country. We could live a life like religious, like brothers, and our prospects are better here than in Maryland where there are too many religious already. We are willing to defray a part of your travelling expenses, if not the whole, if you should stand in need of it. Provided Knoll has nothing to do with it, just say that you will come. Please consider that with Fr. Theodore and answer soon for we must take some decisive step soon.[15]

All during the first year and a half of Fr. Meagher's assignment at Marlboro, he was constantly importuned by Fr. Heimann to bring his men to Kansas and to accept the leadership there. On August 14, 1869, Meagher had been named as "praeses" or local superior of the Kansas communities. Knoll as commissary general was to remain the authoritative voice for American Carmelite affairs, but Meagher was to be the immediate superior in Kansas,[16] One gets the impression from the correspondence that Meagher was willing enough to accept a nominal appointment from the prior general but was loathe to get involved again with the contingent of German Carmelites.[17]

In 1869 Heimann wrote that Knoll had resigned as commissary general. This story supposedly was passed to Miege, in Rome for the First Vatican Council, by the Carmelite prior general.[18] Miege reportedly relayed the news back to Heimann in Kansas.[19] Evidently Knoll also heard of the rumor. He knew that should Miege, obviously favorably inclined to the priests in Kansas, bring the prestige of his office to bear on the prior general, Savini might hear him out. Schooled in the art of persuasion, Knoll wrote to Savini warning him that "Heimann was threatening to give everything to the Bishop."[20]

The numerous complaints received from the Kansas Fathers and the direct testimony of Bishop Miege obviously convinced the prior general that the situation in Kansas was critical. The solution envisioned by Meagher's appointment the previous August should have been a happy compromise. What made the solution so very palatable and seemingly quite viable was the fact that Fr. Meagher was supposedly a friend both of Knoll and Heimann. But, Meagher was not anxious to become the center of controversy. He never assumed the leadership in Kansas. The prior general, then, was forced to name Heimann as superior of the Carmelites in Kansas on May 23, 1870. At the same time, he made Fr. Albert directly responsible and subject to himself.[21] For all practical purposes, the Fathers in Kansas had been removed entirely from the jurisdiction of Knoll. What hurt Knoll was that he learned of this latter appointment only indirectly through Fr. Xavier.[22]

In the meanwhile, the building of the new St. Joseph's church continued until dedication day, June 18, 1871. Bishop Louis Fink in his first official act since his consecration as co-adjutor to Bishop Miege one week earlier, performed the ceremony.[23] The erection of the 650 seat church had cost $45,000;[24] interest on the debt ran ten to twelve dollars on the hundred.[25] As the parish grew, the number of children in the parish school had increased. In 1869 the Sisters of Charity were asked to assume charge of the teaching. Heretofore, the school had been taught by the pastor, by occasional lay teachers, by a Carmelite brother, and at intervals, by one of the sisters from the Academy on Kickapoo Street.[26] Once the parish needs had been set in order, Heimann was free to concern himself with establishing that part of the Carmelite Order now under his leadership on a sound basis.

New Foundations: Upper Marlboro Missions

The castaways from Cumberland seemed to be prospering quite well. It was in early February 1869, that Frs. Meagher, McDonald and Br. Simon Edenhoefer went to Upper Marlboro, Maryland about 21 miles from Washington, D.C. Marlboro was to be the headquarters for the various missions throughout Prince George County, the more important stations being at Piscataway, Oxon Hill and Rosaryville.[27] The community remained subject to Fr. Cyril as commissary general and was always on speaking terms with him even if the relationship was somewhat strained at times.[28] The commissary evidently was resigned to the fact that the Irish members would function more successfully if allowed to pursue their separate destiny. Within five years, they too were essentially independent.

Fr. Meagher in describing the early days of Upper Marlboro shows a trace of bitterness:

> When I left Cumberland, now nearly a year ago, I was set adrift without even a dollar to pay my fare. I was obliged to raffle my watch which I brought from Rome, and for which I must confess, on that account, I had a great affection. I received a little money in that way and also by the assistance of a few friends I was able to set out. Trusting in God and my dear Mother Mary I soon found a resting place. I was poor but unencumbered. I made a beginning and thank God succeeded far beyond my most sanguine expectations. I have secured a small but valuable piece of property of about five or six acres of land on the edge of the town and have erected thereon a beautiful residence just now finished. And, what is better, it is paid for except the small sum of $13 which I intend to pay soon. But God only knows how I struggled and how many days of anxious care and self-sacrifice it cost me. But now, thank God, I feel happy; everything is progressing favorably.[29]

During the years 1869 and 1870, Fr. Meagher and Fr. McDonald were at St. Mary's, Marlboro and attended St. Ignatius, Oxon Hill.[30] There were only a few Catholic whites in the area, but winning some 2,000 black former slaves to the Church offered a real challenge. In a day when ecumenism was not a byword, the enthusiasm of the Methodists posed a serious challenge to convert making.[31]

At the close of the Second Plenary Council at Baltimore in 1866, the bishops realized the problem posed by the Emancipation Proclamation.

Therefore, they admonished the faithful in their pastoral letter:

> We must feel, beloved Brethren, that in some manner a new and most extensive field of charity and devotedness has been opened to us by the emancipation of the immense slave population of the South . . . We urge upon the clergy and people of our charge the most generous cooperation with the plans which may be adopted by the bishops of the dioceses in which they are to extend to them that Christian education and moral restraint which they so much stand in need of.[32]

Legislation during the Council had produced a decree, *De Nigrorum Salute Procuranda (Ensuring the Welfare of the Negro)*. The decree embodied an earnest plea:

> We entreat and beseech priests, through the bowels of the mercy of our God that they devote to this work their labors, their time, and if this can be done, their whole life. Let superiors of religious orders select some of their members to come to the aid of the Bishops; let secular priests, whom the lord has called to this work, offer themselves wholly.[33]

Facing the problem squarely, the Council went on to decree that every means be implemented for the religious care and instruction of these former slaves. Anyone neglecting to provide these means would, said the bishops, "merit the strongest reproach."[34] But, it was far easier to exhort than to win effective action. Through a combination of racial prejudice, timidity, and scarcity of manpower and resources, the chance for large-scale conversion of the Black Americans to Catholicism after the Civil War was to slip away gradually.

A few bishops, however, saw the immensity of the problem and were fortunate enough to be able to cope with it. One of these was Archbishop Spalding, who a year before the Secondary Plenary Council had met, told the Archbishop of New York: "It is a golden opportunity for reaping a harvest of souls which neglected may not return."[35] After the Council had fashioned its decree, Spalding urged the pastors of his archdiocese to put forth every effort of enlightened zeal to secure for the ex-slaves Christian instruction. He desired that separate schools be established for them, "since experience proved how difficult it was to impart religious instruction to those who could not read."[36]

The three Carmelites at Upper Marlboro had not been discharged by Knoll with the sole intent on undertaking missions to American Blacks. On the other hand, they had clearly followed the mandate of the Second Plenary Council and come to the aid of Bishop Spalding. After submitting a request to him for work in the diocese, they willingly undertook the task offered in the missions to former slaves. Once assigned, Knoll quite willingly approved of their work. These early Carmelites needed not be given excessive praise for their action, but they should not be deprived of due laud for accepting a difficult endeavor. Spalding was fortunate to have these volunteers. They were in a true sense among the pioneers in this virgin apostolate thrust upon the Church by the Civil War. It was not until 1871 when the Mill Hill Fathers were introduced into Baltimore that Spalding would receive any further sizable assistance for the Black population in Maryland.

The Marlboro foundations began to prosper; the prior general in Rome aided their growth by directing new candidates to their threshold. Angelus Dwyer entered the novitiate on July 16, 1869;[37] Brocard Murphy, a professed cleric, came in 1870.[38] Fr. Joseph Walsh arrived in 1871[39] and Fr. Cyril Feehan came in December of 1872.[40] Prospects grew even brighter with the aid of good friends. On June 18, 1872, Eliza G. Graham deeded seven odd acres to the Carmelites on the condition that should the Fathers withdraw their pastoral care, the land and improvements made on it would be ceded to the Archbishop of Baltimore.[41]

Carmelite Life in Cumberland

In the meanwhile, Fr. Cyril was busy at Cumberland caring for the needs of his St. Peter and Paul parish. During the year following his arrival, Knoll had the altars in the church embellished. The old school house which the Carmelites bought from the Redemptorists was sold to the congregation for $544.87 and a contract for a new school building given to Buchholz and Fugtman.

On the 16th Sunday after Pentecost, September 28, 1868, the solemn ceremony of laying the cornerstone of the new school building took place. The subscriptions and house-collections for this building, whose estimated cost was set at $6,947, had already netted $2,067.10. Monthly contributions from August to December brought another $1,092.75.

The erection of the building was steadily progressing but on the twenty-fourth Sunday after Pentecost several members questioned the prudence of using the type of masonry utilized on the new building. This criticism came at a time when Knoll was already embroiled in the dispute with his community. In consequence of this dissatisfaction, the new building was examined by persons supposedly expert in such matters. No fault was found, except that the western and the eastern main walls were one fourth inch out of plumb, the former inclining and the latter declining. The defect was considered to be of no serious consequence. The masonry was judged to be solid and perfect in construction. The following Friday, however, an unexpected hurricane lashed against the structure near nine o'clock in the evening and the rear gable-wall collapsed. Despite these delays, the school was able to be dedicated on May 30, 1869. By Ascension Thursday 1869, $5905.07 had been contributed toward its cost.[42]

In April 1870, a cornerstone for a sisters' residence was laid. The building which cost $1200 was completed that October 23.[43] On April 6, Knoll formally petitioned the archbishop to secure some Ursuline sisters from Kentucky to staff the school. Sisters Mary Boniface, Mary Xavier and Mary Margaret were a beneficial replacement [44] for the lay teachers whose poor caliber[45] of instruction had been compounded by some personal scandals.

In Lent 1872, the enlargement and adornment of the church building was taken under advisement with the congregation. The old rectory occupying the space in the rear of the church was torn down and improvement was begun on the north side. A sacristy, extending nine feet, of two stories was built on each side of the sanctuary. In May 1873, the renovation of the church was begun on weekdays after the morning Mass at half past five. The interior of the church was completed by the feast of All Saints. Two new side altars with beautiful zinc statues of the Blessed Virgin and St. Joseph were procured. New stations, a new organ and pulpit and twenty-five new stained glass windows were also placed in the church. The old organ was sold to the less wealthy Methodist Church in Cumberland for $500. The new organ cost $3200. The total expense of the renovation and improvements amounted to nearly $21,800. This exterior and interior adornment at the same time was matched by the introduction of a variety of religious services.[46]

Knoll began a number of excellent devotions suited in their appeal to the mentality of his day. Among the most prominent of these devotions was the novena to St. Joseph as patron of a happy death. This consisted of attendance for nine successive Wednesdays at the religious services on those days. Solemn High Mass was chanted in the morning. In the evening an edifying and fervent instruction was given on St. Joseph. Quite naturally, devotion to the Scapular of Our Lady of Mt. Carmel held a conspicuous place among the spiritual exercises of the congregation during the Carmelite administration. Fr. Cyril was a good instructor in the truths of theology that lay behind the devotion. Another intensely Catholic devotion led by the Carmelites was the practice of praying for

Chapter Three: Separatists Movements   81

the dead. The pious custom of visiting the graveyard on the afternoon of All Saints was introduced just a few months after their arrival in 1867.⁴⁷

The early summer of 1871 found the congregation at SS. Peter and Paul's in preparation for major festivities. On July 2, the Vicar Apostolic of North Carolina, Bishop James Gibbons, was to confirm one hundred and sixty candidates.⁴⁸ The year 1871 also witnessed the celebration in honor of the twenty-fifth anniversary of the Pontificate of Pope Pius IX. The *Cumberland Daily News* gave a graphic description of the event:

> The demonstration here was a wholesale affair. There was no lukewarmness, disaffections or jealousies to be seen; it was one common, fervent effort to truly render the occasion an honest, heartfelt, outpouring: of love and veneration for the good Old Pope and Church. Saturday evening, as previously announced, was set for the time of illumination, when the houses occupied by persons of the Catholic faith were to be illumined. During the afternoon on every hand could be seen preparations making for the display. Windows were decorated with flowers and wreathes entwined about portraits of the Pope. Many houses were beautifully festooned with evergreens, flags and bunting. In several localities throughout the city festoons were extended across the street.
>
> As evening approached, the sky was overcast with clouds, threatening rain; but still preparations for the illumination went on. At an early hour in the evening rain began descending and continued falling in a heavy shower for several hours, which necessarily prevented many persons from witnessing much of the illumination. By previous arrangement, the bells of St. Peter's and Paul's and St. Patrick's churches rang out the hour of nine o'clock, when, simultaneously, the houses of Catholics shone in brilliancy. Lights were profusely placed in windows in every quarter of the city. All persons interested did their best to make the occasion a success. The towering four-story brick, and the lonely hamlet with its little pane, sent forth brilliant lights.
>
> We should like to particularize some of the dwellings so handsomely decorated and lighted up, but where their (sic) were so many worthy of mention we might omit some of the most deserving; consequently we can only speak in general terms. About nine o'clock the rain slackened a little, and thousands of our citizens availed themselves of the opportunity to take a stroll through the principal streets to witness the sights, which added to the flying rockets and bursting fire crackers, made a lively and interesting scene. At about ten o'clock the lights began to be extinguished and soon darkness and quiet reigned supreme. Upon the whole, the illumination was very creditable, and everybody seem pleased.

On Sunday afternoon, the members of St. Patrick's, St. Edward's, St. Peter's and Paul's and St. Joseph's Beneficial Societies, and many school children of both sexes and hundreds of citizens assembled on Centre Street in front of St. Patrick's church, and forming in line, with two bands of music, the Mt. Savage Brass Band and the Cumberland German Silver Cornet, discoursing their best music, took up the line of march through the principal streets of the city. The procession was one of the largest that has taken place here for years. After the principal streets had been traversed the procession returned to St. Patrick's church, where as many as could gathered in the edifice to attend vespers. After the benediction by Father Brennan, the procession again formed and proceeded to St. Joseph's Hall, near the German Catholic Church, where resolutions expressive of the event and appropriate to the extraordinary occasion were read to the people and heartily approved, after which the multitudes were dismissed to depart to their respective homes.[49]

Yet, despite the seeming progress of the Cumberland foundation, Fr. Knoll was daily faced with the decision of abandoning the monastery. Part of the problem lay in the scandals caused, several years before, by some of the novices in the monastery. Knoll had agreed to pay the debt of the monastery by saying Masses for which the Redemptorists retained the stipend. Eager to have the debt paid, the Redemptorists in turn encouraged many wandering priests of ill repute to seek the Carmelite monastery as a place of refuge and reform. While correcting their mistakes and beginning anew in a place where their former errors would be unknown, these priests could say Mass in the monastery for the Carmelites in exchange for the shelter the monastery afforded. History can only judge that Knoll showed too great an optimism in receiving some of these men. Conscious that his debt must be paid, yet no doubt sincere in his belief that the men were ready to begin a new, useful and sincere life, he received all applicants. Such optimism was unfounded; for scandals arose from the actions of some of these well-meaning but still wayward priests.[50]

The resultant action had been that the bishop felt forced by the infamy to take away the mission stations attached to the monastery upon which Knoll was so dependent. It was at this time also that some of the Fathers fled from the scandal-ridden monastery to make a new beginning in Marlboro. For other reasons, the Kansas group had also been able to free themselves completely from Knoll's jurisdiction. Knoll decided prompt action was needed. The monastery debt was due in 1872 and the parish of SS. Peter and Paul's could hardly pay the cost. Moreover, the debt was due to Knoll personally as the property was deeded in his name. He sought new mission stations necessarily outside the domain of the archdiocese of Baltimore, yet close enough to Cumberland to be staffed easily from there. He had to act promptly, while the men in Marlboro were still under his jurisdiction. Though they maintained contact with Knoll, he knew they were in communication with the Kansas group and sought to be free from him. Had they been able to place themselves outside of his jurisdiction, he would have had no one to staff any new mission stations he might have acquired.

Those who admired him personally but were discontent over the situation viewed Cumberland as a hopeless place where the Carmelite name had been slandered to such a degree that it could never regain its luster. Knoll, however, seemed to maintain his optimistic spirit through the entire crisis and planned to continue to use Cumberland as a novitiate. Perhaps, it was a more realistic spirit which told him that he had already invested time and money into this house. Practically isolated from all other Carmelites by 1870, he had no other choice but to retain this monastery if he were to adhere to his original dream and commission of establishing the Carmelites firmly in America. To establish the Carmelites he needed a novitiate to attract new candidates. Assuming a new location and a new debt in some other locale was out of the question.

New Foundations in Pennsylvania

Initial inquiries for suitable mission stations brought offers from the Bishops of Wheeling and Louisville. However the first new foundation Knoll accepted was about 30 miles from Cumberland in the diocese of Pittsburgh at New Baltimore, Pennsylvania. Fr. Norbert Bausch, so recently ordained, was sent there along with two brothers.[51]

New Baltimore had its beginning as a Catholic colonization experiment.[52] Certainly it never enjoyed the publicity of a Ghent or Fulda, but it was an important forerunner of these and many more settlements later promoted by Archbishop John Ireland in the German triangle of the West.[53] Undoubtedly, New Baltimore had received its impetus from Gallitizin's successful community at Loreto.[54] Situated on the eastern slope of the Allegheny chain, New Baltimore appeared to have metropolis potential. It was no more inaccessible than any other nascent town. Pittsburgh was less accessible from New York and Philadelphia than was New Baltimore, which had two main thoroughfares nearby——the Glade Pike and the Pittsburgh Pike. Immense herds of cattle and flocks of turkeys were driven to market on these roads. Hence, the land between the two pikes seemed to be the logical and profitable location for a settlement.⁶⁵ In a diary notation, Bishop Francis Kenrick described some of the history surrounding the social experiment:

> There is a mission eighteen miles distant in a place called Harman's Bottom. Two thousand acres of land, the gift of a Mr. Riddlemoser of Baltimore, adjoin the church "which has "been erected there. But no income is derived from this land as yet: and the rector complains of the heavy burden of paying taxes. Of recent years however many Catholic families have settled in this place. They take up the land, paying almost nothing for it, with this condition only, that, after a number of years, they are to pay an annual rent. The number of Catholics residing there is not large; and their worldly wealth is very little.⁵⁶

The original plans for the colony were quite ambitious. The Bedford *Gazette* even carried a detailed article outlining the erection of a Catholic university on the land.⁵⁷

The first subscription toward the building of a church in the colony was begun in Bedford, Pennsylvania in 1816. The first logs were set in place in 1820.⁵⁸ The church was not completed until 1824. On January 1, 1826, the Reverend Thomas Heyden, a future biographer of Bishop Kenrick, officiated at the dedication ceremony.⁵⁹ When the bishop visited New Baltimore on July 12, 1842, the parish numbered one hundred families.⁶⁰ Within the confines of the colony there were several grist and saw mills, wagon and blacksmith shops, a cooper's shop, and four distilleries. Mention must be made of the altar furnishing establishment of Henry Engbert which in its day supplied many churches in the diocese of Pittsburgh with equipment.⁶¹ The first serious challenge to the prospect of a prosperous trade center at New Baltimore was offered when the main line of the Pennsylvania Canal was erected in 1834. The 394 mile trip from Philadelphia to Pittsburgh took four days and cost $7.00. It was made possible by the Allegheny Portage Railroad. Thirty-six miles of incline and level road were the connecting link between the eastern and western portions of the Pennsylvania Canal System, which lifted boats, passengers and freight over the bold escarpment of the Allegheny Front. The building of the canal sounded the death knell to commerce on the pikes.⁶² The colony was already on the decline, when it received its first resident pastor in 1850, Fr. Joseph Gozowsky, a Discalced Carmelite.⁶³

RETURN TO KENTUCKY: FOUNDATIONS IN LOUISVILLE AND WESTERN KENTUCKY

While the Marlboro and New Baltimore foundations began to develop satisfactorily, negotiations for a house in the Louisville diocese brought a favorable reply. The area offered to the Carmelites, the whole western section of the state, comprising eight counties: Marshall, Calloway, Graves, McCracken, Fulton, Hickman, Carlisle and Ballard—is still known as "Jackson Purchase." In 1818, General Andrew Jackson and Isaac Shelby had bought these 2100 square miles from Chief Paduke and the Chickasaws, naming the settlement "Paducah" in honor of the fine old chief. Of all the river towns which emerged with the healthy signs for the future—Hickman, Columbus, Wickliffe, Wadesboro and Smithland, the town of Paducah offered a location most convenient for both the inland farmers and the river merchants. It was Paducah's good fortune also to be the first town in Western Kentucky to be reached by the railroad. In 1871, the city's population was about 7,000 but there were strong indications that it could double in a very short time.[64]

The first Catholics in McCracken County, Kentucky, settled in 1839 at St. John's, Kentucky, a German colony nine miles south of Paducah. In 1830 descendants of the original Maryland Catholics who settled the state, established themselves at and around Fancy Farm in Graves County. The Catholics of Paducah were first visited by Fr. Elisha J. Durbin, probably the greatest of the early circuit riders who used the home of John Grief on the south side of Kentucky Avenue, west of Sixth Street, for religious services.[65] The first church was built in 1849 under the patronage of St. Francis de Sales.[66] In his two years as pastor, 1869-1871, Fr. Ivo Schacht built the second church at a cost of f 10,000 and converted part of the church into a rectory.[67] What rooms remained unused were put into service for the school.[68] It was then to these buildings that the Carmelites, came on January 1, 1871, with the hope, according to Knoll, of conducting a seminary there for students.[69]

The original community at St. Francis de Sales had Fr. Peter Thomas Meagher[70] as superior and Fr. Aloysius Kammer as an assistant in the parish.[71] On January 25, Fr. Benno Jansen[72] arrived from Cumberland with two novices, Anastasius Kreidt[73] and Bernard Fink,[74] and two clerics, Anselm Duell[75] and Brocard Murphy.[76] Jansen was named pastor and novice master. Besides duties at the church and school, the Carmelite priests were chaplains to nearby St. Mary's Academy, staffed by the Sisters of Charity of Nazareth, Kentucky. They also undertook the parochial duties at Fancy Farm and Hickman and at the mission stations in Mayfield, Fulton, Smithland and Columbus.

Fancy Farm was established by Sam and John Willett, the first Catholics in the Purchase. The name was given to their development in 1845 when the post office was established; the government inspector adopted the name as a compliment to the new postmaster for his evident skill on his holdings. Fr. Durbin built the first log church in 1836, dedicated to St. Jerome. A resident pastor arrived in 1843.[77] The second church, the one used by the Carmelites, was dedicated in 1858.[78] The other mission stations the Carmelites attended were small and dependent. Sacred Heart Parish at Hickman, for example, did not merit a resident pastor until 1879. The church Fr. Durbin built at Smithland, St. Stephan's, was used as a stable by Federal troops in 1863 and was so ruined that it had to be razed in 1870.[79] In the center of the Purchase was Mayfield, saved from extinction by the advent of the railroad. There were many Catholics in the area but St. Joseph's church was not built until 1887 because Fancy Farm was only ten miles west.[80]

The beginnings of the Carmelite foundations in Kentucky could not have been launched under more ideal circumstances. The three priests who began the care of souls in the Purchase, Meagher, Jansen, and Kammer, were eager and dedicated. The superior, Meagher, was indeed a talented person. His biographer described him as "a splendid teacher and organizer, a man of winning ways, an excellent leader."[81] A Fr. Joseph Walsh was assigned to the community in early March and Anselm Duell was ordained on March 26.[82] True, the parishes were poor and the distances to be covered on horseback were great. Yet, correspondence of the community reflects a feeling of security in being assigned an area of such extent as one's sole responsibility. But tragedy struck the young community early—the beginning of the many misfortunes which in ten years were to bring the whole project to naught. Fr. Benno Jansen was attacked by cholera and, although reported as recovering in April, he passed away in July.[83] This loss put an additional burden on Fr. Meagher's shoulders as pastor, teacher and novice master as well as superior. Unfortunately, not very much detail about the parishes has come to light. But some indication of the size of the parishes can be seen in the confirmation statistics for the year 1871: Fancy Farm, 42, Paducah, 60, Hickman, 20 and Columbus, 17.[84]

The second year in Kentucky was blessed in several ways. Fr. Brocard Murphy, who spent his time as a student at the Preston Park Seminary, was ordained on June 21.[85] The old St. Francis church which had been converted into a rectory was remodeled into a two story building, providing ample space for school and living quarters for the postulants. It was during 1872 also that the Carmelites built a two-story frame building on the east side of the church facing out to Broadway. This building served as a school for boys during the remaining years of the Carmelites' stay in Paducah. The Carmelites had been called to western Kentucky by Bishop

Chapter Three: Separatists Movements

William McCloskey on the condition that they open such a school.[86]

While Fr. Knoll was in Europe during the summer, Fr. Meagher had to act also as pastor at Cumberland, Maryland.[87] He returned to Cumberland again in December with Fr. Kammer to get the news from Europe as well as to discuss the possibility of opening a house in Louisville. At this meeting, Frs. Knoll and Meagher discussed the idea of reassigning the novitiate to Cumberland. Knoll was hesitant as his letter to the prior general indicates: "Fr. Peter Thomas is willing to come here to be novice master, but I don't dare ask him to live here as he is the cause of the disorder between the Irish and the Germans."[88]

Apparently, the trip Knoll made to Europe and Rome had gained support for him from the prior general. The correspondence between the commissary and the prior general at this time indicates that Savini was more than willing to seek advice on American affairs from Knoll. Savini appeared eager to support the decisions taken by Fr. Cyril also. Shortly after Knoll had visited Rome, the prior general wrote to Fr. Albert Heimann in Kansas requesting him to resign as superior of the Carmelites in the Midwest. The prior general intimated that all the American Carmelites should once again place themselves under Knoll's jurisdiction. The Kansas Carmelites were not quite ready to seek such a reconciliation and their reply to Rome represented a vague refusal to follow the prior general's wishes. They were willing to obey any commissary who would live in Kansas; they were willing to submit directly to the prior general's jurisdiction. If these two proposals were not acceptable, the *status quo* was the only alternative.[89]

The hand of God touched the little group for the second time in the death of Fr. Brocard Murphy on February 11, 1873. During the fierce epidemic of Yellow Fever that year he was a true martyr of charity and was especially remembered for many years by the Sisters of Charity who beheld the zeal of this young twenty-seven year old priest with their own eyes.[90] In April, Fr. Meagher also had been attacked by the fever and on April 30 was considered dying.[91] Almost miraculously he recovered enough to be active again but the hidden infection continued to wreak devastation on his mind and body. Physical suffering was a heavy cross, added to the already great anxiety and concern for the future of his foundation in Kentucky. Fr. Walsh, too, was taken ill and suffered much from the after-effects.

But all was not sadness. On July 16, Fr. Meagher was awarded the degree of Doctor of Divinity by the prior general.[92] By the time this news reached Paducah there was another letter announcing Bishop

McCloskey's permission for a Carmelite church in Louisville. To undertake this new foundation, Meagher assigned Fr. McDonald as pastor and Fr. Feehan as his assistant.[93] Both of these priests had been stationed in the Upper Marlboro missions. Their reassignment was influenced by new developments in the archdiocese which saw Bishop Bayley of Newark installed in the see of Baltimore on October 13, 1872.[94] It was Bayley who had given Smits his assignment on the condition that Frs. Peter Thomas Meagher and Theodore McDonald work in his diocese. But instead they had accepted missions in Upper Marlboro.

In the June following his installation, Bayley had made a tour of the southern part of the state. He found the church at Upper Marlboro one of the most active and prosperous in the diocese and was more than pleased with the work of the Carmelites. The archbishop was impressed with the large confirmation class of 281 which included more than two hundred black converts.[95] In his diary he noted the fine care given to the former slaves and especially complimented Mrs. Eliza Graham whose kindness had opened the door of the Church to her former slaves. It was quite unusual to find former slaves still attached to their former master. Bayley noted that

> Generally, the negroes will not remain on a plantation where they have been slaves, no matter how kindly they may have been treated, or how high the wages offered—they do not think that they are really free until they go somewhere else.[96]

Despite the archbishop's favorable reaction, the Carmelites were made to understand that they would never receive title to the mission[97] though Archbishop Spalding had inferred they would.[98] Realizing that such an arrangement could only eventually strain the relation with the archbishop, already prejudiced by past history, the Carmelites at Marlboro began to plan for the day when they could withdraw entirely from the missions. The arrival of Frs. McDonald and Feehan in Louisville marked the first step.

In 1873, Louisville, with a population of over 100,000, was at the peak of its importance in relation to the rest of the country. Its vitality was near the top. Through the Louisville and Nashville Railroad a virtual monopoly of the traffic south had been established. The railroad, the city government, and business, represented frequently by the same persons who placed a sculptured locomotive on the City Hall, had cooperated closely to preserve and to enlarge this monopoly. The destruction of the plantation system in the far South had resulted in the erection of general stores everywhere. Louisville wholesale houses and jeans makers sent their salesmen as far as Texas, making long circuits on horseback before the railroads crossed the state. By 1870, the exports of Louisville doubled the imports."

The quickened pulse of trade necessarily led to a rapid population explosion in the city. The boundaries of the city were continually being extended especially in the areas along the river. It was this accelerated expansion that prompted a real estate salesman, Thomas Slevin, to donate to Bishop McCloskey a tract of land originally set aside as a park in a new development area known as the Slevin's Western Division. It was Slevin also who suggested that the Carmelites be approached to organize the new parish.[100] It may be presumed that there were high spiritual motives in the Slevin gift, but there was also the desire to make the church and school an added attraction to buyers interested in the remaining property along the river. Choice lots sold for $7.00 a foot, but the area failed to develop despite such publicity stunts as free dinners, Irish oratory, and outdoor food stands.[101]

The deed for the new church on St. Cecilia Street was dated August 18, 1873 in favor of Bishop McCloskey. For the sum of one dollar a section of land, valued at $12,000, was given by the Slevin family, in addition to $1,000 in cash.[102] Four Catholic churches were erected in Louisville in 1873, creating a total of sixteen churches.[103] The Carmelite Order saw fit to reward the donors with an official letter of affiliation with the Order on September 8, 1874.[104]

Sixteen days after the property was actually secured, the cornerstone was laid on September 7 by Bishop McCloskey. The stone still bears the name of Theodore John McDonald.[105] In announcing the event, the *Catholic Advocate* praised the work of the Carmelites and their intention "to use the building now about to be erected for a college, when they will have means to build another church." The editor asked that a big crowd attend and be generous in the collection for the necessary work of Catholic education of youth.[108] Fr. William J. Dunn preached the sermon extolling the sacrifices of the people in raising a house of God. Reaching oratorical heights typical of the day, he proclaimed the glories of the Carmelites in the Old Testament, in Ireland, and in America, especially in connection with the Brown Scapular.[107]

Several reasons prompted Fr. Meagher to go to Europe in 1874. Expansion of the Kentucky foundation necessitated the recruitment of candidates. The novitiate at Cumberland could not be counted on to supply the demand. The horizon in Kentucky also seemed to offer an opportunity for unlimited expansion to those who were willing to seize upon it. Meagher hoped to convince the Carmelite prior general in Rome that Knoll's disinterested control of the Kentucky Carmelites acted as a brake rather than a spur to expansion. The income he envisioned as forthcoming from the various churches in Kentucky seemed to indicate that a Kentucky Commissariat separate from the jurisdiction of Cumberland would be financially viable.[108] But most of all, perhaps, Fr. Peter Thomas simply sought a few months in Europe to regain his fading health among his loved ones in Ireland and Rome.[109]

He left at the end of February with Bishop William McCloskey and returned in the fall with four postulants for the Sisters of Charity and several students for the Carmelite novitiate at Paducah.[110] The money spent on this trip and in paying for the passage of the others became a bone of contention with several of the Carmelites in Paducah and eventually caused them to seek a transfer. This loss of manpower as well as that caused by sickness and death, eventually led to the collapse of the Kentucky Commissariat.

While Fr. Meagher was away, the first Mass was celebrated in the new St. Cecilia's church on the first Sunday of June, 1874, by Fr. Joyce, pastor of the neighboring St. Patrick's, with Fr. McDonald as assisting deacon and Fr. Feehan as subdeacon.[111] The building was 115 feet long and 50 feet wide and 42 feet high, costing about $28,000. It was a combination church and school but because of the debt, the school downstairs was not furnished at the time.[112] The church pews had to serve as school benches and the heating system was just one small coal stove. A few coal oil lamps provided the only light. The priests lived in two little rooms above the sacristy and their table depended on the charity of the parishioners from day to day.[113] It was a miserable beginning but to be located right in the heart of such a big city promised much for the future.

In the summer of 1874 Bishop McCloskey asked the Sisters of the Third Order of St. Francis of the Immaculate Conception of the Blessed Virgin Mary to take charge of the school. This community had been founded by a group of local ladies at Shelbyville, Kentucky near Gethsemani and had several houses throughout Kentucky, one of which was at Fancy Farm. The sisters worked under indescribable hardships until they could stand them no longer and then migrated to Clinton, Iowa in June 1876. Their departure was so sudden that no delay in plans could be allowed even for two sisters suffering from pneumonia.[114]

The first day of school in September 1874 brought forty-five pupils of various grades. "Classes began at eight a.m. and continued until four in the afternoon. After classes were dismissed, the daily chores such as cleaning the school and the lamp-chimneys and bringing up the next day's quota of coal were scheduled so that is was seldom that the children reached home before supper time." Tuition at that time was only 30 cents a month but few of the families could afford such an expense.[115]

Fr. Feehan became pastor at St. Cecilia's in July 1874 when the work and the worry became too great for Fr. McDonald, who then went to Fancy Farm.[116] The Louisville church was dedicated on August 24 with the usual ceremonies. Fr. Leander Keening, O. Carm., preached the German sermon. He had come to Louisville from Cumberland to conduct the annual retreat for the Ursulines.[117] To formally inaugurate the advent of the Carmelites to Louisville, Bishop McCloskey was awarded a letter of affiliation to the Order.[118]

On the same day this award took place, September 8, 1874, Fr. Meagher was appointed commissary general for Kentucky.[119] This action, removing the Kentucky and Marlboro Fathers from Knoll's jurisdiction, made formal what was already an arrangement *de facto*. The appointment seemed necessary, as was the separation of the Kansas Carmelites from those in Maryland, because of the distance between Knoll and the Carmelite houses in Kentucky. To aggravate this problem of distance, Knoll had left Cumberland and taken up residence in a parish at Butler, Pennsylvania the previous year.

Still every indication pointed to a new and glorious future for the Carmelites in Kentucky. A new commissariat had been launched under the most auspicious conditions. The expanded activities of the Carmelites in Kentucky had also attracted vocations both from Europe and the surrounding environs of Louisville and Paducah. At the beginning of 1874, Albert Murphy, the younger brother of Brocard Murphy, applied for admission. Albert finished his training at the Carmelite seminary in Knocktopher, Ireland, and upon his arrival in Kentucky entered the Preston Park Seminary.[120] He was to prove to be a fine representative of the Kentucky Commissariat, one of the most outstanding community conscious men in the early history of the province.

4
Chapter Four: UNIFYING FOUNDATIONS

New Carmelite communities were founded in Pittsburgh, New Jersey, and Niagara Falls, while the Carmelite foundation in Cumberland, Maryland was sold and those foundations in Kentucky were returned to the bishop. It was slowly becoming obvious that unification of the six Carmelite foundations still extant, with a single seminary system was needed for the Order to prosper in the North America.

Departing from Cumberland - Arriving in Pittsburgh

WHILE the Kentucky foundations showed prospects for progress, ominous clouds shrouded the monastery at Cumberland. In June of 1873, Knoll was so pessimistic that he wrote to the prior general that the Carmelite Order as such could not be said to exist in America. There were in his view only priests wearing the Carmelite habit on the American scene. He deplored the deficiency of novices and to remedy this shortage sought two men——one to be novice master and one to be the new commissary general, a job Knoll now wanted to part with.[1] As the Marlboro and Paducah foundations slowly receded from Knoll's influence, their value in helping to contribute financially to the community at Cumberland slowly passed from view. The Kentucky Carmelites did, however, furnish funds regularly for paying off the existent debt on the monastery at Cumberland. In anticipation of the possible loss of all revenue from the Kentucky foundations, Knoll also assumed parochial duties of St. Peter's church in Butler, Pennsylvania, in 1873,[2] while a new brick rectory was being built at New Baltimore that same year.[3]

The withdrawal of the Kentucky foundations from the jurisdiction of Knoll in 1874 dealt a final blow though to financial and manpower resources at Cumberland. It made the upkeep unbearable and unfeasible. The paucity of the candidates seemed to further argue that the 50 bed monastery there would never be reasonably occupied. There were only two or three priests with Fr. Cyril at this time.[4] Furthermore, the somewhat strained relations between Archbishop Bayley and the Carmelites did not hold out any prospects of a bright future. Motivated by these circumstances, Knoll decided to sell the Cumberland monastery in July 1875 without consulting anyone for $21,000.[5] The Carmelite prior general in Rome was somewhat disturbed over the fact that he had been notified of the transaction only after the transfer had taken place. He thought the reasons adduced for the sale were somewhat fabricated.[6] The monastery was sold to Capuchins from the Westphalian Province of Muenster. Lashed by the waves of the *Kulturkampf*, they had sought a safe harbor in the American continent.[7] On July 17, 1875, Capuchins Anthony Schuermann and Francis Wolf took possession of the Cumberland properties.[8]

The sale had seemed opportune, for Bishop Domenec of Pittsburgh, pleased with the work of the Carmelites at New Baltimore and Butler, asked Knoll to take charge either of St. Mary's church in Alleghany, Pennsylvania, or St. Peter and Paul's church in East Liberty, Pennsylvania. Knoll, however, was tired of financial worries. After his long struggle to pay off the Cumberland monastery, he was hesitant to accept St. Mary's because of the heavy debts the parish had contracted. Furthermore, he would have to build a monastery in Alleghany. If his commissariat was to develop, his cherished dream of a well-founded novitiate and house of studies needed to be a reality.[9]

As for St. Peter and Paul's church, it could not offer the city parishioners which Cumberland culled because East Liberty at that time was only a small village about four miles from the city. Furthermore, although the congregation was supposed to number two hundred and fifty families, the English families were attending Sacred Heart church.[10] The bishop, therefore, offered Knoll Holy Trinity parish on Center Avenue in Pittsburgh, which held out facilities more compatible with the commissary's plans. Thus, by the summer of 1875, Knoll had consolidated his commissariat and centered it solely in the Pittsburgh diocese.[11] The people in the parish had been torn into factions and the style of several of the parish priests had prompted the bishop to make the transfer to the Carmelites.[12] Knoll arrived at Holy Trinity on July 23, 1875,[13] and performed his first baptism on August 1.[14]

Holy Trinity parish had been established on September 21, 1856, at the corners of Fulton Street and Minersville Road. Many of the early Germans, crowded out of the confines of the old St. Philomena parish by the growing business district, and the various industries along the Allegheny River, moved to the "Hill District."[15] They were joined by the waves of new immigrants coming into the newly settled territory known for many years as Riceville. Suke's Run above Pipetown was not a very savory neighborhood. There resorted some of the butchers whose slaughterhouses had been outlawed in the city. The region as far as the present Dinwiddie Street was known as Riceville, and in the sections where the atmosphere was comparatively more inviting were located "Hatfield Garden," famous for its beer and "Social Garden" where the initiated might occasionally witness a bear-baiting.[16]

After a number of preliminary meetings had been held, a formal gathering for the erection of a parish was held on September 21, 1856. At this meeting the Redemptorist Father Scheffler pointed out the necessity of establishing a church and school in Riceville, and upon proper vote and agreement it was decided to buy a parcel of land at Fulton Street and Minersville Road, measuring 128 by 132 feet, from the Hoolship Estate at a cost of $7,000. At a meeting held on October 12, 1856, plans were made to build a brick church measuring 44 by 88 ft., but contracts for this building were not given out until May 26, 1857, because masonry work could not be done in the winter months. Accordingly, a temporary church was used until fair weather came along. The cornerstone of this first church was laid June 7, 1857 by the Very Rev. Patrick McMahon, Vicar General of the Diocese, and the church was dedicated on November 22, 1857, by the Rt. Rev. Michael O'Connor.[17]

The formation of a new parish and the building of a Catholic church in Riceville drew settlers rapidly so that in the course of a few years the building had to be enlarged twice. The future held splendid promise. The Redemptorist Fathers from St. Philomena's were the first pastors but soon withdrew from the parish once it was properly established and gave it over to the bishop who appointed a secular priest, the Rev. Joseph Kauffmann as pastor. In 1865, the Benedictines from St. Vincent's Abbey in Beatty took charge of Holy Trinity. In 1870, the Rev. Jacob Rossweg, another secular priest, was appointed to Holy Trinity and remained but four years.[18] A clerical agitator, the Rev. J. Tamchina, succeeded in getting Fr. Rossweg to abandon the parish by disseminating false reports among the people as to the pastor's sincerity. One of the points raised against Rossweg was that his frequent pleas for vocations was an attempt to scare all young people into convents. He kept his resignation a secret until the last Mass on the Sunday of his departure. During the sermon he made his final point. He would no longer remain in a place that would not produce a vocation.[19]

During the year following Fr. Rossweg's resignation, Fr. Tamchina was pastor. His private ambition hampered his efforts so that the people did not work with him and the parish, as a result, was hurled on the rocks of discontent.[20]

This was the atmosphere at the parish when Knoll arrived. His first task was the erection of a monastery facing out onto a garden.[21] This structure was able to accommodate almost a dozen religious.[22]

The cost of the new priory was $10,000. This sum was paid from the Cumberland funds.[23] Despite the "vocation problem" at Holy Trinity parish, Knoll had expressed his belief that it would be easier to encourage youths to enter the Order there.[24] In those early years at Pittsburgh, four students were members of the community. Bernard Fink and Dominic Peter Rider both attended classes at St. Vincent's Abbey in Latrobe. Dominic Scholl was a novice and Henry Reinhart was preparing to receive the Carmelite habit at New Baltimore.[26] Knoll was most concerned with obtaining a bona fide novice master who could begin to instruct his men in the fundamentals of Carmelite life. "I am ignorant of how to show the novices the fonts [foundations], except for prayers."[26]

School had been opened at Holy Trinity parish even before the first church had been built. As early as October 12, 1856, the school question had been settled, and a certain Professor Henry Mitter opened the first classes. Salaried at $300 a year, he became the first principal. In 1877 the Carmelite commissary invited the Sisters of Divine Providence to teach two classes of the school.[27] In 1874, Knoll also began to function as chaplain at St. Paul's Orphan Asylum.[28] As a mission station, the Carmelites began to attend St. Mary's church in Beaver Falls, Pennsylvania in 1876. Although there was no rectory there, the priests could stay in a few rooms over the local drug store.[29]

CARMELITES IN THE NIAGARA FRONTIER

Out in Kansas, Fr. Albert Heimann was facing similar problems that Knoll had tried to address. To place the Kansas houses that were under his domain on a sound foundation, it was necessary to establish a large monastery. Here religious life could be more regularly observed and candidates for the Order might be more ably trained and educated. He had first thought of establishing such a house at Leavenworth but quickly discovered that the parish of St. Joseph could not support a monastery.[30]

He turned therefore to Scipio. Here Heimann planned to build a new church, a large monastery, and a college for boys. An extensive farm was to be developed. The largest barn in several counties would stand on the property. Besides the ordinary grain crops, there would be cattle, sheep, hogs, and poultry to be cared for. There would also be groves of vineyards and hops for wine and beer. Twenty acres of land had originally belonged to the parish; Fr. Heimann himself, while in the secular priesthood, had brought 160 acres, and he now purchased another 160 acres.[31] Total holdings were later increased to 520 acres.[32]

Heimann foresaw the need for lay brothers to man and care for the farm. Stories passed down through local families suggest that Heimann sent Carmelites to preach at the nearby churches on the brotherhood in the Carmelite Order.[33] This it seems was done periodically and in time these sermons attracted some twenty men to join Carmel, ten of whom persevered. All were older men who had migrated from Germany and most all were skilled tradesmen. The fact that by 1875 the Scipio Community already had ten brothers and candidates for the brotherhood seems to substantiate this bit of local folklore.[34] The service rendered by these men was invaluable.

With the building of the Sante Fe Railroad in 1869, new life and trade flowed into Scipio. A generous supply of timber studded the banks of the Pottwatomie and many citizens realized considerable gain for selling trees for railroad ties. Others profited through rent obtained from the use of their wagons.[35] The dawn of the new growth in the settlement was simultaneous with a great fire; how the fire came to start is still unexplained. It broke out near the creek and an unbounded sea of flames raged through the woods and pastures. In an unbelievably short time, the flames spread towards the old log church. The fire was extinguished before it caused much damage to the church. But the cemetery did not share the same good fortune.[86] The fire was a blessing in disguise, however, for it spurred, plans for a new church edifice.

These were the early prosperous years after the Civil War era. The number of Catholics in the area had increased and money was more in evidence. Trees were cut down, the prairies felt the passage of the plow, and large tracts of land had yielded, year after year, wheat and corn in abundance. Numerous herds of horses and cattle now grazed where formerly the buffalo had its home. With increasing wealth there was also to be expected an increase in the liberality of many towards the church. Heimann had reason to expect with confidence that his plans would be accomplished.

To be on the scene of construction, Heimann first moved to Scipio and had Guenther fill his pastorate in Leavenworth. Then he took out a mortgage on the property of Leavenworth, bought farm implements and plotted the site for the new church on higher ground.[37] Less than one month after the dedication of St. Joseph's church in Leavenworth, the cornerstone for the new edifice at Scipio was laid on the Feast of Our Lady of Mount Carmel 1871. The work progressed at a good speed in spite of many obstacles and was completed in a year. The sum of money ultimately needed for the building was beyond the pocket books and purses of his parishioners. A letter went East to many friends who might be expected to contribute.[38] The best building-lumber had been used by the Sante Fe and now Heimann had to pay dearly for almost every piece of timber —nearly three cents a foot.[39]

Three priests had joined the developing community and eight lay brothers were working on the farm. However, in spite of a strict economy—amounting to privation in food and living comforts—great debts had been assumed to pay for the new buildings and farm implements.[40] For a time things went well. A satisfactory number of boys enrolled in the school and the farm produced good crops in its first year.

Then came disaster! Bad times settled upon the nation—the most severe and protracted depression the country had to endure prior to 1929. Millions of men were thrown out of work. The support of Catholics in the East upon which Heimann had relied shriveled at a time when his school was just beginning to blossom. An ex-Jesuit, Fr. Aloysius Laigneil, had come to Scipio in the spring of 1873 to be named the rector of the new college. About twenty-five students registered to be lodged, taught and fed.[41] The church and monastery, when completed, formed an "L". The frame church, forming the smaller arm of the "L" faced directly north. The monastery, a large rough three story frame building with a double pitched roof containing smaller dormer windows, extended to the west and was topped by a quaint baroque wooden belfry for the Angelus bell. The top story had been converted into use for the "college." The students slept in dormitories there and received the equivalent of a high school education, taught by the priests of the community.

But it was a hard year and their parents could afford to pay little towards their upkeep.[42] Laigneil was disgusted and soon left. Reverend Leander Koenig became the new rector. He was assisted by Frs. Peter Thomas Daily, Felix Link, Ignatius Beerhorst, and others.[43] The crops were poor enough in 1873; but in 1874 they failed completely. Continuous drought and extraordinary heat wilted most of the produce. Cinch bugs devoured more than half the remaining meager corn and wheat and millions of grasshoppers came to complete the destruction.[44]

The college also failed for another reason. Not only was the college supposed to bring a livelihood to the community, which it could not, but it was also supposed to foster priestly vocations among the most promising students. At its peak enrollment nearly forty boys were receiving instruction. It seems that the vocational aspect of the college remained fruitless.[45] The Carmelites themselves were sorely tried. Assistance at mission stations in Greeley, Garnett, Emerald, Holy Cross, Trustland, Humboldt, Burlington, Prairie City, Ottawa, Owl Creek, Westphalia, and Eudora consumed a great deal of time.[46] What the Fathers received in salary and stole fees for their services paid their grocery and clothing bills, but certainly could not begin to reduce payment on their debt and its interest.[47] Nevertheless, Fr. Albert had not forgotten that he was, first of all, a missionary. The Carmelites of Scipio maintained these parishes for miles around and served them well when the bishop had no one else available for his scattered flock. In addition, Fr. Albert had striven to build up the Catholicity of the region by bringing new immigrant settlers from the East.[48] To maintain these mission stations he sought help from more priests. Unfortunately, many of the priests who found temporary lodging at St. Boniface's were poor, unstable men, given to drink. Scipio became known in some circles as *refugium peccatorum* (the refuge of sinners) —an opprobrious title which the Cumberland house had held earlier. Yet, through these men the faith was saved and maintained for many souls during a dismal decade.[49]

The apostolic work in the district sapped much of the Carmelites' time so that often the students went without classes.[50] During these periods, however, the boys were not left idle. They were put to work on the monastery farm. The natural reaction of the parents was either to stop payment of tuition or to withdraw their children from the school altogether.[51] If the children were not receiving an education, they might as well work on their families' farms.

Including priests, brothers and students there were by this time forty-three in the community and it was indeed not an idle question that faced the prior in the fall of 1874: "What shall we eat this winter?"[52] For seven months there was reportedly no bread on the monastery table.[53] All of these hardships in the midst of a depression forced the college to close in June 1875.[54] This was the dark hour for the Carmel in Kansas; complete ruin and bankruptcy seemed inevitable. Creditors foreclosed on the Leavenworth mortgage. The property would have been lost but for Owen Duffy, a generous Catholic who bought the land at auction and retained it for the Order.[55] All means were employed to obtain funds for the beleaguered friars. A curate of the cathedral in Leavenworth, the Rev. Rudolph Mayer [the future Carmelite Pius Mayer], traveled to Europe to appeal in person to the Ludwig Missionsverein.[56] As a consequence, the *Leopolinen Stiftung* granted them 500 gulden in 1875[57] and the Ludwig

Missionsverein sent 1500 gulden at the same time as well as 2400 marks in 1877.[58]

This latter donation undoubtedly was given to cover losses incurred by a plague of grasshoppers in 1876 and by a severe hailstorm in 1877.[59] But the crucial winter was that of 1875. Somehow they survived. The following spring it was decided that a house in the East was needed to secure support for Scipio.

Fr. Ignatius Beerhorst, who had just made his simple profession, and Fr. Leander Koenig were sent to ask various bishops to allow the Carmelites in their dioceses. They received little encouragement though because the country was still in hard times.[60] In the course of their travels, they came to the doors of Bishop Ryan of Buffalo, New York. He himself could not offer them any place, but he told them that Archbishop Lynch of Toronto had wanted to establish a community in his diocese dedicated in a special way to Our Lady.[61]

Following his recommendation, Fr. Ignatius applied to the Archbishop of Toronto, who was no stranger to Carmel. He had attended Mount St. Joseph, the school of the Irish Carmelite Brothers in Clondalkin. There he witnessed the devotion to Our Lady for which he was so noted. The close of the year 1873 found Archbishop Lynch in Europe on business of the diocese. During his visit to Ireland, he enlisted the interest of his former Carmelite teachers to send a band of brothers to his diocese. The brothers were sent to teach in the town of St. Catherines, Ontario, centrally located in the peninsula of Niagara. They were at once engaged in teaching at St. Nicholas Separate School. Already since 1856, the Sisters of St. Joseph had been teaching in St. Catherines, but in 1874 they undertook an extensive program of expansion by the erection of an academy. The brothers took charge of the upper classes of boys. Br. Joseph asked for more volunteers but they never came. The Discalced Carmelite Fathers, who were engaged in missionary work, had sponsored the community in Ireland. At the present time, they were seeking a colony of brothers for Cochin, China. In the same month the Christian Brothers of De La Salle arrived to teach in St. Nicholas' School. Without assistance, the Carmelite brothers could not carry on their work any longer.[62]

Thus, in great need of laborers in his diocese, the Archbishop gave the Scipio applicants a hearty welcome. Under date of July 9, 1875, Lynch wrote to the Vicar Apostolic of Leavenworth, the Most Reverend Louis M. Fink, to make inquiries about the qualifications of the new community. The reply was filled with the highest praise!

The Carmelites of this Vicariate are a first class set of religious—

humble, strict observers of their Rule—zealous priests of the mission. The superior was a special friend of our former good Bishop Miege."

Fink assured the archbishop that he would not be sorry for providing the Carmelites with work.

> They wish to have a mission outside of Kansas because they are so very poor; they have no means of support themselves, owing to our disasters for the last three years. Another reason is namely to get candidates for their Order. ... In Kansas there is not much chance yet of that, owing to the young settlements of thinly settled population ... I am sorry to loose [sic] Father Ignatius—for the present at least, as he has done a great deal of good on the mission.[63]

Acting upon this favorable reply, the Archbishop was more than willing to accept the Carmelites into his diocese. On August 4, he wrote to Fr. Ignatius Beerhorst and gave him faculties in the diocese, directing him at the same time,

> We hereby appoint you to the missions of Flos, Medonte, and Vigo, as principal missionary. ... You will please, Rev. Father, put yourself under the direction of Very Rev. Dean O'Connor for the present till the mission of Flos, etc., be evacuated by the present pastor.[64]

According to his assignment, Fr. Ignatius proceeded to Barrie, Ontario, the residence of the dean, to examine the situation. On August 9, he wrote the archbishop from Barrie saying that he had visited the missions of Vigo, Flos, Medone and was sorry to say that the archbishop had been misinformed about the land in Flos. "Only some Ackers [sic] are middling good. . . . Besides it is the opinion of the good people that they are unable to support a religious community decently because the greatest part of the people are in debt. Your Grace will excuse me if I return the faculties and responsibilities to the archdiocese."[65] Beerhorst suggested that Lynch select another mission in the archdiocese for the Carmelites to staff.

From the letters which Fr. Albert, the superior in Kansas, wrote to the archbishop at this time, it seems that the archbishop now made several new offers to the Carmelites. On August 16, he wrote the archbishop that he was sending Fr. Xavier Huber, who had been collecting alms and was going to make his retreat at the seminary of Our Lady of the Angels at Suspension Bridge, to visit the archbishop and examine the places offered.[66] On August 25 he wrote that he could not praise enough the archbishop's kindness to him and his Order. Fr. Ignatius' abrupt departure was caused by the fear of assuming responsibility in accepting a place from the archdiocese. The letter further indicated that should the Carmelite Order receive a mission in the Toronto archdiocese, it would prefer the location around Niagara Falls offered by the archbishop. Once Fr. Xavier had visited Lynch and approved a location, Frs. Ignatius and Leander, who was able to converse in English, German, French, and Italian,[67] would be sent to begin work.[68]

Fr. Xavier visited the archbishop by mid-September and was pleased with all the arrangements. His report encouraged Heimann to accept the parishes in Clifton [Niagara Falls]and Falls View as well as a mission at Drummondsville.[69] On October 18, he wrote to the Archbishop. "Herewith I send you Rev. F. Ignatius Beerhorst and Rev. P. Leander Koenig; Fr. Ignatius is superior. Fr. Leander who is preaching the jubilee in Allison, Iowa, will be in Niagara Falls next week."[70] With them came Br. Gerard Altendoerfer to cook and to care for the new house.[71]

When the Carmelites arrived at Niagara, they found themselves in charge of a wide frontier thinly settled except for a few families in Clifton and Falls View. Chippewa was within the parish limits also. Falls View was the residence of the pastor. There a shrine to Our Lady of Peace and a stone rectory stood.

The Shrine of Our Lady of Peace could trace its origins to the late seventeenth century. On November 10, 1867, the lieutenant of the French explorer La Salle, La Hotte de Lussiere, and a Franciscan chaplain, Fr. Hennepin, set out from Quebec to find suitable places to raise a fort and to build a ship above Niagara Falls.[72] Landing at Queenston, they scaled up the Heights and travelled several miles along the river beyond the mighty cataract of Niagara Falls to camp at Chippewa Creek for the night. As this place was not suitable for the building of the boat, they decided to turn back to their ship. During the next morning, December 11, 1678, somewhere between the Chippewa and the cataract, Fr. Hennepin celebrated the first Sacrifice of the Mass above the Niagara River.[73] It was at the spot above the Falls, where tradition holds that this first Mass took place, that Fr. Edward Gordon, pastor of the church at Niagara-on-the-Lake, laid the cornerstone on June 13, 1837 for St. Edward's church, which would later become the Shrine of Our Lady of Peace.[74] In that year a census of Niagara-on-the-Lake, Niagara Falls, Chippewa, and Queenston was taken by Fr. Gordon. The registration showed a population of 817 Catholics.[75] The growth of the parish caused Fr. Victor Juhel to erect a frame addition to the church in 1860.[76] This same year, Bishop de Charbonnel of Toronto retired to a Capuchin monastery at Lyons, formally resigning the bishopric of Toronto. His coadjutor, Bishop

Lynch, succeeded him.⁷⁷

Bishop John Lynch had long been stirred with the thought of what a magnificent spot this would be for the erection of an international shrine. This project haunted him until a partial fulfillment of his dream was realized in 1856 when he founded the seminary of Our Lady of the Angels, a few miles from the Cataract on the American side.⁷⁸ On the very year of his succession to the Toronto See, on December 17, he purchased 200 acres of land along the ridge above the Canadian Falls from Colin Skinner, Malone, and others.⁷⁹ These lands were centered around the acre upon which St. Edward's church was situated.

The outbreak of the Civil War in the United States echoed resounding vibrations in Canada. The Niagara frontier became the terminus of the Underground Railroad and the haven of Southern exiles and refugees. This event gave Bishop Lynch the final impetus for the culmination of his great designs.

> It was at the commencement of the American Civil War. Our heart was moved with sorrow at the loss of many lives, and the prospect of so many souls going before God in judgment, some, it is to be feared, but ill prepared. The beautiful rainbow that spanned the cataract, the sign of peace between God and the sinner, suggested prayers and hopes to see the war soon ended; and we called the church 'Our Lady of Victories or of Peace!'⁸⁰

St. Edward's church was thereafter known as the Church of Our Lady of Victories or of Peace. Lynch then obtained special privileges from Rome and made the little church a place of pilgrimage and a spiritual treasure house. The Papal decree of Pius IX read:

> Our Venerable Brother, John Lynch, present Bishop of Toronto, recently made known to us his intention of erecting a place of holy pilgrimage at the Church of the Blessed Virgin Mary of Peace, situated at the cataract of Niagara in the said diocese. For this purpose he addressed to us earnest prayers that indulgences to those of the faithful who should make this holy pilgrimage be granted. We, therefore, proposing in our love and charity to increase the devotion of the faithful and to promote the welfare of souls, do yield to the prayers addressed, to us and mercifully grant a plenary indulgence and the remission of all their sins to all and each of the faithful of both sexes who, after having confessed their sins with true contrition and received Holy Communion devoutly, visit said church on any day of the year they may choose and there address fervent prayers to God and to the Blessed Virgin Mary for the concord of Christian princes, the peace and exaltation of Holy

Mother the Church, the extirpation of heresy and the conversion of sinners. Moreover, on whatsoever day the faithful visit the said church, and there with at least contrite hearts pray according to the intentions mentioned above, we grant them remission of seven years and of as many quarantines of penance as may have been enjoined, or to which they are bound in any other way, according to the customary discipline of the Church. We grant also that these indulgences, remissions of sins, and relaxations of penances may be applied in the manner of suffrages to the souls of the faithful who have departed this life united to God in charity. All things to the contrary not withstanding, these presents are to hold for all time . . . Given at Borne in St. Peter's under the seal of the Fisherman on the first day of March 1861, in the fifteenth year of our pontificate.[81]

In keeping with his designs, Bishop Lynch asked the Ladies of Loretto to establish a convent to the north of Our Lady of Peace. The nuns, led by Mother Joachim as superior, gladly accepted. By 1870 the beautiful convent whose view of the Falls went unrivaled began to be constructed. Mother Mary Teresa Elle Dease, who for forty years was the superior of the Ladies of Loretto in Canada (1851-1889) and whose body rests in the grounds north of the convent, undertook this propitious work.[82]

Upon their arrival in the autumn of 1875, the Carmelites lost no time in acquainting themselves with their new surroundings. On November 12, Ignatius wrote to the archbishop to tell him how pleased they were with the assignment and invited him for a visit.[83] On April 25th of the following year, Archbishop Lynch issued his famous pastoral letter in which he formally introduced and welcomed the Carmelite Fathers to his diocese. He also exhorted the laity to contribute to the erection of their monastery. What the Fathers' functions were to be were set down in this letter:

We have for many years searched for a fervent congregation of men to found a monastery and a church worthy of the place and its destination. Enthusiastic pilgrims of nature's grandeur come here to enjoy its beauty; others alas to drown remorse. We desired to have a religious house where those pilgrims could be attracted to adore nature's God in spirit and in truth, and so would there find, in solitude and rest how great and good God is.

The Fathers of the Order of Our Lady of Mount Carmel, the most ancient in the Church and dear to the heart of our Blessed Mother, have commenced this good work. Our Holy Father Pius IX has been graciously pleased to confer upon the present little church Plenary Indulgences and other favors granted to the most ancient pilgrims of the Old World. The Fathers also propose, when a suitable house is built, to receive prelates and clergy of the Church as well as laity to make retreats; and to provide priests, worn out in the service of their Divine Master, with a home, where they can quietly prepare for eternity.[84]

There were noteworthy signs that the laity was already quite appreciative of the Carmelites' work. In July, Fr. Ignatius wrote to the archbishop that "the fair in Clifton was a success—net receipts, a gold value."[85] July 16, 1876, was a day of pilgrimage to the shrine conjoined with the laying of the cornerstone for the new monastery.[86] A seventeen year old youth, Philip Best, later to be a Carmelite, described the event:

> Sunday, July 16, Carmel Day! The Scapular! Our triumphant entry to Niagara. Hosannas from the laity! I cannot recall the names of the officiating clergy. All I can bring back is crowds of people. We were not of the monastic family—nor of the Clifton parish of St. Patrick's. We boys were only sore-footed pilgrims. We were hungry, but we didn't mind. People came from all parts of Canada and the U.S.A. There was no order all the way from Clifton. Some old folks rode in hacks. Unfortunately I could find no printed record of that important day. There were no local papers. The only ones were printed in Toronto and Hamilton and certainly the worshipful Grandmaster of the Loyal Orange Lodge would not print news of papist pranks.[87]

Several routine letters in the following days seemed to bear out the welcome received by the Carmelites.

In spite of external appearances and assurances, there were significant problems. The community at Niagara had been established to be of assistance to the Kansas foundations, but that assistance was not forthcoming. Perhaps it was not possible for Niagara to contribute anything. Be that as it may, not even a report was issued. In May 1876, Heimann had sent Fr. Pius Mayer to Niagara to investigate and to hold visitation in his name. The findings of the visitator were not very positive. The community was very much in debt and there was no vestige of community life.[88] In fact the Fathers at Niagara refused to give any vital information to the visitator. Fr. Mayer summoned his superior to visit the house personally, with the result that Fr. Ignatius Beerhorst, a priest in simple vows, was sent back to Kansas[89] and Fr. Leander Koenig was summarily dismissed from the Order.[90]

To save the situation in Niagara from complete deterioration, Heimann appointed Fr. Pius Mayer, himself in simple vows, as vicar-prior.[91] Fr. Pius immediately began to assemble priests, students and novices to insure a sound foundation. At the end of October, Fr. Angelus Mallia arrived from Malta, sent by the prior general at the vicar's request. Fr. Mallia was appointed master of novices. The Irish Province sent Frs. Reddy, Grennan and Whitely.[92]

In a very short time the stone rectory on the edge of the escarpment, overlooking the falls, was not sufficient to house the community. The building was half stone, half brick. The first floor served as a study hall, the second as a dormitory. When this proved too small, the students slept in an adjacent building called the ecclesiastical barn, because of the farm stalls on its first floor.[93] According to the new vicar, the archbishop had promised to build a suitable monastery for them at some future date, since the house they were using belonged to him. As a token of the friendship that existed between the Carmelites and the archbishop of Toronto, John Joseph Lynch was affiliated with the Order.[94]

In the meantime, a wooden addition was built to the north, containing a chapel, dining room, study hall, and dormitory. To defray the costs of building and to support the community, Fr. Pius preached missions to the people throughout the diocese of Ontario.[95] In promoting this work, he was encouraged and assisted by the archbishop himself.[96]

Although his difficulties had not entirely passed, the prior in Kansas, Heimann, wrote in 1877 that the Kansas community could congratulate itself on its survival.[97] His surveillance of the scene was supported by the facts. Yet survival was a far cry from the ambitious plans he laid just a few years earlier for his Kansas houses. Now not only had he to close the college of his dreams, but what is more, the only real hope of establishing a successful seminary could be had in the Niagara house.

TOWARD REUNIFICATION OF THE WESTERN CARMELITE COMMUNITIES

During the summer of 1879, Heimann visited his new seminary at Niagara. On his way back to Kansas he stopped in Butler, Pennsylvania, to pay respects to Fr. Cyril Knoll. The folly of the separatist movements in Kansas and Cumberland had taken their toll on both men. They both had spent long years in building a dream only to see it disappear. In Kansas the road looked long and uncertain, almost as if Heimann was starting anew. At this meeting the men reviewed the crises each had faced in the estranged years of separation. Small separate commissariats had brought only heartache. They did at least serve an historic function of warning coming generations of Carmelites that such endeavors would end only in futility. It was resolved that the only sane solution was to reunite the separated houses. Fr. Albert laid down one condition—that he be allowed to retire to Niagara and that it be placed directly under the jurisdiction of the prior general.[98] Niagara held a little of the reality that had been his dream; it showed some success. At the same time, Heimann did not wish to be subject to Knoll in order to avoid an open feud such as the one that had severed their relations ten years earlier.

The arrangement was welcomed by Knoll too, for he had his problems in the Pennsylvania houses. His unpopular characteristics had also plagued his administrative abilities there.[99] Fr. Anastasius Peters, at one time a European school teacher, followed his brother, who was in the community at Boxmeer, in to the Carmelite Order. As an ordained priest, he went to Straubing. His ambition carried him to the United States where Knoll appointed him pastor of New Baltimore. He soon found himself in trouble largely because of the English orientation of the parish. Knoll then transferred him to the German parish at Butler.[100] Just a few months after his new assignment, a number of serious complaints were brought against him so that Bishop Tuigg, a stern man, suspended him. In January 1879, Knoll himself assumed charge of this congregation to save it for the Order if possible. Peters was then given a commission by Knoll to found a monastery in the eastern part of the United States. The letter of commission and recommendation written by Knoll was kept by Fr. Anastasius. Later, it was to play an important role in the establishment of a commissariat of the South. When Leavenworth and Scipio were once more charged to Cyril's care in July 1879, he sent Peters to distant banishment in the prairie missions.[101]

The two leaders returned to Kansas to announce the amalgamation. Fr. Cyril surrendered the Butler parish because of the scandals that had stirred the congregation and their consequent displeasure with the Carmelites. He also hoped to concentrate his efforts on the Kansas houses begun so many years before.[102] Fr. Albert Heimann stayed with his priests a few months until Rome had approved the change. Then he left for Niagara. There he was made novice master and acting prior. Fr. Mayer was away too often on preaching assignments to be able to fill these offices. Fr. Heimann was an exemplary friar who faithfully fulfilled the Carmelite Rule. As a superior he was ever a kind father to those under his direction.[103]

As the separate houses in the western sections necessarily moved to a closer unity, the houses in the eastern sections realized that unification was the only solution to their problems also. No single group by itself could support with manpower or money a novitiate and seminary, the bedrock needed for their growth. Archbishop Bayley, who came to the See of Baltimore from Newark on July 30, 1872, was most anxious to keep the Carmelites in Marlboro. He was, however, unwilling to give the establishment canonical status.[104] His decision was made despite the agreement which Spalding had signed making the foundation "permanent."[105]

Under orders from Fr. Meagher, who then had been appointed commissary general for Kentucky and Maryland, Fr. O'Dwyer and Fr. Walsh prepared to leave the Maryland missions. On April 9, 1875, Fr. O'Dwyer sent his regrets to the archbishop. He declared that he had even gone to Louisville to try to persuade Fr. Meagher from the action, but to no avail. A report of the parish at Upper Marlboro indicated a healthy climate. One curious notation announced that the former slaves had been taught Catholic hymns to counter Methodist propaganda of "hymn festivals."[106] The Carmelites left the missions with an excellent record. They were active centers of Catholic life and freed from debt; their material prosperity was assured.[107] On August 12, 1875, the Mill Hill Fathers assumed charge of the Marlboro missions. Before the Fathers surrendered their stations, Bayley had suggested that the priests join the ranks of the secular clergy. Fortunately Frs. Dwyer and Walsh were too loyal to entertain such a thought. The Carmelites reported to Paducah.

THE SEPARATE FOUNDATIONS COME TO AN END

The year 1875 brought several important changes in the Kentucky Commissariate. When Fr. Meagher wrote to the prior general on February 22 of that year from Louisville, there was a somber report on the state of affairs. St. Cecilia's church had cost much more than anticipated and only a small rectory could be built.[108] On March 15, 1875 the prior general granted permission for the canonical establishment of the Louisville house.[109] But when the bishop, William G. McKloskey, was approached regarding providing the Carmelites assurances about their permanency at St. Cecilia's, he absolutely declined. He was happy enough to have the services of the Fathers but he had no intention of surrendering the title to the property. Fr. Anastasius Kreidt wrote in his diary:[110]

> August 5, 1875. A letter from Pop [Fr. Meagher]. He has suffered— suffered greatly. The Bishop of Louisville has cheated him. After having called him to his city and forced him almost to erect a church and to establish himself there, he refuses to give him the deed of the property, unless he wishes to sacrifice his privileges as a regular. Of course, Pop has refused and left Louisville.[111]

When the news of Knoll's sale of Cumberland was echoed in the Louisville community that year, it came as another shock. Fr. Kreidt wrote:

> August 21, 1875. The general has answered my letter. He knew nothing about our misfortune in Louisville. The old prior of Cumberland did not inform the general of the step he took until the thing had happened irreparably. The general finds the three reasons adduced to excuse the sale as very weak and insufficient.[112]

The Kentucky Carmelites felt that at least $5,000 of the money from the sale should have been given to Paducah. Besides the fact that the money was desperately needed to support the students, Meagher felt there was a question of justice. They had all worked to help pay off the Cumberland debt; Marlboro and Paducah had offered 1200 Masses for Knoll, plus the donation of over $1,000 in cash gifts and some $3,000 in salaries.[113] The first steps were taken toward initiating a civil suit when, to Fr. Meagher's dismay, the lawyer discovered that the Cumberland property was in Knoll's name. The title had never been registered for the corporation even though the Carmelites had gone through all the legal requirements.[114] Fr. Knoll appealed to Archbishop Bayley to prohibit any further civil action, but the Metropolitan would have nothing to do with the problem.[115] As a court of last resort, Knoll wrote to the Cardinal Protector of the Order. He stated his case. He had paid the Kentucky Carmelites' passageway over. They had furthermore worked with him only a year. After that, they chose to separate, a decision which worked considerable hardship to Knoll. The contributions sent to support his Cumberland foundation in view of their action had actually been due in justice. There was no need for any retribution now.[116] Too far distant to understand the complexities of the situation, the Cardinal supported Knoll as a matter of principle.[117]

The quarrel over Cumberland erected a wall of separation between the Kentucky Carmelites and Fr. Knoll. The fact that the Cumberland mortgage was paid by February 19, 1874, was in no small part due to their efforts. They had trusted him when the legal corporation was set up, but once they realized what had taken place, they made a complete break and set up an independent commissariat. Their troubles were actually just beginning. When the missions at Upper Marlboro were closed, Fr. Meagher discovered that Frs. Dwyer and Joseph Walsh had kept no financial records and that both had been sending money to their parents without permission.[118] Both men were suspended. Fr. Dwyer left to become a secular priest,[119] but Fr. Walsh went to New Baltimore where he was reinstated. Fr. Forrestal, in the meantime, had left Paducah, physically ill from the effects of yellow fever and very emotionally disturbed at Fr. Meagher's practices and policies. He went to Pittsburgh where he died on March 1, 1878.[120]

These were hardships difficult enough for a man in robust health to bear and all the more debilitating to Fr. Meagher in his weakened condition. But he continued on bravely. He went to supervise the construction of the new church at Columbus[121] and helped Fr. Feehan at Paducah open the academy once again.[122] With Dwyer, Walsh and Forrestal gone and Fr. McDonald soon to leave for Europe because of ill health,[123] there were only three priests left: Meagher at Paducah, Feehan at Hickman, and Francis Walsh at Fancy Farm. This meant, as Meagher sadly explained to the prior general, that when he went out on quests so that the students might eat, there was no one at home to teach them.[124] His situation mirrored the problem in Scipio.

But despite all these set-backs, his own failing health, and the twelve students to be supported,[125] Meagher continued his work at Paducah. On October 27, 1878, he paid $900.00 for land for a parish cemetery and named it "Mount Carmel." He had the remains of Fr. Brocard Murphy and Sr. Ursula removed from St. John's cemetery and transferred to the new burial ground. He was quite confident that the Carmelites would be working in Kentucky for many years and should have a community burial plot.[126] In December, Fr. Albert Murphy took over Fancy Farm; Fr. Walsh moved to Columbus while Fr. Feehan remained at Hickman.[127]

The yellow fever epidemic that year was unusually severe. In the Columbus area Fr. Walsh was the only clergyman and Dr. Luke Blackburn the only doctor who stayed, tending the sick and dying heedless of personal safety. Later on the two heroes were honored at a public testimonial. So popular did Dr. Blackburn become that it was quite easy for him to later be elected governor of Kentucky.[128] Fr. Walsh died from the effects of the fever three years after that epidemic. At Hickman, population 1950, 454 cases were reported with over 180 deaths.[129] The epidemic, however, was less severe than in many other southern areas. For example, it proved more disastrous to Vicksburg than had the bitter siege of that city during the War Between the States. One report there listed 1,040 known cases of fever with 326 deaths out of a total population of 2,500.[130]

The diocesan clergy and religious women in Mississippi displayed the same rare heroism that the Carmelites had in Kentucky and that, indeed, the clergy throughout the country evidenced. Considering the fact that the Diocese of Natchez numbered at the time only twenty-five priests and that the first community of sisters had arrived only thirty years previous to the epidemic of 1878, the loss of six priests and sixteen sisters was indeed a great one.[131] Bishop Elder reflected this courage when he summoned the Sisters of Mercy: "My dear sisters: We are facing a dread pestilence; we must meet it with entire confidence in God and submission to his Holy Will. ... We must remain here together to be organized into bands for the visitation of the sick and the comfort of the dying. I bless you all and I, myself, will stay to share your danger. Be of good cheer; God is your helper and protector. . . ."[132] The Carmelite contribution in Kentucky, therefore, was by no means singular. It only typified a deep dedication that marked the religious ranks throughout the country.

The arrival of Fr. Anastasius Kreidt in Paducah in mid-July 1879 revived hope of life once again for the Kentucky Commissariat. He brought great personal talent and energy to the mission. Unfortunately, he worshipped Fr. Meagher, whom he affectionately called "Pop." In his diary, Kreidt penned the most sentimental effusion about him. When, through daily association, this idealism wore off, Kreidt became quite melancholy. He then sank into almost abject despair as he was accused by Meagher of withholding money from the community. It was with bitter sadness that young Anastasius obeyed the commissary's order to exchange places with Fr. Feehan.[133]

The great change in Meagher and the explanation for the strange things he said and did at this time could be attributed to the increasing ravages of the yellow fever attack he had suffered. Death came unexpectedly at 5:30 p.m. on August 2, 1880, from a stroke while he was resting at St. Mary's Infirmary in Cairo, Illinois. He was only forty years old.[134] Frs. Feehan, Kreidt, and Murphy went to Cairo and returned with the remains to Paducah.[135] In his diary Kreidt wrote a most anguished memorial of the man who was the inspiration of his life despite their late in the relationship misunderstanding: "He died far from home—no one of his brethren was near him. He died suddenly. When the priest came, he was dead. He did not die in the habit, not even a small scapular was found on him. Good God! What a death."[136] The funeral was on August 4; the burial was in Mount Carmel cemetery. On August 9 the *Paducah Daily News*, carried a memorial editorial, probably written by Fr. Feehan, on the life of Meagher. It is a beautiful tribute to a holy and zealous man in which the writer explains the virtues of the "son" by an eloquent account of the "father" "... whom the penner of these lines saw daily assist at the sacred functions ... in Ireland."[137]

Two days after the funeral, all five priests of the commissariat—Feehan and Reddy from Paducah, Walsh from Columbus, Kreidt from

Hickman and Murphy from Fancy Farm—addressed a joint letter to the General announcing the death of Fr. Meagher and begging that one of their number be appointed superior.[138] Such unanimity did not actually exist. They had hardly dispersed to their respective stations when each one began to analyze how the turn of events might affect him personally. Walsh wrote to the prior general on August 9, warning him that the situation was quite desperate financially. He also noted the existing rivalry between Kreidt and Feehan.[139] Kreidt wrote on August 23 recanting the proposal made in the group letter. He now hoped no one would be appointed superior.

Union with the other Carmelite houses was not only sensible but absolutely necessary. In Kentucky everything belonged to the bishop and the Order was actually carrying a debt of 25,000 lira. The mission stations were too distant and too poor. Fr. Walsh at Columbus, over sixty miles away, had only twenty poor families. Fr. Murphy at Fancy Farm, nearly twenty-five miles distant, had just a rural parish. At Hickman, close to one hundred miles from Paducah, Kreidt cared for only twenty families. He was living with the parishioners, as he could afford no rectory. As he saw it, there was no future in these places, no possibility of getting novices and the continued lack of community life was more than he cared to endure any longer.[140] Five days later he actually received a letter from Dominic O'Malley who had gone to Niagara for ordination. Heimann and Mayer were eager to have the Kentucky Carmelites join the ranks at Niagara.[141] Feehan clearly opposed such a plan.

Fr. Feehan evidently presumed he was to be the next pastor and superior. On August 13 he moved his library to Paducah and ordered Kreidt to Hickman.[142] The appointment from the prior general, dated August 24, 1880, did, indeed, name him as superior, but noticeably the appointment was as prior of Paducah only, and then only *ad nutum* ("at the prior general's pleasure").[143] However, he assumed command of the situation at once. He intended to prove there was still a great deal of vitality in the Kentucky Commissariat.

One can see a reflection of his activity in the many announcements that now began to appear in the local newspaper. An ice cream festival was held on August 26th. On Sunday, September 19, a solemn Mass was celebrated with a procession of various church societies to open the forty hours devotion. On September 30th Feehan visited Graves City for an undisclosed reason. On the seventh of the following month, Bishop McCloskey administered confirmation in Paducah. On the thirtieth of the same month, Fr. Feehan returned from giving a retreat at the parish of his brother, Fr. Richard Feehan, in Holy Cross, Crittenden County. All Souls Day Masses were scheduled for 6:30 and 9 a.m. Fr. Durbin, the oldest parish priest in Kentucky, paid Feehan an important visit on November 20. Christmas in the Catholic community would be celebrated with a special ceremony. A Solemn Mass would begin at 6 a.m.; low Masses were scheduled for 7 a.m., 8:30 and 9:30.[144]

Despite this flurry of announced activity, the fate of the Kentucky houses was already sealed. Yellow fever, tough economic times, a paucity of Catholics in the Purchase and the lack of vocations capable of completing higher educational studies, the competing needs of Carmelites in Cumberland, and administrative policies of a bishop and of the Carmelite commissary all contributed to ending Carmelite ministry in Kentucky in the 1800s.

FOUNDATIONS IN NEW JERSEY JOIN A REUNITED AMERICAN COMMISSARIAT

The new year of 1881 was not very old when the word came from the Carmelite prior general, Fr. Angelus Savini, that the Kentucky missions were to be joined with the house at Niagara Falls as well as those of Englewood and Tenafly, New Jersey, under the jurisdiction of Fr. Anastasius Smits. This union of English-speaking houses on January 8, 1881, was only practical.[145] It was natural also to select the man to lead the unification who had for all practical purposes conducted the most successful of the four separatist movements. Financially, he was not much more secure than the other leaders though. Nor had he attempted to establish a seminary—the bedrock of any true religious movement. He viewed the duplication of Carmelite seminaries throughout the country as a costly and unnecessary folly.

Smits was slightly above average height, of slender body, with a thin ascetic face. He was fastidiously clean and neat in person and surroundings. As pastor or prior he insisted on the same methodical neatness and cleanliness in monastery, church and school. He spoke Dutch and German as well as English with the exactitude of an Oriental scholar trained at an English university in a strong though somewhat toneless voice. In sermon and conference his facial expression and voice expressed a pleading which was well nigh irresistible to the audience. Every natural topic had a supernatural point. In a sense he was doctrinaire. He distrusted the spiritual methods of others. Later in life as a novice master, he refused to let any one else take charge of his novices when he was called away on business.

Sincerely and solemnly he announced his views and then considered the matter finished. "We have promised God and Our Lady poverty, which means detachment; we have not promised economy, which means spending becomingly." When the Chapter had appointed him master of novices, he held that the local superior had no right to send him out to conduct missions or give retreats. In the twilight of life he said: "We must pray now very much; we have for a General just a secular priest who does not understand religious life. But, after him there will be another General."[146]

In 1869 Smits had been made pastor of the Madonna church at Fort Lee, New Jersey. He owed the assignment to the recommendation of Fr. J. P. Poels, the pastor of St. John's in Newark. Smits appeared wearing a secular cassock.[147] He explained: "Bishop [James Roosevelt] Bayley of Newark . . . advised me to secularize and stay with him. I said nothing but remained where I was at Englewood alone for several years. In the meantime, hearing from no superior, Holland considered me secularized."[148] Again in the evening of life he writes: "Bishop Bayley of Newark . . . advised me to secularize. Fr. [Sebastian Gebhard]Messmer, afterwards Archbishop of Milwaukee, urged me in the same way." When Bishop Michael Corrigan, afterwards Archbishop of New York, urged him to secularize, Smits said: "I told him that I could not do so, as I had taken my vows to keep them." It seems difficult to reconcile these words with the facts. Apparently he yielded to suggestions of these bishops at least insofar as to take what is conceived to be the first step towards secularization, laying aside the habit.[149]

The appointment Fr. Smits received on May 4, 1869, made him pastor of Fort Lee and all the territory lying east of the Hackensack River. Besides the mother church at Fort Lee, there were in this district missions at Englewood, Tenafly, Carrieville, now called Northvale, and a "station" at the home of Mr. Frank J. Mills in the present Borough of Haworth, then called "The Old Hook." Left without assistance and unable to care for the entire district, Smits requested the Bishop to free him from the charge of Tenefly and Carrieville. This was done by the appointment of a secular priest who made his residence at Tenafly. In later years when Fr. Smits was no longer alone and when some parochial disturbances had arisen in Tenafly, both that mission and the one at Carrieville were returned to the care of the Carmelite Fathers.[150]

Within the first year of his appointment Smits transferred his residence from Fort Lee to Englewood. Within another year he was to be relieved from the care of Fort Lee so that he could devote himself entirely to the growing population of Englewood and the missions attached to it.[151] The extent of his assignment thus north to south was from the New York State line above Closter to the neighborhood of Little Ferry and east to west from the Hudson to the Hackensack River. From the heights of West Fort Lee, Madonna church overlooked the broad valley, drained by Overpeck Creek and the Hackensack River, extending twenty miles in depth west to the picturesque Ramapo Mountains and north to the New York State Line. In midsummer of the same year a fellow Carmelite from Kansas, Angelus Kempen, joined Smits in the parish work. Englewood was growing fast.[152]

To Fr. Kempen was left most of the work at Fort Lee; Smits was offered free living quarters by a retired Englewood business man, Mr. Eiremann in 1870. The combined income of both the Fort Lee and Englewood parishes when Smits took charge was not much more than a thousand dollars a year.[153] In the summer of 1870, Kempen received a dispensation from his vows and thus left Fort Lee, which was then removed by the bishop from the care of the Carmelites.

The library assembled by Smits and his companion priests at St. Cecilia's reveals that they were men of unusual discernment and kept well abreast of topics of their day. In 1870, Fr. Smits found it necessary to say Masses each Sunday in Englewood because of the rapidly growing Catholic population in that village. Madonna church was then served for a time by the Passionist Fathers of West Hoboken, and later by priests of the Capuchin Order.[154]

In 1869, the diocese of Newark was only sixteen years old. The northern half of New Jersey had been under the jurisdiction of the Archdiocese of New York. In 1853, however, Bishop James Roosevelt Bayley was assigned the task of forming a new diocese that embraced the entire state of New Jersey.[155] He had but twenty-six priests to serve over 40,000 Catholics.[156] The religious organization of northern Bergen county, a deserted and untrampled wilderness of the diocese, was slow. On May 26, 1859, however, the Northern Railroad of New Jersey whistled in a new era in the area.[157] The long steel rails, like arteries, brought fresh blood, youth and vigor to the hitherto sequestered valley. Englewood was the most rapidly developing of the many communities that had sprung up within the northern district, then known as the English Neighborhood.

In 1863 Mass was said in a building known as the lock-up on Van Brum Street in Englewood. A Protestant denomination had equal privileges to the temple of worship so that there was a race every Sunday between the minister and the priest. As the priest was too poor to own a horse, he had to walk all the way from Fort Lee. The arrangement was first come, first served. The last to arrive with his flock had to cool his heals outside until the first religious service was finished.[158] The first Catholic church building, fifty feet by twenty-five feet, was dedicated on November 11, 1866. Bishop Bayley named the church in honor of St. Cecilia.[159]

Smits testified that the generosity of the congregation was overwhelming. It was they who furnished the old church with the vestments and altar necessities. When he assumed charge there was but one old vestment on hand in a trunk behind the altar. As soon as the parishioners realized that Smits would remain as a resident pastor, construction was begun on a rectory. The sum of $2,100 was spent on securing property on which to build an $8,000 rectory. This was at a time when greenbacks were low in value, whereas labor was steep in cost. Smits noted that the parishioners had to pay masons building the basement $5.50 a day. A mortgage of $5,000 was made. The house was furnished one room at a time by the personal gifts of the congregation.

In those early years, the parishioners enlarged the church, installing confessionals and regular pews. The Temperance Society of the parish also erected a recreational club for parish use.[160]

One of the proudest chapters of the history of Carmel in America is that which tells of its early endeavors in the field of Catholic education. The nineteenth century demanded the existence of Catholic schools. The Catholic Church had a delicate responsibility of converting its huge immigrant flocks to American ways, while guarding their cherished Catholic traditions. The Catholic school system was a definite answer. The Carmelites had seen this necessity and taken the initiative in providing Catholic education for the souls under their care.

In spite of the legislation of the First and Second Plenary Councils of Baltimore in May 1852 and October 1866 on the necessity of Catholic children attending Catholic schools in order to safeguard their religious faith, large numbers of Catholic children continued to go to the public schools. A number of American bishops felt this as a heavy burden on their conscience and, therefore, solicited from the Holy See a directive to the hierarchy for the purpose of correcting the situation. As a consequence the Congregation of the Propaganda of the Faith sent an instruction dated November 24, 1875. This instruction was intended to emphasize the danger to Catholic children enrolling in public schools and to strengthen the hands of the bishops with their priests and people in their efforts to provide more Catholic schools.[161] The emphasis on the Catholic school system was further underscored in 1884. The Third

Plenary Council, then meeting in Baltimore, made a great effort to lay down a school policy for the whole country. Carmel, however, had not waited for these mandatory decrees.¹⁶²

The establishment of schools must have been an integral part of the plans, adopted by Fr. Smits when he entered the Englewood scene. It is recorded in *The Catholic Church in Englewood* that the first classes had been scheduled by Fr. Cody in 1867. But the first Catholic parish school in Bergen County dates from 1874. In that year, Fr. Smits and the Board of Trustees of St. Cecilia's church voted to erect a school on the parish property, facing Division Street. The new building included living rooms for the four Sisters of Charity whom Mother Xavier of Convent Station had promised to assign as the first teaching staff.

The new school was formally opened for classes in the fall of 1874. The number of pupils increased so rapidly that it soon became necessary to take over the entire building for classrooms and to purchase a nearby dwelling for use as a convent. The new home of the sisters was limited in size; yet it served for many years their gradually growing numbers.¹⁶³ It became the home also of the two sisters who were assigned to the school established in 1879 in Our Lady of Mount Carmel Parish, Tenafly. Fr. Theodore McDonald, then Carmelite pastor of the mission in Tenafly, two and one half miles north of Englewood, had promised the parishioners he would equip a school for their children "even if he had to sell his only coat." This homely and ingenuous pledge, which is recorded in the parish annals, speaks more eloquently of his zeal than it does of his business sense.

McDonald's earnestness must have registered heavily with Mother Xavier for she agreed to let two of her sisters make the arduous trip daily from Englewood to Tenafly. According to the first arrangement, only one of the Tenafly teachers was to receive a token monthly stipend. The second sister, outside of storing up other worldly credit, gained nothing but the exercise and the experience. The records are silent about the sale of "Father Mac's" coat or the amount of money realized on the same.¹⁶⁴

During the early period of St. Cecilia's grammar school when the number of children attending was about two hundred and twenty-three, there were only two families whose children went to the public schools. Fr. Smits always gave catechetical instructions on Mondays, Wednesdays and Fridays in the school. On Tuesdays and Thursdays a special eight o'clock Mass was attended by the children. Under these conditions no Sunday school was necessary. Smits was extremely well liked by his parishioners, Kreidt attested to this popularity and noted "at long last I have for the first time met an enemy of Smits here."[165]

In the spring of 1877 Smits finally received help with his parochial burdens.

> Whilst I was in that abnormal situation at Englewood, Fr. John McDonald, tired of Ky., had obtained permission from the Gen. (sic) to be transferred back to Ireland. On his way to the steamer at New York, he called on me at Englewood and liked it so well, that he asked me to let him stay with me. I consented on the condition that he do nothing to have me join again the scandalous crowd of American Carmelites of Cumberland and Kansas. There were no other then. He wrote for permission to the Genl. (sic) and got it in 1878. Thereupon, some trouble arose in the church of Tenafly with an Italian Priest. I had to take it back and have Fr. McDonald attend it.[166]

McDonald for his part demanded that they form a regular community and wear the Carmelite habit.[167]

Early Catholics of Tenafly walked to Englewood to hear Mass. The first Mass in the Tenafly Borough was offered in Coyte's barn on Railroad Avenue on June 2, 1873.

Ground was broken on the old Faley Reservation in the early part of September 1873 for the first church. The cornerstone was laid October 26 of the same year. The first building was not much. It was one of those square, box-like frames. The lot was brought for $1,000 and the building was erected complete for $2,720. The boundaries of the original parish extended north to Tappan, N.Y. and embraced all those towns which in more recent years became separate parishes—Norwood, Northvale, Closter, Demarest and Bergenfield.[168]

The appointment of Smits in 1881 to head the Commissariat of Kentucky and New Jersey and Niagara Falls must not have come as a complete surprise. On October 27 of the preceding year Knoll had actually suggested this arrangement to the prior general.[169] The plan united all the English-speaking houses and separated them from the German-speaking houses which had been united under Knoll. Fr. Smits could see no future in Paducah and advised the bishop there that the Carmelites would withdraw from the missions as of August 1.[170] Fr. Kreidt went to Englewood on August 9. Fr. Walsh went to Scipio where he died on August 1, and Fr. Feehan, Fr. Reddy and Fr. Murphy went to Niagara. In the twelve years of the Kentucky and Marlboro foundations (1869-1881) sixteen priests had been directly involved. Of these five died while the Commissariat was still operating: Frs. Jansen, Brocard, Forrestal, Meagher and Francis Walsh. Two priests joined the ranks of the secular clergy: Frs. Dwyer and Kempen; and the other ten (Frs. McDonald, Feehan, Elias, Mayer, Kreidt, O'Malley, Reddy, Brady, Walsh and Duell) all went on to do work in other places.

Despite the fact that the Leavenworth community had a debt of $24,000 once Knoll arrived there, he decided to build a decent place in which to live. He took the money remaining from his sale of Cumberland and started the building of a small monastery. At the same time he had to appoint a new prior to succeed Fr. Albert at Scipio. On the advice of Boniface Peters he chose his brother, Anastasius. Boniface himself was made master of novices.[171]

For the erection of his new monastery, it was agreed that each house should contribute a certain amount of money to Knoll. But the house at Pittsburgh obstinately refused. Fr. Louis Guenther was sent as a visitator to New Baltimore and Pittsburgh where he was received with discourtesy. When he first requested to see the financial ledgers he was refused. They would clearly show that the city parish had large resources banked which John Verhayen, the prior,[172] refused to contribute to his commissary.[173] In the meantime Knoll had been busy penning a note to the Ludwig Missionsverein for funds to pay the debt on St. Joseph's church, Leavenworth, whose interest was running between eight and ten percent.[174]

The Pittsburgh incident ran deeper, however, than financial concern, for it revealed that Knoll was not trusted by his community. The complaint once again was with his administrative policies. It was a well-founded one in the light of Knoll's present and previous actions. Elias Van Riel of the Pittsburgh convent had discovered that Knoll held the deeds to the convent in his own name and that excess funds were under a personal account.[175] Fr. Theodore McDonald supported this charge and claimed that Knoll had nearly $1,500 that he planned to leave in his will to friends outside of the Order.[176]

Concern over private investment of the commissariat's funds was nurtured by the financial scandal that had just occurred in the archdiocese of Cincinnati. During the financial panic of 1837 when there was almost a universal suspension of payment by banks and a general distrust of the money market, the sterling honesty of Archbishop Purcell and his brother, Fr. Edward Purcell, had induced thousands of their fellow citizens to urge them to receive deposits and use them for the needs of the diocese. In the days of the Civil War other sums were added and Fr. Purcell's notes promised six percent, the legal interest in Ohio.

In the period of Reconstruction, Purcell ceased taking loans and tried to free himself from the burden of earlier deposits, but the people insisted on leaving their money in his hands. In 1878-1879 there were a series of financial crises. Banks which held diocesan funds either as loans or deposits were closing their doors. A run on the notes offered by Purcell could not be met and many people lost lifetime savings. To the credit of the archbishop, he made all the cash, collateral, and property of the diocese available to the creditors. Unfortunately, the loss had been too great.[177] The Carmelites in Pittsburgh feared that Knoll's handling of savings would disappear in a similar disaster.

McDonald suggested that the Pittsburgh community was so disturbed, realizing what had become of Cumberland, that he thought it would be best were the Pittsburgh Carmelites placed under Smits' jurisdiction. Pittsburgh at the time was the wealthiest and most influential house. As the summer wore on, tensions mounted. Knoll hoped this new dissension would be forgotten. On the feast of Our Lady of Mount Carmel, he laid the cornerstone at Scipio for the new church which Fr. Peters had begun to build.[178]

Far-sighted prior and pastor, Fr. Albert Heimann had already in 1874 commissioned Br. Michael Purdy, who had arrived at Scipio in that year and did not have a trade, to begin work on a sandstone quarry that was discovered southeast of the monastery. Purdy spent most of his time at the quarry year after year. He pried the stones loose, chipped, graded and bevelled them. By 1881, Anastasius Peters had enough stone to begin building the fine church still standing in Scipio today. The baptismal font, the holy water stoop and the cemetery cross were fashioned from stone taken from this same quarry.[179] In spite of cheap building material, immense sums of money still had to be expended in the construction of this church. The monastery would soon see its fiscal resources completely exhausted.[180]

When Knoll had realized the deep discontent in the Pennsylvania houses with his administration, he became thoroughly disgusted and sent his resignation to the prior general at Rome. He urged Angelus Savini, the prior general, to unite all the houses in the United States under Smits as commissary general.[181] Thus, on September 24, 1881, the houses of Kansas and Pennsylvania were also put under the jurisdiction of Anastasius Smits.[182] Fr. Anastasius Peters immediately objected to the appointment on the grounds that Smits was unfamiliar with the principles of religious life. He had lived too long outside the monastery by himself.[183] The German Carmelites, in the houses formerly under Knoll, highly disapproved of the announcement and sent a formal communique to the prior general:

> We do not rejoice over the designation of the Commissary of the Irish for the German, convents . . . The Germans were here first; our customs and languages widely differ. They follow a different set of Carmelite Constitutions than we do. Wherefore, Most Reverend Father, so that charity can prevail among us and religious observance be fostered, so that destruction of the Order can be averted, we beg you to allow us to exist as a separate commissariat with either Father Cyril Knoll or Father John Verheyan as superior.[184]

The prior general, nevertheless, was unswerving in his decision. Thus were brought to a close seventeen years of difficult effort, filled with just about every conceivable hardship in the physical and spiritual order. Knoll had lost control of the organization he had begun. But that organization was now assured continued existence. From four comparatively weak separate movements came forth one relatively strong commissariat.

From the Archives

(Above) **Sketch of St. Francis de Sales Church in Paducah, Kentucky.** The parish became the center of the Kentucky Commissariat which included several churches serving nearby towns. The Carmelites also built a parish church, St. Cecilia's, in Louisville, the city the Carmelites had first settled in when they came from Germany in 1864. (Below) **The interior of St. Francis de Sales Church**, decorated for the Christmas season. *(Photos courtesy of the Archives of the PCM Province)*

From the Archives

(Above) **St. John's Catholic Church and the original Carmelite monastery in New Baltimore, Pennsylvania**, in 1885. The Carmelites arrived at St. John's, the oldest Catholic parish in Somerset County, in 1870. The tall steeple had just been completed on the church when this picture was taken. Fr. Norbert Bausch was the first Carmelite pastor. The church was later replaced and the monastery expanded. (Below) **The students at New Baltimore** assemble in front of the newly expanded monastery building in New Baltimore for a photo to record a visit by the provincial, Pius Mayer (center, seated), in 1893. *(Photos courtesy of the Archives of the PCM Province)*

From the Archives

The original Carmelite residence in Niagara Falls, Ontario, on the bluff overlooking the falls. The left section was the original stone rectory for Our Lady of Peace parish, with a lean-to added by Ignatius Beerhorst in November 1875. The rest of the additions were begun on July 16, 1876, and completed under Pius Mayer to house students and novices over the years. The building was torn down for the construction of Portage Road. *(Photo courtesy of Archives of the PCM Province)*

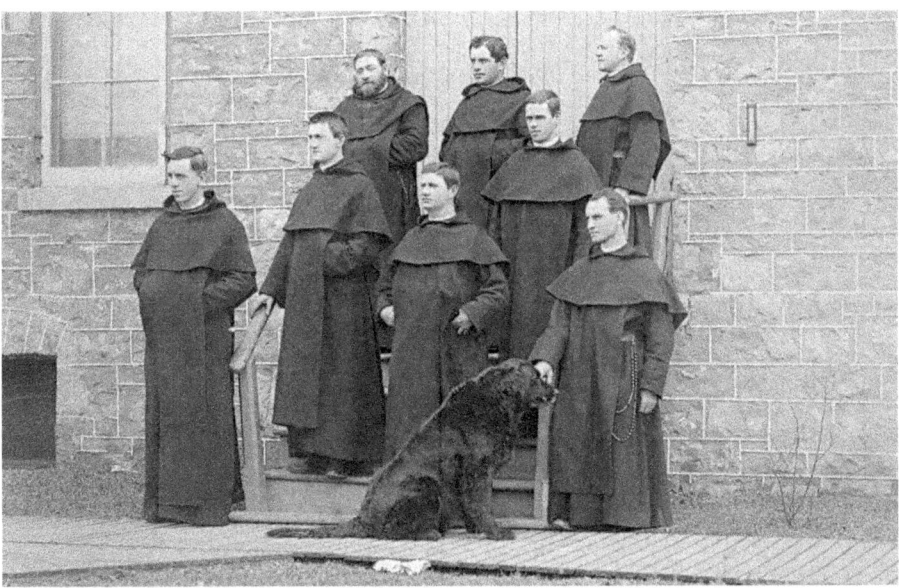

The Carmelite community of Our Lady of Peace Monastery, 1883 (Left to Right - Top Row) Alphonse Brandstaetter, Cyril Feehan, Otto Wiedemann; (Middle Row) Cyril Kehoe, Dion Best; (Bottom Row) Anastasius Smits, Avertanus Brennan, Berthold Lauzau, and Rex the dog *(Photo courtesy of the Archives of the PCM Province)*

The Hospice of Mount Carmel in Niagara Falls, Ontario, constructed as a place for retirement for priests and a place of refreshment for pilgrims to the Niagara area. Much of this original building was destroyed in the 1967 fire. *(Photo courtesy of Archives of the PCM Province)*

Our Lady of Peace Shrine, Niagara Falls, Ontario, founded in 1837, as it appeared on the occasion of its 100th anniversary. The church cemetery now covers most of the ground shown. The name of the church comes from Pope Pius IX in reaction to the threat of civil war between the US states. This new title was due to the location of the Church "by the sight of the beautiful rainbow that spans the cataract the sign of peace, between God and sinner" During hostilities between Mexico and the United States in April 1914, talks between the two governments were held in Niagara Falls. An agreement resulted which averted war. On May 24, all the delegates and their families attended a special mass at Our Lady of Peace. In 1996 a delegation from Japan participated in a prayer service and presented a peace symbol known as "The Peace Poll" which is on display in the vestibule of the shrine. In 1998 the Canadian Conference of Catholic Bishops concluded their annual meeting with a Mass for "World Peace" in the church. *(Photo courtesy of the Francis J. Petri Historical Collection)*

From the Archives

First Provincial Chapter
Holy Trinity Monastery, Pittsburgh, Pennsylvania
May 1-7, 1890

Members of the First Chapter of the Most Pure Heart of Mary Province in 1890 - The Chapter took place at Holy Trinity Parish in Pittsburgh, Pennsylvania. Standing left to right: Cyril Feehan, Dominic O'Malley, Otto Widemann (substitute for Cyril Knoll), Bernard Fink, Anastasius Kreidt, Leo Van der Heuvel. Seated left to right: Albert Murphy, Pius Mayer, (prior provincial), Albert Heimann, Louis Guenther.
(Photo courtesy of Archives of the PCM Province)

The American Commissariate had been canonically erected as a province in the seventh session of the General Chapter, held in Rome, Italy, in October 1889. The Holy See gave its apostolic indult on February 9, 1890. The province was given the title the Most Pure Heart of Mary.

The first chapter was held at Holy Trinity monastery in Pittsburgh, Pennsylvania, May 1-7, 1890. Pius Mayer, the commissary general, was appointed the first provincial. At the chapter's second session, the definitors (counselors) as named by the prior general, following the provisions of the apostolic indult, were declared. They were Cyril Knoll, Albert Heimann, Leo Van der Heuvel, and Dominic O'Malley. (Otto Wiedemann attended the chapter as a substitute for Cyril Knoll.) In the third session, the provincial selected Anastasius Kreidt as the assistant provincial. All priors and vicar-priors would remain in office for the following three years. The fourth session dealt with finances. The fifth session resulted in a number of resolution: all postulants (pre-novices) were to be members of the Third Order first; priors were to reside continuously in the house they were prior of; the novitiate was transferred from Niagara Falls. Ontario, to New Baltimore, Pennsylvania; each Carmelite priest was to celebrate 324 Masses each year according to the intention of the sacristan or prior of the house; an archives was to be started in every house of the province; Anastasius Kreidt was to be the chronicler of the Province and each prior was responsible to insure that a diary of the house was maintained; and funds were to be collected for the construction of a retreat house.

The sixth session also approved some propositions: a postulant needed to know Latin in order to be received, unless his parents paid part of his tuition (exceptions were to be made for the poor); during the following year, a Carmelite would be sent to Europe to recruit vocations; the provincial was to prepare an annual supplement to the Roman Ordo containing all the differences between the Divine Office of the Roman rite and that of the Order.

The seventh session declared that the celebration of the Feast of the Blessed Virgin of Mount Carmel would be celebrated on the Sunday following July 16th.

The final session was mostly ritual. The priors received their letters of appointment. A requiem Mass was celebrated for the deceased members of the province. The presiding office, Pius Mayer, imparted General Absolution and the chapter was adjourned.

Second Provincial Chapter
St. John the Baptist Monastery, New Baltimore, Pennsylvania
May 24-29, 1894

Members of the Second Provincial Chapter, 1894, at St. John's, New Baltimore, Pennsylvania Sitting (left to right): Paul Ryan, Ambrose Bruder, Dionysius Best, Pius Mayer, Leo Van der Heuvel, Angelus Lager. Standing: (l to r) Anastasius Kreidt, Theodore McDonald, Anastasius Smits, Louis Guenther, Cyril Kehoe, Otto Wiederman, Avertanus Brennan, Dominic O'Malley. (Paul Ryan and Angelus Lager were not *gremiales* (voting members) of the Chapter. *(Photo courtesy of Archives of the PCM Province)*

The second provincial chapter of the PCM province began with the naming of the officers of the chapter. During the second session a Mass of the Holy Spirit was celebrated by the prior provincial, Pius Mayer. The members then elected the definitory (councilors): Otto Wiedemann, Cyril Kehoe, Anastasius Smits, and Ambrose Bruder. This was followed by the election of the prior provincial, with Pius Mayer being reelected.

The third and fourth sessions elected Theodore McDonald and Anastasius Smits as delegates to the General Chapter. The rest of the sessions dealt with finances.

In the seventh session, on May 28, propositions were discussed and voted on. Those approved were: a call for uniformity in the financial accounts of the Carmelite houses throughout the province (procurators were to be instructed in the proper procedures); each house was to hold a chapter meeting at least once a month; the office of prior and pastor were to be separate with the pastor only able to spend church funds under the supervision of the prior; some students would be sent to Rome to complete their theology studies; the monastery and land at Leavenworth and Scipio were to be sold, and a more suitable location obtained; the novitiate house would be enlarged to care for the growing number of students; provincial money was to be deposited in banks under the name "Carmelite Fathers" (Money belonging to the parish should be depostited in accounts under the name of the parish); with the permission of the prior general, Anastasius Kriedt was to take out a loan for $35,000 to complete the hospice at Niagara Falls, Ontario; the *Carmelite Review* was to be recognized as the magazine of the province and should be supported by all of the members of the province

In the eighth session, the definitory elected Ambrose Bruder as the provincial procurator and appointed the priors and procurators of the houses. The definitory also agreed that in the future, Carmelites would be allowed to attend the funerals of their parents.

In the final session, on May 29, 1894, it was agreed that the next provincial chapter would take place at Our Lady of Peace in Niagara Falls, Ontario.

Third Provincial Chapter
Our Lady of Peace Monastery, Niagara Falls, Ontario
July 5-9, 1897

Members of the Third Provincial Chapter, 1896 at *The Hospice, Niagara Falls, Ontario* First Row: Dominic O'Malley, Gabriel Browne, Paul Ryan; Middle Row: (l-r) on middle steps: Otto Wiedermann, Theodore McDonald, Anastasius Kreidt (incoming provincial), Louis Guether, Ambrose Bruder, Alphonsus Brandstatter; Third Row: (l to r) Ferdinand Van der Staay, Cyril Kehoe, Pius Mayer, (outgoing provincial) Anastasius Smits, Berthold Lauzau. *(Photo courtesy of Archives of the PCM Province)*

At the first session, the outgoing provincial, Pius Mayer, gave a report on the status of the province. He reported that the Roman Congregation of the Propaganda had decreed that the remnant of the extinct Commissariate of the South be transferred to the province. The province, however, would not assume the assets nor the liabilities of the Commissariate. The congregations of Carmel, Louisiana and Fort Davis, Texas were to be turned over to the local bishops. The Carmelites at Marienfield were to continue their missions until the bishop could find substitutes for them.

The province was made up of 33 priests, nine students with solemn vows, 13 with simple vows, 16 lay brothers, five novices, and four students without vows. Four of these students were in Rome while the rest where in New Baltimore.

Mayer then showed the decree that the prior general had named Anastasius Kreidt as the presiding office of the chapter. Kreidt then appointed the officials of the chapter.

The second session began with a Mass of the Holy Spirit. The *socii* (the delegates from various houses) presented their letters of election. The chapter then preceded with the elections which had the following results: Anastasius Kreidt as prior provincial, and Otto Wiedemann, Theodore McDonald, Ambrose Bruder, and Anastasius Smits as definitors.

In the third session, Anastasius Smits and Pius Mayer were elected as delegates to the general chapter. Mayer was also elected as definitor of the province to the general chapter. Otto Wiedemann was elected *custos* of the province, with responsibility for the province while the prior provincial was attending the general chapter. The session included financial reports for all six houses of the province.

In the fourth session, the chapter accepted the following propositions: that the medicine know as *Carmelite Spirits* (*Karmeliten Geist*) be produced to provide for the upkeep of the novitiate and the house of studies; that when necessary, the definitory may permit the same person to be both prior and pastor; that a German edition of the *Carmelite Review* be published in order to increase provincial revenues. The provincial also announced that he had selected Dominic O'Malley to serve as assistant provincial.

In the fifth session, Ambrose Bruder was reappointed as provincial procurator and Otto Wiedemann was selected as novice master. The definitory then appointed the priors of the houses.

In the final session, the Acts of the Chapter were read and approved. The next chapter was set to be held at Our Lady of Peace Monastery in Niagara Falls.

5
Chapter Five: PROVINCE AND PROSPECT

The 1880s were focused on the re-formation of the commissariat-- a move not readily accepted by all the Carmelites. Some men left to attempt a new reality in Texas. Only when the third Commissary General for North America was appointed did a more cohesive bonding between the foundations occur. By 1889, the number of Carmelites dictated that the commissariat move to the status of a province of the Order. The 1890s saw a continuing organizational development, the initiation of new creative ventures, including a band of itinerant preachers and new publications illustrating the spiritual dimension in everyday life. A few days after Cyril Knoll died, the new year and century began. It marked the end of the era of Carmel's early founders and foundations.

Commissary General Anastasius Smits

GREAT things were expected of the new arrangement whereby a supposedly capable administrator, alert to the times, adroit with the customs of the country, and capable in the native tongue, governed a relatively large number of men and houses seemingly united in purpose. But expectations did not come true. The external bond created by the amalgamation could hardly weld the internal spirit of unification between all the houses and men needed so that the commissariat could operate effectively. Smits well understood the task that lay before him. Referring to his new assignment he wrote: "I did by no manner of means relish the appointment, knowing as I did, the component parts of the whole. ... But having consulted various religious friends and superiors, all agreed in telling me that I must accept and try to find means to establish unity and discipline, and, if I could not succeed, to report to the Holy See directly."

Smits was sincere in his desire to establish the Carmelite Order in the United States. He wanted more than just a group of men wearing the Carmelite habit. He wanted his men to be well trained in the spirit of the Order and to carry on Carmelite religious life as it should be lived. The rigors of the early missionary period were over and it was his hope that more regular discipline could be established. With this in mind he began a visitation of all the convents to see at what level observance actually stood.[1] It seems that he was not aware of Fr. Anastasius Peters' resistance to his appointment, nor for that matter the objection raised by the German Carmelites against the appointment of an English-orientated commissary.[2]

His reception at Scipio was anything but cordial. Peters raised his objections again. He argued that Smits' appointment could not have received the approval of the prior general because Smits had been guilty of apostasy while in Englewood. Peters demanded to see papers from the prior general that would confirm the commissary's assumption of power.[3] The confrontation was serious. The insubordination which this figure of leadership posed in the only Carmelite seminary of the West where twenty men[4] were stationed necessitated his removal. Smits immediately urged the prior general to remove Peters as superior. To support his petition, Fr. Anastasius noted that parishioners in Kansas had complained of the prior's drunkenness and over-familiarity with a young lady of the parish.[5] The prior general had appointed a commissary and he put full confidence in his judgments. He acted without hesitation. On June 24, 1882, Louis Guenther was returned to Scipio as superior. But far from quieting the explosive situation in Kansas, the action spurred further insurrection. Peters prepared to lead an open revolt. He had been collecting money for the new church at Scipio. He had also received money after selling a herd of cattle and arranging a loan at St. Louis. These funds were devoted to his new scheme.[6]

Peters now planned to establish a colony of German families in Texas. He hoped to lead a group of impatient Carmelites to this new community, thus being able to maintain his leadership. Smits had sent Peters a letter of obedience transferring him to Pittsburgh. The transfer was timed so as to remove him from Scipio before Guenther arrived. Since Peters refused to acknowledge Smits' leadership, he did not obey. Knowing what the final outcome of his action would be, Peters began to seek a way out of the Order by applying for missionary assignments. By July 31, 1882, he had been twice refused release from the Order for this purpose.[7] John Konz, an immigrant farmer at Scipio, hoped to lead a group of Catholic settlers to virgin farmlands offered by the Texas and Pacific Railway. Considering the plight he found himself in, it was not hard for Fr. Peters to be encouraged by Konz to accompany the first settlers. After some preparation, on the night of August 5, 1882, Fr. Anastasius Peters, Br. Anton Keber, and two novices, Albert Wagner and Andreas Fuhrwerk, set out for Texas. Carmelite chronicler Reichwein's description of the adventure is too colorful to omit.

> It was the night preceding the feast of the Transfiguration of Our Lord when some of the monks did not go to bed. One of them, most likely to have an excuse in case the scheme would fail, had asked for some pills, claiming to have some stomach trouble. The rest of the monks, not suspecting any of the schemes and plots

that were to be enacted that night, slept the peace of the just, but the rebels were busy in packing their trunks, filling them with the best spoils of the library and sacristy. After midnight the wagon arrived; so quietly did they approach that nobody else but the conspirators themselves is aware of what is going on—the transfiguration of holy monks into vagabond ecclesiastics. The signal is given, "All's well" and in a few moments the wagon is loaded with the trunks containing the spoils of their poor brothers which they are leaving behind. What do they care whether others suffer—they snap their fingers at the Church's excommunication which they incur at this moment. They continue to say Mass and go to Holy Communion as if nothing had happened.[8]

By the time the prior general was prepared to bring formal sentence against them, the Bishop of San Antonio had interceded for their cause.[9]

Of all the separatist movements that occurred across the span of Carmelite history in America, the Texas Commissariat had the least influence on the history of mainstream Carmelite activity. To trace the interesting story of this Commissariat would be to follow a tangent divergent to the purpose of this study. Nevertheless, a summary study of this movement needed to be recorded, if only to provide the reader with data reflecting a more virtuous tinge than the beginning of this excursion would seem to augur.[10] The Carmelites who worked in this apostolate erected the first Catholic church in West Texas.[11] There were mission stations in one part of the territory that distanced three hundred miles apart. Their work was a thankless one with poor Indians, Spaniards, Blacks, and Mexicans.[12] Driven by drought[13] to the bayou country of Louisiana, the Carmelites began anew and actually conducted a successful seminary and mission.[14] Plagued, however, by the dreaded fever, riddled by exaggerated press reports of a shocking incident within the community, victimized by detraction resulting from the scandalous actions of only a few of the members, this separatist movement eventually suffered the same fate as all others.[15] When the prior general of the Order commanded the suppression of the Commissariat of the South in the last decade of the nineteenth century, the community was left either to return to Europe from where a number of them had emigrated or to join the mainstream of Carmelite life in the United States.[16]

Set aside the advances made by the commissariat united under Smits, the Commissariat of Texas gave one more proof of the failure of a separatist movement to prosper. As was noted, Smits began a visitation of his new commissariat to restore discipline where possible. In his first comprehensive report to Savini in Rome on July 1, 1882, from

Englewood, he gave a detailed account of the religious discipline in each house. His overall summary concluded: "There is not yet a Carmelite spirit of prayer, solitude and mortification because the active life and parish life make it difficult."[17] The revolt at Scipio had certain nationalist overtones which gained wide backing among the German element throughout other houses. In fact Fr. John Verheyen who had been the German Carmelites' alternate choice as commissary of the West refused, as prior of the German habitat at Pittsburgh, to give Smits some surplus funds. This refusal was based solely on the national disfavor evidenced by the Germans of the province. Previous to his appointment, Smits had been a close friend of Verheyen.[18]

The commissary was too anxious to create perfection out of a group of men and houses that had until recently been able to give little consideration to even a minimal amount of religious discipline. As his drive toward this goal grew, he concentrated in himself, besides the office of commissary, that of local superior, novice master and confessor and pastor. He tended also to deprive many a local superior of responsible freedom of action. His stock appeal with the German Carmelites never increased for he often expressed his wish to sell Scipio since he considered it a loss.[19] One of the reasons for his displeasure with this house was the fact that the Bishop of Leavenworth had agreed to pay 80,000 francs for the new church. So far Smits had received only 20,000.[20]

KARMELITEN GEIST

Because he had contracted large debts on quarters that were too small for habitation, Smits received severe criticism. But the most serious accusations questioning his fiscal capability centered about the manufacture of *Aqua Santa Maria della Scala*, more commonly known as *Karmeliten Geist*. The financial returns from the sale of this product did not even pay for initial cost outlays.[21] Smits had procured the formula for the "medicine" from his Dutch confreres. Br. Augustine Van Snepsen and Br. Gregory Van Der Erf were entrusted with the secret formula.[22] His concern over the sale of this product is evidenced by the fact that he secured a patent from the United States Patent Office in 1878.[23] *Karmeliten Geist* was a distillate from a dozen aromatic herbs which were allowed to stand each in separate tanks filled with wine. The explanation of the product in English from a label submitted to the Patent Office well proclaims its supposed attributes:

AQUA A SANTA MARIA DELLA SCALA
(KARMELITEN GEIST)

This Medicine was first prepared by the Order of the Carmelites, (a society of Monks) and has been known for its excellent qualities in Rome and Italy, for several hundred years. It is highly appreciated by all who have used it and is especially recommended by the Medical profession. It contains nothing but pure herbs. The Carmelites in the State of Kansas, U.S., by their Superior in Rome have been made familiar with the secret of manufacturing this preparation (and is their exclusive property) for the purpose of introducing the same into this country. The price is so extremely low, as to place this medicine within the reach of all.

DIRECTIONS

This preparation is especially adapted for the cure of Indigestion, Weakness of the Stomach, and all other Stomach disorders. For these ailments take 30 drops on sugar together with some water every 2 or 3 hours.

For Asthma, Palpitation of the Heart, Fainting and Fits, take 30 drops every half hour until relieved.

Headache, Nervous or Rheumatic, will be cured instantaneously by applying the preparation on the fore-head and temples. It can also be used by pouring some drops in the hand and inhaling the Flavor.

For Weakness of the Eyes apply the preparation upon the Eye-lids and around the Eyes.

Inflamed eyes will rapidly be cured, by mixing 12-15 drops in a wineglass of rain water and bathing the eyelids and parts around the eyes with this mixture several times during the day.

For Weakness and General debility it is unsurpassed. In case of sickness, a few drops sprinkled over the room will absorb all bad smell and create in the room a fragrant odor.[24]

Nevertheless, Smits' concern for building the Order was sincere and well meant. Furthermore, his emphasis did offer a constructive impetus toward improvement of the caliber of Carmelite life. He frequently expressed his desire to build a good commissariat by training the young men in the spirit of religious discipline. The lack of priests often worried him. Manpower shortage necessarily reduced his ability to give the candidates a proper formation and doctrinal education. He often said, "It is the lack of knowledge which holds us back." Some of the priests he claimed did not even know how to say Mass properly. Smits had conceived of sending the students to Innsbruck, although these plans never materialized. He felt that a good vocation was a rare one in the United States, and hence he often chose to postpone the reception of solemn vows to see if the candidate was really worthy.[25] This, indeed, marked a different approach than that followed by Knoll, who had sought expansion at the expense and sacrifice of qualified men. For his service as commissary, Smits was rewarded with the office of Titular Provincial of Scotland.[26] This province no longer exists but the titular title gave Smits legal standing in the Order. His attempts at reform at length proved too severe. With nearly half the men of the commissariat opposed to his regime, he was forced to retire from his leadership role.

Commissary General Pius Mayer

On August 31, 1886, the prior general appointed Pius Mayer as the new commissary of the American houses.[27]

Pius was a large man, measuring more than six feet. He had large features and his bearded face gave the impression of great power, both intellectual and emotional, so that in any gathering of men, he was an outstanding figure. Despite his great height and weight, his movements were quick. He marched to the altar with the decided stride of a soldier about to mount guard. An excellent preacher with an unhesitating flow of words, he spoke rapidly, yet intelligibly, adhering always to fundamental doctrine, simple, concise and direct. A ready speaker in three languages, possessing a most extraordinary fund of information of Church history, the lives of the saints, and also of public affairs, he was able to meet a demand at a moment. Able to speak out on topics of the day, but his sanguine nature often led him into sweeping judgments which the facts did not warrant. He found it hard to view problems from different angles. At official gatherings he defended his policies with vigor.[28]

Like Smits before him, Mayer set out on a complete survey of the province to analyze the manpower and resources at his command. He was most concerned with putting more order in all the aspects of the commissariat's life. His reports were thorough and covered every aspect of conditions. Initial surveys were concerned with the financial standing of every house. Mayer was quick to point out corporation law and the need for the various houses to follow correct legal procedure in their monetary affairs. A close study was also made concerning financial relationships between the monasteries and the churches cared for by each. A survey of the various sources of revenue, and a thorough analysis of the fiscal policy of each house were presented.[29] This original survey also noted that under Smits' regime several priests had left the Order, namely, Moerland, Bausch, and Van Riel. In view of the financial deficit of some of the houses and loss of manpower, Mayer expressed the view that it might be wise to return some of the parish sites to the bishops.[30]

His survey was actually a prelude to the first formal organizational meeting held in 1887 at Pittsburgh. As a result of that conference Mayer was authorized to enter negotiations with the Vogler Company of Baltimore about the possible sale of the formula for *Karmeliten Geist*.[31] Far more important, however, was the gathering convoked just two years later. With the permission of the prior general, Mayer called a three-day meeting of all the superiors in Pittsburgh on April 9, 1889.[32] Not only was this convocation timed with an eye to organizing affairs of the American houses, but it was staged just prior to the general chapter scheduled to be held in Rome later that year. Mayer had been assured a seat to represent the American cause by his appointment the previous October 5 as Titular Provincial of Saxony.[33] Like Smits, being named Titular Provincial of Scotland, Mayer's appointment gave him legal standing in the Order.

Of the many resolutions passed and approved at the Pittsburgh session, two especially enacted a uniform and central discipline on all members. Resolution 15 set down a *horarium* to be followed with few deviations in all of the houses. It guaranteed that choral obligations with regard to recitation of the Divine Office would be fulfilled and it established formal meditation periods. Resolution 17 spoke out on decorum in the dining room and the need for spiritual reading during two meals. But most telling was Resolution 18 that sought to enforce the Constitutions of the Stricter Observance upon all members. A long list of articles had been carefully selected from these constitutions. Their observance was made obligatory. This was a prudent move, placating those not used to such discipline by not enforcing the whole code upon them, yet requiring that the essentials be observed. Mayer paved the way for the time when the entire code would be acceptable. There were also special resolutions regarding the house of studies.[34]

When Mayer assumed his office as commissary, he found his former friend, the Archbishop of Toronto, had turned against him. Smits had been jolted by the prior general's decision to replace him as commissary. Before retiring from the office, he persuaded the archbishop to refuse Mayer faculties, should he move to Niagara.[35] Furthermore, though the archbishop had planned to turn over the deed to the Niagara property to the Carmelites, he was encouraged to refuse to sign this for Mayer.[36]

The addition Mayer had joined to the Niagara house in 1878 proved too small to handle the professed students, so that Mayer was forced to send them to New Baltimore and use Niagara as a novitiate. In 1888, the commissary even reopened Scipio as the novitiate for western vocations because of the distance of the Kansas house from Niagara.[37]

Among the first six resolutions of the Pittsburgh meeting, there were proposals to open a central postulant house for young candidates rather than allow them to spend this period in the individual houses. It was noted also that the New Baltimore house of studies needed to be enlarged because of the numerous applicants seeking admittance. Since the property at Niagara was in a questionable state, resolution three directed the commissary to look for a new foundation. The Bishop of Kingston, Ontario hoped the Carmelites might conduct a high school on the grounds of a college there. If this offer were accepted, the novitiate and scholasticate could be transferred there. An invitation had also been extended by the Hamilton diocese.[38] A final resolution suggested that the scapular devotion and confraternity were to be promoted as a means of spreading devotion and the Order's name in America.[39]

As Mayer departed for the general chapter, he was armed with impressive statistics and plans. Furthermore, the growth in manpower of the commissariat was healthy. A census of the houses revealed: Scipio: five priests and six brothers; Leavenworth: three priests and one brother; Pittsburgh: five priests and one brother; New Baltimore: three priests, three clerics and two brothers; Englewood: six priests; Niagara: six priests, four novices and four brothers.[40]

Mayer came to the general chapter in Rome, representing six monasteries. He hoped to prevent a recurrence of the situation that had already occasioned the loss of other houses and was threatening a new disaster in the Texas commissariat. The problems he faced were probably not exclusively limited to the American scene but the legislation adopted by the chapter was very much needed and applicable in the United States. The legislation provided that: 1) Individuals were forbidden to promote new foundations; 2) The authority for any new monasteries was limited to the provincial chapter or to the definitory (provincial council); 3) Any new members accepted were to be affiliated to the province and not to only a certain monastery. 4) Members of another province, unless transferred by the prior general, were to have neither active nor passive voice in the province where they were temporarily living. 5) The provincial, with the consent of the provincial chapter or his definitory, was empowered to transfer money from one account or convent to another at his discretion. Two resolutions were of great import to the Carmelites in America. The new prior general, Aloysius Galli, was directed to send a visitator to Marienfeld, Texas. The chapter also approved of elevating the American commissariat to the status of a province, dedicated to the Most Pure Heart of Mary.[41]

From Commissariat to Province

In the twenty-six years of Savini's reign[42] he had been faced with the destruction of the Order as the anti-clerical movement spread over Europe, suppressing monasteries and confiscating Church property. Unfortunately there were many bishops whose loyalty to the Holy See left much to be desired. In Italy, the political idea of unification swept the religious issues aside and the saintly "Pio Nono" was hard put to steer a prudent course. His early sympathy with the liberals was retracted after the turn of events despoiled the Vatican of the papal states. His efforts at defending the political and theological interest of the Church left him little time or taste for political leadership in the burning social and economic issues. Savini had understandably been anxious to counteract the misfortunes of the Order in Europe with new foundations elsewhere even at the expense of a lessening somewhat in religious life and observance. The problems which nearly destroyed the American foundation might never have arisen or would not have been permitted to endure very long if the central administration of the Order in Rome were not itself in difficult times.

On February 9, 1890, the decree went forth formally establishing the American Carmelite Province of the Most Pure Heart of Mary.[43] On the 28th of March, the letter of the commissary went forth calling for the First Provincial Chapter to be held at Pittsburgh on May 1. The opening sessions witnessed the usual check of credentials and Mass of petition. Following the directives of the Apostolic Indult, the prior general had wisely appointed most of the leading figures of the commissariat to retain their positions. Pius Mayer was named prior provincial and Knoll and Heimann were rewarded for their efforts on behalf of the American houses with appointments as first and second definitors. The obvious balance of power in favor of the German element in the province was highlighted by the fact that the chapter was held in the most prosperous house—the German monastery of Pittsburgh. To the list of officials appointed, Mayer requested that Anastasius Kreidt be selected as assistant provincial. The definitory then agreed with the proposition of the new provincial that the priors and vicar priors who were holding office at the time should be reappointed.

The fourth session held on Saturday, May 3, at 9 a.m., examined the report and condition of each of the houses of the province. Although financially all the accounts were favorable, yet the outstanding debts attached to most of the houses allowed only the Pittsburgh community to appear as offering any real prospect for prosperity. This convent was able to report an income for the year of 1889 of $9,351.33, with outgoing expenses listed at $5,438.10. Both these figures were slightly misleading, however, as a perpetual foundation amounting to $2,100 had been given to the house. Furthermore, the convent had lent the province $3,550 for purposes of expanding the house at New Baltimore.

That same session heard sixteen proposals made for consideration; decisions for these were postponed until the following session on Monday at 9 a.m. Of the resolutions, three and four were concerned with the reception of brothers, suggesting that they be allowed only to make simple profession. All the postulants to the brotherhood should first be received into the Third Order, it was further suggested, making no distinction between those who were skilled and those who were not. Later, the provincial and the members of the convent where the postulant resided could decide on a candidate's fitness. Resolutions five, six, and seven sought a perfection of religious observance. History had taught a lesson. There was a strong exhortation not to send men of ill standing to the province.

Resolution eight merely allowed the novitiate to be transferred from Niagara Falls to New Baltimore, which both in its adaptability and environs was ideal for a novitiate. The accommodations at Niagara were too small, too little adapted for regular observance and too accessible to visitors. Along with this regulation went the third resolution of the sixth session stipulating that postulants should not be received if they lacked knowledge of Latin, unless their parents would pay at least part of their tuition. Exceptions should be made only in favor of intelligent boys whose parents were poor. All of these resolutions showed an effort on the part of the Fathers to build a healthy religious community for the future. There were even resolutions pointed towards the collection of documents and the writing of a history of the Province.

But perhaps the most significant resolution was saved until the end of this fifth session. It read:

> that since from the beginning of the foundation at Niagara Falls it was the intention both of the archbishop and the Order to erect a retreat house for the clergy and laity, and Archbishop Lynch, of happy memory, made this intention known in his pastoral letters to the diocese and to the whole city, but because of the scarcity of priests this work could not be begun, now alms be collected and the construction of the contemplated retreat house, proportionate to the alms received, be undertaken. After the house has been con-

structed, that the domestic care be entrusted to our Third Order sisters, provided this meets with the approval of the Archbishop and Father General.[44]

The resolutions of the first provincial chapter were approved on June 25, 1890.[45]

The prior of Niagara was the young and gifted Fr. Kreidt,[46] who threw himself energetically into the task of bringing the hospice to realization. Kreidt immediately wrote of his plans to the new archbishop of Toronto, John Walsh, who gave his heartiest approval.

TORONTO, May 23, 1890

Rev. A. Kreidt. Prior, Monastery of Our Lady of Mt. Carmel, Niagara Falls, Ont.

Dear Father Kreidt:

I am glad to hear that you intend to begin, as soon as means will allow you, the construction of a house for spiritual retreats at Niagara Falls, in the archdiocese. I sincerely hope that your appeal to a charitable public for the furtherance of this most praiseworthy and meritorious object will meet with the success it so eminently deserves. A retreat house, conducted by your zealous fathers, could not fail to do much good for the salvation and sanctification of souls, especially in a place and amid surroundings where nature itself invites solemn thought and serious reflection, and where, in very deed, one hears: 'The voice of the Lord upon the waters, the God of majesty hath thundered: the lord upon many waters.' (Psalm xxviii)

Wishing your pious undertaking the divine blessing and a happy issue,

I am, dear Father Kreidt,

Yours sincerely in Christ
JOHN WALSH
Archbishop of Toronto[47]

The hospice was to be a combination monastery and retreat house, each in a separate wing of the building, with a large monastic church in the middle, dividing the two wings. Kreidt at once devised schemes to collect funds.[48] In the late summer of 1892 he obtained an apostolic blessing for all those who would contribute to the building and for those who would subscribe to *The Carmelite Review*, a magazine he planned to publish.[49] He received testimonials of approval for the first issue of the *Review* in 1893 from Cardinal Gibbons, Archbishop Janssens of New Orleans, and Archbishop Phelan of Pittsburgh.[50] A building and loan association was also formed in which the laity could safely place their savings at a moderate rate of interest. Kreidt thus was given a source of funds from which to make his own investments.

A pious union or an association for sharing in the fruits of Masses said in the Carmelite monasteries was organized. Twenty-five cents given yearly until the hospice was completed entitled the donor to a perpetual share in the pious union. One project that also received attention was the creation of a stamp bureau.[51] People throughout North American were petitioned to send cancelled stamps to be sold for the benefit of the new hospice.

At the same time, Kreidt issued a circular letter to all the sisterhoods in the United States and Canada asking them to forward scapulars and religious articles as their contribution to the Carmelite project. The scapulars and religious articles were then awarded as premiums to the generous benefactors who had collected the stamps. Within the first year, the stamp bureau realized a profit of nearly one thousand dollars.[52] To say the least, the initial steps in the building program seemed auspicious.

An unexpected event took place that seriously disturbed the peace and calm of Carmel and threatened to bring the whole project of the hospice to ruin. A dispute arose between the Carmelites at Niagara Falls and the Most Reverend Archbishop of Toronto concerning the ownership of the Niagara lands. The event was well summarized by Br. Andrew Cavanaugh in his memoirs:

> In April 1876, (sic) Bishop [John Joseph] Lynch invited the fathers to build a monastery at Niagara. He gave the Carmelites two hundred acres of land as an unattached gift, but, alas, the grant was made orally. This failure to have the donation recorded in writing permitted Bishop [John] Walsh, successor to Bishop Lynch, to charge one hundred dollars an acre for the land, i.e., $20,000.[53]

The dispute began in April 1893, when the archbishop attempted to sell certain lands which the Carmelites had been using for farm purposes.[54] At first, the dispute was with the local prior, but later the archbishop carried it to the provincial, Fr. Mayer, then at New Baltimore, and later to the apostolic delegate in Washington. First indications of the gravity of the affair were seen in a letter dated June 13, 1893, from the chancellor of the archdiocese refusing confessional faculties for a member of the Carmelite community "until ... the community will have fully withdrawn its unfounded claims to our diocesan property."[55] The issue was clearly exposed. On July 4, 1893, the archbishop wrote a caustic letter to Fr. Mayer in which he set forth the claims of the Diocese:

Toronto, July 4, 1893
Very Rev. Pius E. Mayer, O.C.C. Provincial
New Baltimore, Somerset Co., Pa.

Very Rev. Father:

In your communication to me of the 19th of June you refer to a letter of Vicar General McCann to Father Best, in which the Vicar General speaks of the unfounded claims of your community at Falls View on the property of our Episcopal Corporation and you go on to say that in the absence of any official communication of my Chancellor to you, you can only guess at the meaning of the phrase. You cannot of course honestly pretend to he ignorant of the fraudulent claims repeatedly made by Father Kreidt in April and May last on the property of the Archdiocese at Niagara Falls. However, in order to do away with all excuses I will give here a summary of the facts that have led up to the fraudulent claims in question, although these facts must be as well known to you as to me.

Some thirty years ago Archbishop Lynch purchased two hundred acres of land more or less at Niagara Falls. This property he paid for out of diocesan money.

In 1876 the Archbishop invited your community to settle at "the Falls" and in a letter to Father Ignatius, superior of the young institution, he promised that he would give one hundred acres of the land there in trust for the use and benefit of the young community.

In 1882 he fulfilled the promise by giving your Community a lease of 100 acres or thereabouts, so long as you remained at the Falls.

4. You yourself who were then Prior of the Community here, in a letter dated March 16, 1882, and which is in our possession, professed yourself perfectly satisfied with the lease in question and made no further claims.

5. In the meantime you cropped and grazed the 100 and odd acres not included in your lease but remaining in the absolute and unquestioned right of the Episcopal Corporation. You were allowed this privilege out of pure kindness and good will because the land in question was not required or available for diocesan purposes.

Matters continued in this position until the month of April of the present year when I got an opportunity of selling that land at a satisfactory price, intending the proceeds for the establishment of a charitable Institution.

Soon afterwards to our painful surprise, I learned from our purchasers that your prior at the Falls, Father Kreidt, had employed a Protestant Solicitor to forbid in his name that our purchasers should attempt to buy the lands in question from us and prohibiting them from entering such lands or dealing with them in any way, on the ground that the Carmelite Fathers had acquired title by the length of possession in accordance with an act of civil law to that effect. It is necessary to remark that many things sanctioned and approved by civil law are unlawful and unjust in a court of conscience and in the courts of the Church; but in this case we do not admit that you have a valid claim even under the civil law.

Again and again in the course of several weeks back your prior at the Falls claimed title to our said lands, purely and simply on the ground of rights derived from length of possession. You have no other claim or title. Although at first the solicitor engaged wrote as if acting on the sole instruction and responsibility of Father Kreidt, the latter fell back on the authority of you, his Provincial, for the stand he took in the matter, and referred to you repeatedly as having the entire matter in your hands now, and as being responsible for the present shameful situation.

As I do not wish to bring this matter into civil court, in order to avoid an enormous scandal, I have placed the matter in the hands of Msgr. Satolli, Apostolic Delegate to the United States.

However, you have it in your power to undo the wrong done us by Father Kreidt, by causing the Carmelite Corporation at "the Falls" to withdraw in a formal and legal manner the claims put forward to our property, and I ask you in the name of our holy religion, and in the name of justice and honesty to do it.

If you do this act of common justice and honesty it will be possible to re-establish relations of good will between your Community at the Falls and the Archbishop and the Clergy of the Archdiocese.

If you refuse to do so, I will make use of all lawful means to protect the rights and property of the Archdiocese. In the long run it will, I think, be found in this case, as in all others, "honesty is the best policy."

I am Very Rev. Father,

John Walsh
Archbishop of Toronto[56]

The position of the Archbishop Walsh was clear and unmistakable. He felt the Carmelites were not only wrong in their claims but that they were knowingly being fraudulent. He is very clear that if the Carmelites want to be in good relation to the Archdiocese of Toronto, they will cease with their claims on the property. In a clear sign of those times, the archbishop is very insulted, "a painful surprise," that the Carmelites had engaged a non Catholic lawyer to pursue their case against the archdiocese.

The position of the Carmelites can be learned from the following letters of Fr. Pius Mayer, Fr. Anastasius Smits, and of the first apostolic delegate to the United States, Monsignor Satolli.

> June 3, 1893
> St. Cecilia's Rectory
> Englewood, N.J.
>
> Very Rev. and dear Fr. Provincial:
>
> Your favor concerning the Falls-land questioned received. I beg to return the following reply.
>
> 1. I cannot remember ever to have uttered any expression to either Archbishop Lynch or Walsh that could be construed into meaning that we held all the land for use only. I am morally certain I never did. My conversation with Archbishop Walsh on the subject was limited to a few words only, incidental to a general talk on various subjects. I remember very well that I tried to be very careful in my expressions on these different points.
>
> With reference to Archbp. Lynch the facts are the following in the matter: I requested him to make good his promise of the 100 acres by giving us a formal Deed to that effect since we were incorporated and empowered to hold a Title. To which he at once assented and ordered Mr. O'Sullivan to draw up the Deed. The Deed was properly drawn up as they generally are when religious Communities receive by way of donation diocesan property. I wanted to have a clause put in giving us the right to demand at any time a warranty Deed in fee simple upon payment of a small sum of money, so that we might be free to leave any time without loss of the improvements made. We could sell to any other religious Community. Without this clause, we could not sell, but on leaving, all would revert to the Diocese again, compensation being compulsory only for what the Archbishop might consider to be of value to the diocese.
>
> Mr. O'Sullivan put the price we were to pay for this warranty Deed, at $200.00 an acre. To that I objected, telling the Archbishop that it made his original promise void, looked like sharp practice, and reduced our labour and our outlay to nothing. He said that I was perfectly right, that Mr. O'Sullivan had done so without his knowledge, and that he would put it at $50.00 per acre. He said he would gladly give it for a dollar, but was not sure that he had any right to do so.
>
> I had the second Deed (Corrective of the first) made out, together

with a formal, agreement between the Archbishop and the Order to concede the parishes of the territory, we then attended, to the Carmelites. These papers he was to sign and execute at the time of our young men receiving Minor Orders; but hearing of the changes mentioned in your letter he would not sign.

I left all these Documents properly wrapped and marked at the Falls, before I left for Europe. Not knowing at the time that I was not to come back there, I took no further precautions to have them kept safe. I have no correspondence on the matter, for everything was transacted orally, mainly because his correspondence was generally so unsatisfactory.

I have only 2 or 3 times seen the map you mentioned, and do not know where it can be; unless Mr. O'Sullivan took it when he drew the first Deed and never returned it. However, it appears to me that I saw it once since.

I would have written before now, but I could not possibly manage it. With Best wishes, I am fraternally,

A. J. Smits, O.C.C.[57]

+ + +

New Baltimore,

June 6, 1893

My dear Fr. Prior:

I am painfully surprised at the news about your health. May God grant you a speedy convalescence. I send you James, so that your work may not be interrupted. The enclosed letter contains the information which Fr. Smits is able to give regarding the land question. It looks like deliberate fraud on the part of J. J. Lynch.

Yours devotedly.

Pius B. Mayer, O.C.C. Prov.[58]

+ + +

New Baltimore, July 14, 1893

Dear Father Prior:

I am glad you feel so well and hope it will be lasting. Concerning James I wrote the AB. telling him, that our quarrel and Jas. Faculties had nothing in common, and announcing an appeal if he did not give faculties. He then forestalled me by appealing to the Delegate on account of our opposition to his sale of the land. I answered explaining matters and demanding a deed in fee simple for 100 acres, after which we would release the other hundred, repudiating at the same time the deed of 1882 as a sham. The same I wrote to A. B. Walsh. I did not hear of the matter since then. We cannot do anything but wait. In regard to your building I would give builders a chance to offer bids, but do not accept any or commence building, until our quarrel is settled. May the Bl. Virgin help us.

Kindest regards to all.

As ever.

Yours sincerely,
Pius B. Mayer, O.C.C.
Prov.[59]

+ + +

Washington, D.C.
July 4, 1893
Apostolic Delegation
United States of America
No. 503

Rev. Father:

The Archbishop of Toronto has brought to the attention of this Apostolic Delegation that Archbishop Lynch now deceased has granted 100 acres of land to the Carmelite Order at Niagara Falls, but had reserved for himself another 104 acres of property, although he allowed the Religious the use of this property since 1882. Now, however, when the Archbishop wished to sell this land, the Fathers had notified the purchaser in writing- not to take possession of the property, alleging: that they had obtained the right of ownership in this land by prescription. Since all these matters now rest in the hands of our Lordship, the Archbishop has had recourse in law to this Apostolic Delegation, inasmuch as one having residence in the United States is subject to this Apostolic Delegation. The Archbishop asks that you desist from your opposition and that you direct your subjects in the aforesaid monastery no further to oppose obstacles to the Archbishop in the free exercise of his right. I do not know on what solid grounds the Carmelite Fathers and you, my Lord, rely in contending that they have acquired dominion over the other 104 acres of land which the Archbishop did not grant; but in whatever way this case is to be handled, if indeed it cannot be settled otherwise, it must be before an Ecclesiastical tribunal and not a civil one. Therefore be kind enough to furnish me with suitable information concerning this matter and to let me have your own opinion.

Your Lordship's humble servant, etc.[60]

\+ \+ \+

Washington, D.C.
July 12, 1893
Apostolic Delegation United States of America
No. 658

Rev. Father:

I have received your letter written to me on the seventh of this month, and I am grateful for the points of information which you have presented to me concerning the cases now pending between the Most Rev. Archbishop of Toronto and the Rev. Carmelite Fathers. Furthermore I am confident that this case can be peaceably settled between you and the Archbishop without the intervention of Ecclesiastical Authority. If, however, the case should have to be taken to higher Authority, it would be necessary for you to submit the following documents:

The earliest agreement either in the original or in an authentic copy.

A copy of the Pastoral letter in which the Archbishop made known the execution of his gift.

A map including the boundaries and a description of the land.

The document drawn up in 1882 in which the Archbishop declares that he acknowledges the right once granted the Fathers, of preference in purchasing the land in case the part reserved to the Archbishop should be sold.

Finally also all the letters and other documents which may appear suitable to you to safeguard the rights of the Order.

In conclusion I will not omit to point out that the Apostolic Delegate cannot interfere in the case "of the approval of the new Superior, Singler," as explained by you, since the Archdiocese of Toronto, and therefore the Archbishop, is not subject to the jurisdiction of this Apostolic Delegation.

Your Lordship's humble servant, etc.[61]

\+ \+ \+

New Baltimore,
July 17, 1893

Dear Fr. Prior:

I received a letter from the Auditor of the Apostolic Delegation. He counsels peaceable arrangement with the Archbishop. In case of judicial treatment he calls for a number of documents, none of which is in existence save the infamous lease of 1882. The more

I think of the matter, the more I become convinced that we must lose the battle, as we cannot prove our assertions. All the witnesses except myself are dead and *Unus testis, nullus testis*. Besides as I told you already in April here, you really went too far, in claiming the whole farm. Therefore I direct you to inform the Archbishop that we are ready to release the hundred acres in question. If we had expenses for improvements, we also had the fruits for 17 years.

The lease of 1882 is not according to the original agreement, and if Smits had sense enough to take me along when the deed was made, it would have been made differently, or not at all. But as it is, there is nothing left, but to accept the inevitable.

But I hope, that conciliatory overtures will be met in a conciliatory spirit. Nothing new here. Regards to all.

Yours fraternally,
Pius R. Mayer, O.C.C.
Prov.

P.S. I would consider it best, if you saw the Archbishop personally.[62]

+ + +

From a study of the foregoing letters it is evident that the Carmelites were making a twofold claim: first, a claim in fee simple to one hundred acres of land described in a deed of March 11, 1882; second, the ownership by prescription, of one hundred acres, more or less, which the archbishop had not included in his deed of March 11, 1882, but which the Carmelites had used without hindrance of any kind since they came. They based their alleged rights on the promise Bishop Lynch is reported to have made to Fr. Ignatius Beerhorst and Fr. Albert Heimann, the superior in Kansas.[63] The only documents the Carmelites could produce were the Pastoral Letter of Archbishop Lynch of April 26, 1876, and the deed so often referred to in these letters and given by Lynch on March 11, 1882. The former makes no mention of any grant of land. The latter is well worth deep study.

After a lengthy legal description of the land[64] the archbishop grants the lands just described,

> ... reserving from out of said last premises one acre of land known as the Church lot TO HAVE AND TO HOLD unto to said parties of the second part their successors and assigns to and for their sole use forever subject nevertheless to the reservations, limitations and conditions expressed in the original grant thereof from the Crown. And subject also to the Provisio that should the parties hereto of the second part ever abandon the premises hereby con-

veyed with the permission of the Holy See the said premises are to revert to the parties hereto of the first part.

The said parties of the first part covenant with the parties of the second part that they have the right to convey the said lands to the said party of the second part not withstanding any act of the said parties of the first part and that the parties of the second part shall have quiet possession of the said lands free from all encumbrances and the said parties of the first part covenant with the parties of the second part that they will execute such further assurances of the said lands as may be requisite and the said parties of the first part covenant with the parties of the second part that they have done no act to encumber the said lands save as herein after mentioned and the said parties of the first part release to the parties of the second part all their claims upon the said lands subject to the provisions and conditions herein mentioned.

And it is hereby covenanted to by the parties of the first part that proper compensation as far as any improvements made may be of value to the Diocese shall be made by them to the parties hereto of the second part whenever the said parties of the second part are permitted as aforesaid to relinquish the premises hereby conveyed and have executed further assurances as may be deemed necessary.

It is hereby further covenanted by the parties of the first part that should the parties of the second part desire to raise money by mortgaging a portion of the premises hereby conveyed for making improvements thereon they the parties of the first part will obtain such discharges and conveyances and otherwise perfect the title to the parties of the second part as may be necessary for that purpose provided that the clause is not intended to be an absolute release of such portion of said land to the parties of the second part.

The parties of the first part further covenant with the parties of the second part that they the parties of the second part can purchase absolutely any of the three parcels hereby conveyed in payment of two hundred dollars per acre but not less than one entire parcel to be sold at any one time and after any such purchase the next proceeding- clause is not to operate.[65]

From even a very cursory reading of the conditions under which the Carmelites received title to the land, it is evident that they received not outright ownership, but only the use of the land for as long as they would remain in the diocese. The archbishop promised not to encumber the land and if the Carmelite Fathers wish to raise a mortgage, he would do what is necessary in law to enable them to do so. If they should with proper permission from Rome wish to withdraw, the diocese would recompense the community for the improvements of use to the diocese. The Carmelite Fathers had the option of buying outright at any time any or all of the three parcels of land at $200.00 an acre.

As to whether the Fathers at the time at which they received the grant understood the transaction as an outright gift or only a perpetual lease, it is hard to hold that they understood it as anything more than a perpetual lease. The following letter which passed between the superior of the Carmelites at Niagara in 1882, who was none other than Fr. Pius Mayer, and the lawyers will shed light on the question:

O'Sullivan & Perdue
Barristers, Attorneys-at-Law

Toronto, March 13, 1882

My dear Father Pius,

R.C. Epis. Corp.
&
Carmelite Fathers

I was too busy all day on Saturday to write you and will be equally so today in order to get the Archbishop's affairs in shape. I went to Welland, saw all the papers there (the declaration of incorporation was received here this morning) and went through the title. It was fortunate I did so because the title was not in the Epis. Corp. at all but in the Archbishop—notwithstanding a large mortgage was made by the Corp. I immediately had a deed of the property made by his Grace so as to perfect the title and went to see him with the deed to your Corp. After a long interview we adjusted the clause about compensation and about a complete title to you for the purpose of mortgaging which is satisfactory. As Father Schmitz (sic) was anxious to purchase some of the land so as to be your own absolutely I got a covenant that you could buy out and out any of the three parcels at the rate of $200 per acre. The 17 1/3 acre block on which the church stands could thus be placed in a way, that you could mortgage it to any extent you please and could sell to any person if necessary. I thought this clause valuable and so I will prepare the deeds of that block and if your Corp. chooses to buy in that way you can do so. If not, there is no harm done. If not availed of then whenever you abandon the premises with the consent of the Holy See the property reverts to the Epis. Corp., compensation being made to you for the improvements made by you as far as they are of value to the Diocese.

There is a large mortgage now on the property but it is collateral security to the debts of some parishes north of Toronto. In case you think well of buying, your money will go to release the portion bought. You would do well to consider carefully before putting an expensive building on any land which you have not a good title. I may say you can purchase any of the three blocks at any time and if you do not wish to raise money on it by mortgaging there is no hurry. The Episcopal Corp. will be bound at any time to convey it to you on the above terms.

In case I see His Grace today I will write to you again—if not or in any event I will send you over the deeds so that you can see them before registration.

Yours truly,

D. A. O'Sullivan[66]

+ + +

Rev. Father Pius
Superior Carmelite Fathers
Niagara Falls, Ontario

March 14, 1882

My dear Sir:

We send you by post in this deed, from His Grace the Archbishop, to R.C. Epis. Corp. so as to complete the title in this: deed of transfer to your Corporation. We also return the papers handed us by Father O'Malley. His Grace did not wish to sign the deed for the sale of the 17 1/2 acres to you and even if he did I would have held it till I was satisfied that you desired it done that way. We send over this deed to you so that it can be used when necessary. The deeds drawn at the request of Father Schmitz are also enclosed but they are of course useless now. We have marked the important clauses in the deed to you so that you can see your position. In case you register them you must register the one from His Grace to the R.C. Epis. Corp. as well. We referred to the mortgages on the property in our last letter. We are told that the only encumbrance is the mortgage to the Acme Savings & Loan Corp. here for about $5,000 and it is collateral to mortgages on other Church property.

There is no hurry about registering the deeds but when you are satisfied of the best course you will do well to get the registered title in yourselves by registration of the new deeds just mentioned.

We will charge you half fees—parts of these three days being devoted to these matters and $5.00 disbursed—say $26.00.

Yours truly,
O'Sullivan & Perdue[67]

+ + +

Rev. Father Pius
Carmelite Fathers
Niagara Falls, Ontario

March 16, 1882

Revd. Sir:

Your letter received. You will see that Father Schmitz (sic) will not be surprised at the terms of the conveyance to you. It is better than he got at the time he was His Grace. You had better appreciate your position fully as I intimated to you before any expense in buildings.

D. A. O'Sullivan

P. S. Thanks for the remembrance of Mrs. O'S.[68]

+ + +

There is no document extant to explain the Carmelite claims to the undeeded property which they possessed by prescription. According to the existing law of the Church, they required a plausible title, undisturbed use for forty years. At length they bowed to the inevitable. On November 9, 1893, the Apostolic Delegate Satolli from Washington was visiting Niagara University. He then made a call at the hospice construction at which the Archbishop of Toronto was present.[69] On November 15 Archbishop Satolli issued a letter praising the hospice and *The Carmelite Review*.[70] No doubt the whole matter was discussed and on December 4 the archbishop proposed to sell the entire plot of two hundred acres, more or less, to the Carmelite Fathers at $100.00.[71] This was tantamount to giving them without charge the land deeded by Walsh on March 11, 1882, and of receiving $200.00 an acre for the land claimed by the Carmelites by right of prescription. The prior, Fr. Anastasius Kreidt, accepted the offer on December 18th,[72] calling the terms moderate, and the deed was issued on February 9, 1894.[73]

Thus was the acrimonious dispute settled, but it took all the cash that had been collected for the erection of the hospice to pay for the land. The community assumed a small mortgage; the rest was paid in cash.

The yearlong argument in no way exhausted the energies of Kreidt. In fact he directed his fiery spirit to polemics against anti-Catholicism. In 1893 the agnostic Robert Ingersoll in the last years of his life visited Niagara Falls with his doctrine.[74] Kreidt made note of the event in his and went on to attack certain other undesirables:

> Niagara Falls is the favorite haunt of freaks and notoriety-hunters. To the species must be added the pest of every decent commu-

nity the so-called "ex-priest and escaped nun." The genuine article lately made its appearance in this vicinity. It is an outrage that the custom officials, who with paternal anxiety guard public morals in confiscating indecent literature, should have allowed this recent adventurer to escape their vigilance ... His subjects were "The Convent Unveiled" and "Secrets of Romanism" .... He made remarks reflecting on our monastery and the convent in the neighborhood .... The whereabouts of the A.P.A. may be unknown to those outside of the disreputable brood of scoundrels who bring this class of lecturers among respectable citizens ... .[75]

Kreidt directed his readers' attention to a still further attack on the Carmelites:

> A fanatical preacher named Bosworth who has probably found his exchequer at a low ebb after the return of his family from their summer vacation has been endeavoring to re-fill his purse by showing audiences in the maritime provinces how he can make Rome howl. After he had stirred up the usual cesspool of misrepresentation against our holy religion and its devout practices he brought down the house by producing a Scapular. The papers quote the speaker as saying that "to it was attached two small cards. A picture on one represented Mary and the infant Christ, but with the crown on the head of the former. Mr. Bosworth then read out of a pamphlet written by the most Rev. John Hughes, D.D., late Archbishop of New York, statements to the effect that those who died without this Scapular would surely go into everlasting torment. It was a power unto salvation..."[76]

Even before ground was broken for the new building, Kreidt had collected ten thousand dollars. This sum represented one-fourth the cost of the building. Dean Harris, who was a generous contributor to the hospice fund, wrote of Kreidt at this time in his *History of the Catholic Church in the Niagara Peninsula*:

> The present superior, the Very Rev. Anastasius J. Kreidt, is a man remarkable for his scholarly attainments, his religious zeal and indomitable energy. Trusting in the Providence of God and in the generosity of the people, he began this great building, confronted with obstacles and difficulties that would have discouraged a less energetic and enterprising man. Overcoming all discouragements he has succeeded beyond the expectations of his friends and will undoubtedly carry his great work to a successful finish. This exceptionally talented and large-hearted priest established a few years ago *The Carmelite Review*, a well-edited monthly magazine, which already has reached a circulation of four thousand and is slowly and steadily widening its circle of readers.[77]

NEW DEVELOPMENTS IN THE 1890s

Ground was broken for the hospice on August 21, 1893, even though the question of ownership of the land had not been settled. After settlement, the archbishop and the Carmelites were soon on friendly terms again, and on the feast of Our Lady of Mt. Carmel 1894, Archbishop Walsh laid the cornerstone in the presence of a large crowd of visitors.[78] Kreidt continued to labor for completion of the project. In July 1896, the third provincial chapter gathered in the new hospice. It was only fitting that the splendid work of Kreidt which provided housing for the voters should be rewarded. Thus, he was named provincial.[79] In the same month, the famed Cardinal Merry del Val paid a visit to the hospice.[80]

On June 15, 1899, the first section of the new building which had been completed was solemnly blessed by Archbishop Denis O'Connor of Toronto, successor of Archbishop Walsh who had died on July 31, 1898.[81] The sermon was preached by Bishop Richard A. O'Connor of Peterborough, a former pastor of Our Lady of Peace church.[82] The first retreat for the priests of the Toronto Archdiocese was held in the hospice from July 24th to July 29th, 1899.[83] Six school teachers were present for a retreat conducted for them in August of the same year.[84] But unfortunately the hospice, a retreat house, failed in its main purpose. To Father Kreidt's disappointment very few retreatants responded to the invitation for spiritual refreshment. Perhaps, it was due to the fact that lay retreats had not yet become popular.

The yearly pilgrimage to the shrine of Our Lady of Peace on the hospice grounds had in the meanwhile continued to increase in solemnity, beauty and in the multitudes who attended. By 1895 many of the elements peculiar to the format of the pilgrimage today had been incorporated. In 1892 the Holy Father, Leo XIII, animated by the desire to increase devotion to Our Blessed Virgin Mary under the venerable title of Our Lady of Mount Carmel, enriched the churches and chapels of the Carmelite Order with a precious privilege for their Scapular feast day, July 16. The text of the papal letter that granted the *Toties Quoties* indulgence reads:

> In order that the devotion and piety of the Faithful towards the Blessed Virgin of Mt. Carmel, whence flow the most precious and salutary fruits, may increase, we with pleasure yield to the pious request of our beloved son, Aloysius Maria Galli, Prior General of the Order of Our Dear Lady of Mt. Carmel of Ancient Observance, and have determined to enrich the churches of the Order of Carmelites with an especial privilege. We therefore grant trusting in the mercy of God and in the authority of the

Holy Apostles Peter and Paul to all the Faithful of both sexes, after they have with true repentance confessed and received Holy Communion in each year on July 16, the day on which the feast of the virginal Mother of God of Mt. Carmel is celebrated, from the time of the first vespers of the feast until sundown of the day designated (July 16), whenever they piously visit one of the churches or public chapels of the Monks or Sisters of the entire Carmelite Order, those of the calceated as well as those of the discalceated, wherever it may be, and there address pious prayers to God for peace between Christian sovereigns and for the extirpation of heresy, for the conversion of sinners and the advancement of our holy mother the Church. As often as they may make this visit, we grant to them a plenary Indulgence and forgiveness for all their sins. We also grant that these Indulgences and this remission of sins may be bestowed upon those who departed this life united in love with God. And we grant this, not withstanding Our own and the Rule of the Apostolic chancery, relative to the non-granting of Indulgences *Ad Instar* or any other Apostolic constitutions or decrees that may conflict herewith, and all others, they may exist.

We decree that this grant shall constantly continue in force, and we desire that the same belief, as would be given to the Original Belief, were it exhibited, be also bestowed to all transcripts thereof whether they be printed or otherwise copied, provided that they are signed by a Notary Public and bear the seal of some Dignitary of the Church.

Given in Rome, at St. Peter's under the Ring of the Fisher, on May 16th, 1892, in the fifteenth of Our Pontificate. (L.S.)[85]

The Shrine of Our Lady of Peace was thus able to extend this benefit to its pilgrims.

St. Albert's Blessed Water had by this time also become very popular at the pilgrimage. This water, blessed with a relic of Saint Albert, a Carmelite saint whose patronage was invoked against fevers and diseases, was for the use of the sick. The basis for the use of such water is traced back to an account in St. Albert's life. Attacked with a grievous sickness, Albert, according to tradition, had recourse to the Blessed Virgin, who appeared to him holding a crystal cup filled with water, which she offered him to drink. St. Albert implored her to bless the water and upon tasting it, he was immediately cured. Inflamed with love for his neighbor, he asked our Blessed Lady to attach a healing power to all water which he would bless in her name and in that of her Divine Son. Apparently, his prayer was granted. Since his death in 1306 Carmelites believed his intercessory power was present in connection with water blessed with his relics.[86]

The usual pilgrimage day began with a solemn Mass at the church of Our Lady of Peace. Holy Communion was distributed at all hours of the morning. For those who had communicated or planned to spend the day at the pilgrimage, ample accommodation was made to supply necessary refreshments. As early as 7:30 a.m. pilgrims began to come from Buffalo and Niagara Falls, N.Y. A special pilgrimage train chartered by nearly a thousand German devotees from Buffalo arrived at 8:00. The pilgrims from Toronto under the directorship of the rector of St. Michael's Cathedral, the Reverend Francis Ryan, the archbishop's personal representative, arrived at the Shrine just before the solemn High Mass. A procession in the late afternoon wound its way around the monastery grounds and came to rest near the little Shrine. Various sermons on Our Lady of Mount Carmel and her Scapular were delivered by celebrated and honored clergymen. The German pilgrims were also thrilled by a sermon given in their own tongue. This was followed by solemn benediction of the Most Blessed Sacrament. Later the pilgrimage officially ended with a papal blessing of the pilgrims.[87]

The pilgrimages at the turn of the century were headed by Archbishop O'Connor of Toronto, the Very Rev. Dean Harris of St. Catherines and Fr. McHale, president of Niagara University.[88] In 1898 two long trains of the Michigan Central Railroad, each with sixteen cars, left Exchange Street Depot of the New York Central and arrived at Falls View fifty minutes later with pilgrims willing to pay fifty cents for the round-trip ride. Children rode for half fare. From Rochester, New York, an early train came to Niagara Falls, N.Y., and the pilgrims trudged over the upper Suspension Bridge to catch the Niagara Falls Park and River Electric Railway alighting at the hospice crossing, just below the hill behind the monastery. From Toronto lake boats carried the passengers to Niagara-on-the-Lake where they caught the Michigan Central to Falls View arriving in time for the 10 o'clock Mass. Hamilton, Ontario visitors took the Grand Trunk Railway to Clifton and the Park Electric Railway to the monastery. St. Catherines and Thorold visitors rode the Niagara Central Railroad.[89] At the 1899 pilgrimage it was estimated that over 1600 German Catholics from Buffalo attended. In that year several new features were introduced. Cold cuts and cake were served in tents to shade the many visitors from the sun. The grounds were as yet poorly landscaped.[90]

The advances outlined above, attained through the force of unification of the houses, were not the only signs of a more prosperous foundation in the United States. The original work begun by Frs. Smits and

Mayer on a home mission band was vastly enlarged. The resulting effects of such mission tours in New York, New Jersey and Pennsylvania by many of the Carmelites helped spread the name of the Order. Moreover, they also served as an ideal outlet for the Carmelite apostolic spirit.

The moving force behind the travelling mission band was the new provincial, Anastasius Kreidt. He often liked to quote Brownson's famous dictum to preachers: "Imitate the models not by saying what they say, but by doing what they did."[91] He brought to his sermons a vast knowledge culled from an avid habit of reading. Within a brief fifteen day span, for example, in 1903 he managed to read *The Pit, The Count of Monte Cristo, The Ruffians, An Arkansas Planter, Mrs. Wiggs of the Cabbage Patch, Green Pastures and Picadilly*.[92] And all this in the midst of a rigorous mission which he and Fr. Best were conducting, during which he heard over one thousand confessions.[93] The names of the early missionaries were familiar ones in the history of the province such as, Avertannus Brennan and Basil Kahler.[94] In Fr. Basil, his superior, were recognized for all those sterling characteristics so essential to the successful missionary. Possessed of a robust physique together with an oratorical charm that stamped him as an ideal pulpit personality, he carried the Carmelite message to the public with effectiveness.[95] There were men like Philip Best who kept a storehouse of information on file on all areas of theology, history, science and art.[96] Even Theodore McDonald with his low pitched voice and too quick recitation joined the band for a while.[97] In their day these men were polished and capable orators. Their material may seem outdated but in the context of their decade, it was pertinent and captivating. Mayer often spoke on the Blessed Mother. Reproduced below are extracts from one of his favorite themes:

> "Behold from henceforth all generations shall call me Blessed"
>
> Dearly beloved, the Church applies to Mary the words taken from the Book of Proverbs: 'The Lord possessed me in the beginning of His ways before He made anything from the beginning. From eternity I was ordained, before the hills I was born. Happy the man that hears me and watches before my doors daily. He that finds me finds life and gains salvation from the Lord.' Mary then existed in the plans of God before creation from all eternity and was assigned to a most elevated position, to a grand office before the Angels were called into existence. Yea; according to the doctrine of the Church, the manifestation of the divine Council of the Incarnation of the Word of God caused the fall of the Angels, as Lucifer considered it too humiliating to adore and serve the God made Man through Mary . . . There never was a mere creature more holy, more united to God; and if we honor the saints of

God for their sanctity, as the world honors its heroes of science, politics or war, we have not only the right but the duty to honor Mary above all others. Certainly the distance between Christ and Mary is immense because He was God, she a mere creature; nevertheless, our veneration for her approaches as closely as faith will allow, to the service rendered to Christ, to whom as God nothing is impossible, whilest Mary can obtain by her intercession, what to her own power would be impossible, as God delights in dispensing his graces through her hands.

The non-Catholic world charges us with Mariolatry, accusing us of worshipping her and depriving God of the honor due to Him alone. But, my dearly beloved, these accusations are mere cant, and base themselves upon an erroneous interpretation of the Bible. The Bible is full of Mary, and our faith, in order to be Biblical, must also be full of Mary. Without her Christianity cannot exist, as the history of the world and of religion clearly demonstrates. Look around among the different sects that call themselves Christian. What do you see? The sect, which, though it does not bestow special honors to the Mother of God, does not dishonor her as much as the others, is the Church of England, established by law. There, we see a gradual turning back to the old faith of Rome; we witness numerous conversions and apparently the day is not very distant, when the Catholic Church in England will assume a prominent position. But among all the other sects we see the reverse; repudiating Mary, they are repudiating Christ and are gradually drifting into infidelity.[98]

By 1903 the Mission Band was one of the principal means of financial support for the province. The chapter of that year named Kreidt to head the band. Regular speakers in the group included at that time Paul Ryan, Cyril Kehoe and Berthold Lauzau. Supplementary help came from Anastasius Smits, Cyril Feehan, Dionysius Best, Vincent Metzler, Anselm Werner, Francis Krebs, and Jerome Reichwein.[99] The activity of the early mission band was now at its peak as is reflected by the numerous organizational directives issued at this time. One such decree, issued by the provincial, Ambrose Bruder, reflects the severity of discipline that was imposed on the men:

RULES AND REGULATIONS FOR OUR MISSIONARIES

In order to avoid friction and to enhance the efficacy of the missionary staff inaugurated at our last Provincial Chapter, the following regulations are laid down:

1.—The fathers will reside in the monasteries to which they may be assigned by the provincial and will not change their residence unless ordered to do so by him.

2.—All applications for missions, retreats, etc. are to be forwarded to the Superior of the Missions, who will distribute the work among the staff.

3.—The money received by the members of the staff is to be forwarded to the Superior of the Missions.

4.—The Superior of the Missions will forward the checks to the provincial, unless otherwise instructed.

5.—An itemized statement of all expenses entailed by a mission is to be sent to the Superior by the responsible head of a mission.

6.—No pocket money is permitted to missionaries. They are to turn over whatever traveling money they may have to the procurator of the house where they live.

7.—When a mission is closed, the missionaries are to take the train to their respective houses on the day of the closing. Since missions usually close on Monday morning, this means they are to leave no later than Monday evening. A visit may be made to our nearby houses for a short time. However, to remain over night, a written permission from the provincial is necessary.

8.—The use of distilled liquors in any form is prohibited during a mission.

9.—When the missionaries return to their houses, they are excused from choir exercises and other duties during two days. Then they follow again the regular exercises. They may be employed by the prior for any work, subject however to the call of the Superior of the Missions.

10.—The missionaries are not to forget their own spiritual wants, keeping in mind the well known words of St. Paul bearing on that subject.

11.—The superior of the mission staff is answerable to the provincial for the observance by the different missionaries of the above regulations.[100]

Mention must be made also of the development in the apostolate of written communications. The province, under the impetus of Kreidt, published both *The Carmelite Review* and the *Rundschau vom Berge (The News Magazine from the Mountain)*. The *Rundschau* was first published in 1894 and copies were printed monthly until 1902 when it went to the graveyard of most German periodicals of the time. Fire had raged through the printing office of the journal on Sunday May 15, 1898. *The Carmelite Review*, a well-edited monthly magazine, reached a circulation of over

4,000 by the turn of the century.[101] *The Review* first appeared in January 1893. Kreidt appointed Fr. Philip Best as editor. He had been employed in a Hamilton newspaper office before he entered the Niagara Carmel. Br. William Quigley, and for a time also Br. Augustine Van Snepsen, acted as agents for the journal. Both were successful in obtaining subscriptions. *The Review* was growing fast in popularity and was rated highly among the new sociology magazines.[102] It was the first major publication to carry an extensive review of the life of James A. McMaster, editor and publisher of the *Freeman's Journal*, after his death.[103]

The editorial policy and purpose was clearly stated in the first issue:

> This magazine is to be devoted to the Queen of Carmel ... It shall be our duty to honor Mary, the Flower of Carmel, to unfold the beauty of that lovely flower, to spread its sweet fragrance far and wide, and to screen it from every foul breath that would dare pollute it. We shall endeavor to bring to light everything that will enhance the loveliness of this flower par excellence, which will be a worthy posy to offer our Queen, and a sweet smelling nosegay for her clients ... *The Carmelite Review* will likewise be a medium of inter-communication between English speaking Carmelites ... From month to month the Reverend superior of the Monastery here at Niagara Falls will have something new to say to his many friends who are interested in our hospice.[104]

The many Catholic publications of the last decade of the nineteenth century could attribute their foundation to the pronouncements of the Third Plenary Council of Baltimore and the encyclical letter, *Longinqua Oceani*, issued by Pope Leo XIII on January 4, 1895. The strength of Catholic publication then is registered by the fact that the first Catholic editors' convention was held in Chicago in 1893.[105] Nevertheless, there were signs that the state of Catholic journals was not entirely sound. *The American Ecclesiastical Review* of February 1894, carried an article by Louis W. Reilly entitled "The Weak Points of the Catholic Press."[106] In reality, it was generally recognized that Catholic journalism at the time was a losing financial venture. Journals rose and were soon swallowed up in bankruptcy. Sometimes, too, many journals tried to cover the same territory.[107]

In 1903 the definitory decided to transfer the office of the *Review* to the new Carmelite college in Chicago. A secular priest, Rev. Aeneas B. Goodwin, who had just joined the teaching staff in Chicago, became the new editor. The journal was printed by the *Chicago Daily Calumet*.[108] The magazine was labed *The New Carmelite Review* and given a new purpose:

> ... Eleven years ago the *Review* was founded by the Carmelite Fathers to fill a want that had long been felt in Catholic literature.

> Before that time there had indeed been many Catholic magazines of high standing and of great influence but there had been no Catholic magazine that aimed especially at influencing and moulding the actual daily lives of the people by showing them the practical influence of religion on life, and in fact the inseparable union that exists between real religion and life . . . It is then in accordance with the success that we have obtained and with the assurance of still greater success that the Carmelite Fathers have decided to enter into a wider and more prominent field with *The Review* . . . *The Review* will be doubled in size. It will be made a peoples' magazine. Prominent churchmen, labor leaders, and literary men will contribute. It will be the only religious magazine that will aim to express the wishes of the working people . . . *The New Carmelite Review* will be the working people's magazine.[109]

An article in a 1904 issue on the Iroquois theatre fire by State Senator Clark typifies the new direction of the magazine.

> I was one of the first to arrive at the scene of the holocaust.... My experiences in organizing an emergency hospital will live in my memory during life .... The firemen and police were bringing the burned and crushed victims from the building very rapidly. They were being piled together on the sidewalks—the living with the dead. There was a restaurant next door. I knew its proprietor. (Thompson) I asked him for the use of his restaurant, which he kindly gave, directing' that all of the severely burned be sent there. Approaching the Iroquois Theatre, as the maddened and crazed crowds were leaving the lower floors by the front entrance, I was riveted to the spot by the horror stricken faces. Appealing to Charles Truax, in the name of humanity to go at once through the Reliance and Columbus Memorial building and summon to the restaurant all doctors, I rushed through the Masonic Temple, stopping in the drug store on my way down and giving orders for all bandages and liniment to be had in the neighborhood to be sent ... As each table announced its dead they were instructed to place them on the floor between the tables . . . loved ones stacked as cord wood. Out of 175 that were placed on the tables we were able by the oxygen equipment to save 25 to 30. If our equipment had been at hand when the doctors first arrived, at least 25 more would have been alive today.[110]

But many of the subscribers did not appreciate the new wilderness furrowed by the magazine. Before many months the complaints became so insistent that Fr. Goodwin was dismissed as editor and manager. Fr. Stephen J. McDonald, was asked to carry on in Goodwin's place. The appointment of this Carmelite was little more than a rear-guard action to cover an embarrassing retreat. The mailing list had not been maintained properly. Printing bills had been left unpaid. Furthermore, postmasters in various cities were protesting against irregularities in the mailing lists. In the Federal Post Office in Washington the *Review* had been placed under the heading of fraudulent publications.[111] Finally in 1907 a Mr. Jaegle of the *Pittsburgh Observer* offered to attempt to revitalize the magazine, but the definitory declined.[112]

An extensive building campaign had also been carried on throughout the province aside from that done at Niagara. Since 1881 schools in Pittsburgh,[113] Scipio,[114] and Leavenworth[115] had been erected. New churches were built at New Baltimore,[116] Pittsburgh,[117] and Clifton,[118] and land was purchased in Englewood for the construction of a new church there.[119] The new addition to the house at New Baltimore had also been completed.[120] Moreover, there had been a rapid growth in manpower in the province since 1881. The province now had thirty-five fathers, sixteen clerics, nine scholastics and fifteen brothers.[121]

1900: The Beginning of a New Era

The last years of the century saw many of the founding fathers pass from the scene. Heimann had died on September 16, 1893,[122] and Knoll passed away three days before Christmas 1900.[123] It was, indeed, the end of an era in American Carmelite history. No new foundation had been accepted by the American Carmelites since 1876 when Knoll assumed parochial duties at Beaver Falls, Pennsylvania. But from a Fourth of July definitory meeting in 1899 came the significant decision to attempt to operate a college in the city of Chicago.[124] There was every indication that a new era in American Carmelite history was about to begin. The years spent in undertaking numerous apostolates had already brought the province to life. The years spent in consolidation and unification now brought the prospect of a bright future. The purpose Fr. Cyril Knoll outlined for his immigration to America had been achieved. By 1900 the Carmelite Order had laid a firm foundation on North American soil. Yet, that journey of a thousand miles which began when Knoll took his first step into the Straubing Carmel was far from finished. The challenge of twentieth century American Catholicism awaited a generation of Carmelites yet to be born. To meet that challenge of the future as it had met the challenge of the past, history would record the fact that Carmel, with vigor and commitment, would continue to proclaim the Good News of the Gospel throughout America.

ABBREVIATIONS USED IN THE NOTES:

A.A.B.   Archives of the Archdiocese of Baltimore.
A.A.T.   Archives of the Archdiocese of Toronto.
A.C.N.   Archives of the Carmelite Fathers, Niagara Falls, Ontario,
A.C.R.   Archives of the Carmelite Fathers, Rome.
A.C.S.   Archives of the Carmelite Fathers, Straubing, Germany.
A.C.W.   Archives of the Carmelite Fathers, Washington, D.C. (Archives - Province of the Most Pure Heart of Mary)
A. LMV. Archives of the Ludwig Missionseverein, Munich.
A.U.L.   Archives of the Ursuline Nuns, Louisville.

Endnotes

Chapter One: Transit and Transition

1. A.C.S., *Liber Personarum Provinciae Germaniae Superioris* (Inchoatus 1842) p. 2. This source indicates that Knoll was baptized in honor of St. John the Evangelist. An "*Excerptus de libro personarum Provinciae Germaniae Superioris* (Inchoatus 1842)" is now contained in the Carmelitana Collection, Whitefriars Hall, Washington, D.C.

2. An excellent summary of the effects of the French Revolution and Napoleonic conquests is given by Kenneth Scott Latourette, *The Nineteenth Century in Europe* in *Christianity in a Revolutionary Age* series, (New York: Harper & Brothers, 1968), I: 150-66. This is the source for material mentioned in the introductory paragraphs of this chapter.

3. Klemens Martini, O. Carm., *Der deutsche Carmel* (Bamberg: J. Kirsch, 1926), II: 218-27.

4. *Ibid.,* II: 164-66.

5. *Ibid.,* II: 288.

6. *Ibid.,* II: 354.

7. *Ibid.,* II: 379.

8. *Ibid.,* II: 516.

9. *Ibid.,* II: 97.

10. *Ibid.,* II: 229.

11. *Ibid.,* II: 272-74.

12. Canisius Janssen, O. Carm., *Carmelkluis on Carmelwereld* (Bussum: Paul Brand, 1955), p. 171.

13. *Ibid.,* pp. 174-75.

14. Gundekar Hatzold, O. Carm., *Das Karmelitenkloster Straubing* (Straubing: Joseph Habbel, 1947), pp. 69-81 *passim*. The Carmelites had maintained a monastery at Straubing since 1368 AD. The monastery enjoyed the protection of Duke Albrecht, son of Emperor Louis IV. Albrecht II, son of the original patron, is buried behind the present high altar in a sculptured marble sepulcher that is the outstanding art object of the church. Eamon Carroll, O. Carm., "Visit to Germany," *The Sword,* XV (August, 1952), 325. The community was given property on its arrival in Straubing and soon began building a church and monastery. They also acquired in 1372 the brewery that adjoined the monastery [until 1980], although it is now in private hands. The first church was consecrated in 1430, but not completely finished until 1464. Straubing's trials were also the Carmelites'. Their church was the only one free from interdict when the Hussite heresy threatened the town in 1470. The frontier of Bohemia, the present [Czech Republic], is not many miles to the east of Straub-

ing. When Protestantism was sweeping through Germany, Provincial Andreas Stoss helped keep the faith in the wavering monastery. Saint Peter Canisius was the guest of the community and preached in the Carmelite Church during the Lent of 1558. One-third of Straubing was destroyed by fire in 1780, but the monastery escaped unharmed. The protection was attributed to Our Lady, under the title of her *Gnadenbild, Maria von den Nesseln*. An image of Our Lady received its name from the fact that the statue was discovered in an abandoned place among nettles, near the town of Heilbronn. This statue was moved to Straubing in 1661 where the town received it with solemnity. A great devotion to the *Nesselmutter* grew up. Straubing formally consecrated itself to her in 1703. Hatzold, *op. cit.,* pp. 1-60, passim.

15. C. Cyprian Alston, "Benedictine," *Catholic Encyclopedia,* II: 451.

16. Hatzold, *op. cit.,* pp. 82-97, *passim.*

17. A.C.R., II American PCM I, Albert Weiss to Augustinus Ferrara, April 5, 1847. Letters to the Carmelite house in Rome concerning the American Carmelite Province of the Most Pure Heart of Mary have been preserved in the General Archives of the Order. Letters after the year 1900 are kept in vertical files and constitute a "living" collection, unavailable to consultation. Materials to 1899, about 330 pieces, have been gathered into one bundle under the signature *II Americana PCM I*. A microfilm of this bundle can be found in the Carmelitana Collection, Whitefriars Hall, Washington, D.C.

18. A.C.S., "*Liber Personarum Provinciae Germaniae Superioris* (Inchoatus, 1842)," *op. cit.,* p. 1.

19. A.C.R., II Americana PCM I, Weiss to Augustine Ferrara, April 5, 1847.

20. A.C.S., "Schematiamus Fratrum B.M.V. Carmelo Straubingano in Bavaria Degentium 1856." Materials listed in this study from the Straubing Archives are now available in the Carmelitana Collection, Whitefriars Hall, Washington, D.C. Most of this material is contained on microfilm.

21. "Father Cyril Knoll, O. Carm., Our First Commisary General," *The Sword,* II: 459.

22. A.C.S., "*Liber Personarum Provinciae Germaniae Superioris* (Inchoatus, 1842)," *op, cit.,* p. 2.

23. "Father Cyril Knoll, O. Carm., Our First Commissary General," *The Sword, op. cit.,* II: 465.

24. A.C.S. Knoll Papers, Bavarian Minister of the Interior to Peter Heitzer, September 26, 1846.

25. A.C.S., "*Liber Personarum Provinciae Germaniae Superioris* (Inchoatus, 1842)," *loc. cit.*

26. Ibid.

27. A.C.S., Knoll Papers, J. Oberudorfer to Albert Weiss, November 14, 1848.

28. A.C.S., Knoll Papers, Bavarian Minister of the Interior to Weiss, December 20, 1848.

29. A.C.S., Knoll Papers, Oberudorfer to Weiss, April 20, 1849.

30. A.C.R., II Americana PCM 1. Albert Weiss to Augustine Ferrara, October 16, 1849. "Father Cyril Knoll, O. Carm., Our First Commissary General," *The Sword, op. cit.,* II: 459 suggests: "Father Knoll entered the novitiate at Straubing in June, 1846, "was admitted to simple vows in 1847, to solemn vows in 1850, and was, apparently at once placed in charge of the community." This information obviously was postulated on the fact that records from the Straubing Archives indicate Knoll made solemn profession in 1860. The anonymous author of the *Sword* article reasoned that the period of novitiate and simple vows allowed for today was observed in those times ago. This is not true. Letters from the Straubing house indicate that dispensations from the required time were often given in the case of priest novices. Adjustments were made in view of apostolic demand.

31. A.C.S., Knoll Papers, Oberudorfer to Weiss, June 4, 1851.

32. A.G.S., "*Liber Personarum Provinciae Germaniae Superioris* (Inchoatus, 1842)," *loc. cit.*

33. A.C.R., II Americana PCM 1, Louis Fritz to Joseph Lobina, August 7, 1850.

34. A.C.S., "*Liber Personarum Provinciae Germaniae Superioris* (Inchoatus, 1842)," *loc. Cit.*

35. *Ibid.*

36. A.C.R., II Americana PCM 1, Fritz to Lobina, February 2, 1861.

37. *Ibid.,* Valentin von Riedel to Lobina, April 27, 1851.

38. *Ibid.,* Fritz to Lobina, June 28, 1861.

39. Fr. Joseph Maier was born on March 8, 1819. He was the son of a mason from Klinglbach. Maier entered the Straubing Carmel on March 20, 1850. He was professed on July 20, 1851, and ordained a priest on April 4, 1854. Knoll thought highly of him as a director of seminarians. A.C.R., II Americana PCM 1, Cyril Knoll to Jerome Priori, October 24, 1845. The prior general later transferred him to the Dutch Carmelite Province in 1862. In 1868 he returned to Straubing and died there on July 10, 1880. A.C.S., *Liber Personarum Provinciae Germaniae Superioris* (Inchoatus, 1842), *loc, cit.,* and *Schematismus Fratrum B.M.V. Carmelo Straubingano in Bavaria degentium 1856.*

40. Brother Brocard Bauer was born on September 26, 1822, on a farm outside of Schaltendorf, Germany. He entered the Straubing monastery on September 11, 1845, and was professed the following year on September 29. A.C.S., *Schematismus Fratrum B.M.V. Carmelo Straubingano in Bavaria degentium 1866.*

41. A.C.S., "*Liber Personarum Provinciae Germaniae Superioris* (Inchoatus, 1842)," *op. cit.,* p. 1.

42. A.C.R., II Americana PCM 1, Cyril Knoll to Lobina, August 4, 1851.

43. *Ibid.,* Maier to Lobina, October 22, 1853.

44. *Ibid.,* Knoll to Jerome Priori, June 1, 1855.

45. *Ibid.*, Knoll to Lobina, December 19, 1853.

46. *Ibid.*, Knoll to Priori, October 24, 1854. The anonymous biographical essay in the *Sword* referred to above suggests that Knoll received this honor in 1866, the actual year of the chapter.

47. *Ibid.*, Knoll to Priori, January 20, 1856.

48. A.C.S., Knoll Papers, Unsigned and undated letter from the Episcopal office to Knoll.

49. A.C.R., II Americana PCM 1, Knoll-Priori, October 24, 1854. Necessary permissions were forwarded immediately as indicated by a letter of thanks sent by Knoll to Priori on December 19, 1854.

50. *Ibid.*

51. For a complete description of the shrine, see Wolfgang Schaller, *Unsere Liebe Frau von Sossau* (Straubing: Uttenkoferschen Buchund Kunstdruckerei, 1927).

52. A.C.S., Knoll Papers, Vicar General of Regensburg, Lemberger to Knoll, March 11, 1855.

53. A.C.R., II Americana PCM 1, Knoll to Priori, June 1, 1855. Several images were ordered from Rome as a gift to the Ursulines for their efforts in obtaining Sossau for the Carmelites.

54. *Ibid.*, Knoll to Priori, September 27, 1855.

55. *Ibid.*, Knoll to Priori, November 30, 1855.

56. A.C.S., Knoll Papers, Undated letter of Knoll to King Ludwig I of Bavaria.

57. A.C.S., *Schematismus Fratrum B.M.V. Carmelo Straubingo in Bavaria degentium, 1856*.

58. A.C.R., II Americana PCM 1, Knoll to Priori, December 17, 1856.

59. *Ibid.*, Knoll to Priori, February 21, 1857.

60. *Ibid.*, Knoll to Priori, December 31, 1856.

61. *Ibid.*, Knoll to Priori, February 21, 1857.

62. *Ibid.*, Knoll to Priori, December 31, 1856.

63. *Ibid.*, Knoll to Priori, February 21, 1857.

64. *Ibid.*

65. *Ibid.*, Knoll to Priori, May 10, 1857.

66. *Ibid.*

67. *Ibid.*, Knoll to Priori, June 8, 1857.

68. *Ibid.*, Knoll to Priori, October 22, 1857. Maier records the departure date as September 30, 1857, but Knoll in his own hand marks October 1 as the correct date.

69. *Ibid.*, Knoll, to Priori, May 10, 1857.

70. *Ibid.,* Knoll to Priori, October 22, 1857. As a temporary gesture, Knoll had named Fr. Fritz as vicar and sent Joseph Maier to Sossau.

71. *Ibid.,* Knoll to Priori, December 5, 1857.

72. *Ibid.,* Knoll to Priori, December 27, 1857.

73. *Ibid.,* Knoll to Priori, March 30, 1858.

74. *Ibid.,*, Apparantly Maier did not carry out his threat. He was prior of the Straubing community in 1861. Martini *op.* etc., II: 437. In late 1862, the Provincial transferred Maier for some undisclosed reason to the Carmelite monastery at Boxmeer. A.C.S., "*Liber Personarum Germaniae Superioris* (Inchoatus, 1842)," *op. cit.,* p. 2.

75. A.C.S., Knoll Papers, Knoll to Emperor Franz Joseph, September 27, 1858.

76. *Ibid.,* Austrian Minister of the Interior, Friedeusfelz to Knoll, September 15, 1860.

77. *Ibid.,* Magistrate of Pesth to Knoll, May 30, 1859.

78. *Ibid.,* Undated letter of Knoll to the Magistrate of Pesth.

79. *Ibid.,* Magistrate of Pesth to Knoll, March 16, 1860.

80. *Ibid.,* Knoll to Magistrate of Pesth, March 27, 1860.

81. *Ibid.,* Receipt signed for payment for masonry work by Erhard Lonnocher to Knoll, May 28, 1860. Payment of 1000 gulden was made for complete masonry work. Receipt signed for payment for carpentry work by Andreas Schlimonik to Knoll, May 28, 1860. Payment of 610 gulden was made for the work of the carpenter.

82. *Ibid.,* Lefehl to Knoll, July 4, 1860.

83. *Ibid.,* Contract signed by Erhard Lonnocher with Knoll, March 12, 1860.

84. A.C.R., II Americana PCM 1, Knoll to Priori, December 20, 1860.

85. A.C.S., Knoll Papers, Magistrate of Pesth to Knoll, May 9, 1860.

86. *Ibid.,* Undated letter of Knoll to Magistrate of Pesth.

87. A.C.R., II Americana PCM 1, Knoll to Priori, May 10, 1860.

88. A.C.S., Knoll Papers to the Secretary of Cardinal Seitowsky, September 12, 1860.

89. Carlton J. Hayes, *A Political and Cultural History of Modern Europe* (New York: Macmillan Co., 1947), II: 94, 96, 172-3.

90. Charles Loring Brace, *Hungary in 1851* (New York: Charles Scribner, 1852), p. 37.

91. Jeno Horvath, *Modern Hungary* (Budapest: Magyar Kulugyi Tarsasag, 1923), pp. 133-37.

92. A.C.S., Knoll Papers, Notation, sheet in Knoll's handwriting- listing the personnel of the community at Pesth in 1859.

93. A.C.R., II Americana PCM 1, Knoll to Priori, October 18, 1859.

94. A.C.S., Knoll Papers Notification from chancery office to Knoll, October 31, 1860.

95. A.C.R., Pius Mayer, O. Carm., *Historia Provinciae Americanae*. fol. 5, The original autograph of Fr. Pius is found in the archives of the Carmelite Order in Rome. This manuscript consists of 133 sheets of paper of various kinds, bound into a tablet 25.5 x 17 cm., corresponding in format to other provincial histories in the archives. Only the first 20 pages were actually used. Folios 1-4 are blank. Included in this tablet are certain loose notes which Fr. Pius took from the registers of various Carmelite Generals and which he evidently used in composing his short history. A copy of this brief history was made by Fr. Joachim Smet in 1948 for the Carmelite Provincial Archives at Whitefriars Hall, Washington, D.C.

96. A.C.S., Knoll Papers, Neuhoffer to Knoll, February 16, 1861.

97. *Ibid.,* Peter Koehler to Savini, March 2, 1864.

98. *Ibid.,* Knoll to Emperor Franz Joseph, October 2, 1861.

99. A.C.R., II Americana PCM 1, December 22, 1863.

100. *Ibid.,* Knoll to Priori, January 29, 1864.

101. Fr. Leander Streber, O.F.M., born in Bavaria, entered the Franciscan monastery in Munich as a lay-brother. He came to the United States in 1844 where he first served in Holy Trinity Church, Cincinnati. In 1846 he came to Louisville as sacristan at the cathedral. With the personal help of Bishop Spalding and over the protest of his superiors, he was ordained on March 3, 1850, at the age of forty-two and sent as a curate to St. Boniface's Church in Louisville. When the new parish of St. Martin's was established in 1853, he was appointed pastor. In 1857 he went to Germany in search of help for the diocese of Louisville. In May 1881, he retired from St. Martin's parish and died on August 24, 1882. *The Centenary of the Church of Saint Martin of Tours* Louisville: 1953), pp. 1-8.

102. Sister Mary de Lourdes Gohmann, O.S.U., *Chosen Arrows* (New York: Pageant Press, 1957), pp. 1-54, *passim.*

103. After Cyril Knoll left for Pesth, the Ursulines chose another spiritual director and confessor who was not from the Carmelite monastery in Straubing.

104. A.C.R., II Americana PCM 1, Knoll to Priori, December 1, 1859.

105. *Ibid.,* Knoll to Savini, January 29, 1864.

106. *Ibid.,* Knoll to Savini, December 22, 1863.

107. Assisting Fr. Streber were: Maurice Gipperich; June 6, 1858—October 30, 1858; George Bruner, January 1, 1859—April 10, 1859; Anton Miller, O.C.M., April 22, 1860— December 2, 1860 ; Gabriel Blum, O.S.B., October 14, 1860—August 2, 1863; John Neyhurst, August 9, 1863—March 9, 1876; B. Keller, May 1, 1864—October 14, 1864. *The Centenary of the Church of St. Martin Tours, op. cit.,* p. 6.

108. A.C.R., II Americana PGM 1, Knoll to Savini, December 22, 1863.

109. *Ibid.,* Knoll to Savini, January 29, 1864.

110. *Ibid.,* Koehler to Savini, March 11, 1864. Members of the community included: Peter Koehler, prior; Eliseus Primbs, sacristan; Louis Fritz, procurator; Xavier Huber; Wolfgang Pielmaire, chaplain to the high school; Thomas Handl, director of the Third Order of St. Francis of Straubing; Avertanus Schwegler; Augustine Heindl; Angelus Hofmann, librarian; Gerard Wiesblhuber, chaplain at Sossau; Angelus Traidmer, director for the seminary. Brothers in the community included: Berthold Wartner, gardner; Simon Stock Edenhofer, cook at Sossau; Anastasius Betz, sacristan; Alphonsus Braudl, tailor and porter; Jacob Riepe; Dionysius Kumplinger, cook at the Straubing monastery.

111. A.C.W., Knoll Papers, Savini to Knoll, February 8, 1864. The actual transcription is in the hand of Fr. Eliseo Giordano, secretary and assistant to the General. A.C.R., *Regesta Savini,* f, 20r, indicates that the permission was recorded in the prior general's ledger. The *Regesta* which covers the years 1863 to 1881 is a half vellum volume, 36.5 x 24.6 cm., of 100 paper folios, with 40 lines to the page. It has no title page, but on its back is the inscription in ink: "Rege. ab A. 1863 ad An. 1881." A microfilm copy of the *Regesta* is available in the Carmelitana Collection, Whitefriars Hall, Washington, D.G. Also confer Joachim Smet, O. Carm., "Americana in the Regesta Savini," *The Sword,* XVII (Autumn, 1954), 316-39.

112. John Tracy Ellis (ed.), *Documents of American Catholic History* (Milwaukee: Bruce. Publishing Co., 1962.), pp. 279-88.

113. When the original version of this book was composed as Carmel Came, no scholarly, comprehensive presentation of Carmelite history existed. Since then, comprehensive works have been published. See, for example, Joachim Smet, *The Carmelites: A History of the Brothers of the Blessed Virgin Mary of Mount Carmel.* 4 volumes in 5, 1977-1985 (vol 1 second edition, 1988); Joachim Smet, *The Mirror of Carmel: A Brief History of the Carmelite Order,* 2011; and Leopold Glueckert, *Desert Springs in the City: A Concise History of the Carmelites,* 2012.

114. A.C.S., *Liber Personarum Germaniae Superioris* (Inchoatus, 1842), op. cit., p. 1. *Ibid.,* Knoll Papers, Oberdorfer to Heitser, September 19, 1843. Reichwein indicates that Huber left the novitiate because of doubts regarding obedience. He returned shortly, however, and in view of his personal qualities he was allowed to continue the same novitiate. Once ordained, he was almost employed in preaching and begging. Thus, "he became accustomed to a roaming life, estranged to religious observance and obedience." Jerome Reichwein, O. Carm., *History of the Carmelite Order in America,* f 2r. This manuscript history was written on six folded sheets of ruled paper, 17 x 14. Because of its fragile nature, it has been preserved in the Carmelite Provincial Archives in Washington, D.C.

115. *Ibid.,* An unaddressed school report signed by Obermuller in March 4, 1840. It was probably given as a character witness before Knoll went to work.

116. *Ibid.,* Unaddressed testimonial reports signed by Schmid, pastor of Altotting, January 10, 1842; Muhlthaler, pastor at Riedenn, August 23, 1838, and Hogl, seminary director at Metten, September 10, 1842.

117. *Ibid., Liber Personarum Germaniae Superioris* (Inchoatus, 1842), *loc. cit.*

118. *Ibid.,* Knoll Papers, Vicar General of Regensburg to Koehler, February 20,

1863.

119. A.C.R., II Americana PCM 1, Koehler to Savini, April 1, 1864.

120. *Ibid.*

121. A. LMV., Huber to LMV, April 28, 1864. (LMV Leav. I 3/5). Carmelite material in the archives of the Ludwig Missionsverein has been photostated by Rev. Theodore Roemer, OFM Cap. Fr. Roemer is the author of *The Ludwig Missionsverein and the Church in the United States* (Washington: Catholic University of America, 1933). Prints of the material are now available in the Carmelitana Collection, Washington, D.C. Letters in the archives of the Ludwig Missionsverein indicate that Huber, Koehler, and Savini all sent letters to the Society asking for passage money for Huber. A. LMV., Huber to LMV, April 14, 1864. (LMV Leav. I 3/1); Koehler to LMV, April 12, 1864. (LMV Leav. I 3/2); Savini to LMV, April 23, 1864. (LMV Leav. I 3/3).

122. *Ibid.* Knoll, to LMV, October 13, 1865. (LMV Leav. I 3/7). Also see *Annalen der Glaubensverbreitung,* XXXLC (1867), 278.

123. Gohmann, *op. cit.,* p. 88.

124. A. LMV., *loc. cit.*

125. A.U.L., A letter from the archivist, Sister M. Austin, O.S.U, to the author dated March 30, 1962 indicates this comment is contained in the Annals of the Ursuline Sisters, although no documentation is given.

126. A.C.R., II Americana PCM 1, Savini to the Sacred Congregation of Bishops and Regulars, May 13, 1864. The answer is written on the returned request.

127. A. LMV., *loc. cit.* This directly contradicts the account in the Ursuline Annals which reads: "On the 31st of May the ship safely reached the harbor of New York. Here the missionaries tarried for a few days to attend to some business. On the 6th of June, they left New York and arrived in Louisville on June 8th."

128. A. LMV., *loc. cit.* There is much intrigue concerning the last leg of the journey. In the first place, Knoll himself dated his own arrival in Louisville on June 9. A.C.R., Knoll to Savini, July 13, 1864. Fr. Smits in his schematic history of the early years of the province says: "On the train from New York to Louisville, Ky., where they knew a priest whom they expected advice and help from, they met Fr. Guenther, who as a secular seminarian had just finished his studies at St. Vincent's OSB, PA., for the diocese of Leavenworth and was on his way to Leavenworth. They told him of their intention, and thereupon he persuaded them to go with him to Leavenworth, where Bishop Miege, S.J., would most probably give them a good place." Smits, it should be noted, is vague. He opens his history: "In or around 1863-64 Frs. Cyril Knoll, O.C.C., and Xavier Huber, O.C.C., came from the Monastery of Straubing to America with the intention of starting the Order in this land. . ." Anastasius J. Smits, "Notes," f. lr. This manuscript was written in 1918 by Fr. Anastasius J. Smits at Scipio, Kansas, at the request of Fr. Hilary Doswald, O. Carm. It consists of five sheets of paper, 24 x 15 cm., ruled on one side only, nineteen lines to the page. The text is written in pencil with frequent emendations. The original is in the Carmelite Provincial Archives, Washington, D.C. A copy is available in the Carmelitana Collection, Washington, D.C. Reichwein, who provides interesting details in his brief history, suggests: "From New York he wended his way to St. Vincent's Abbey in Pennsylvania to consult with Rt. Rev. Abbot Wimmer in regard to a place of settlement. Not being able to come to a satisfactory conclusion they went from Pittsburgh with a steamboat to Louisville in company of a young candidate for the priesthood by the name of Kilian Guenther

who advised them to apply to Rt. Rev. Bishop Meige for a place promising at the same time to join their order in case they would come to Kansas. Reichwein, *op. cit.,* f. 2r.

129. *Annalen der Glaubensverbreitung,* XXIV (1856), 397-400.

130. Smits and Reichwein both mention this detail in their sketches. Smits, *loc. cit.;* Reichwein, *loc. cit.*

Chapter Two: First Foundations

1. An excellent review of the mood of Kentucky during this time is given by E. Merton Coulter, *The Civil War and Readjustment in Kentucky* (Chapel Hill: University of North Carolina Press, 1926), pp. 145-65.

2. N.S. Shaler, *Kentucky: A Pioneer Commonwealth* (Boston: Houghton, Mifflin Co., 1888), pp. 287-330.

3. *Cincinnati Commercial,* July 11, 1863.

4. On the day before Christmas 1863, the first cargo of molasses and sugar since the beginning of the war arrived in Louisville from New Orleans. Richard and Lewis Collins, *Collins Historical Sketches of Kentucky* (Covington: Collins and Co., 1882), 1:129.

5. George R. Leighton, *Five Cities* (New York: Harper & Brothers, 1939), p. 58.

6. Jenny Lind arrived in Louisville for a performance at Mozart Hall from April 7-10. The first tickets were sold for $175; other tickets were auctioned. John J. Weisert, Mozart Hall (Louisville, 1962), p. 1.

7. The best summary of life in Louisville before the Civil War is presented by F. Garvin Davenport, *Ante-Bellum Kentucky* (Oxford, Ohio: Mississippi Valley Press, 1943).

8. John Lancaster Spalding, *The Life of the Most Rev. M. J, Spalding,* D.D. (New York: Catholic Publication Society, 1873), p. 263.

9. For a complete review of tolerance toward Catholicism in this period, see Sister Agnes Geraldine McGann, *Nativism in Kentucky to 1860* (Washington: Catholic University of America Press, 1944).

10. Spalding, *loc. cit.*

11. When Knoll and Huber arrived, Frs. John Neyhurst and B. Keller were Streber's assistants. *The Centennary of St. Martin of Tours, op, cit.,* p. 18.

12. On June 11, 1864, Spalding received the rescript. He took possession of his new see on July 31, 1864. Spalding, *op. tit.,* p. 255.

13. *Ibid.,* p. 260.

14. Ben J. Webb, *The Centenary of Catholicity in Kentucky* (Louisville: Charles A. Rogers, 1884), p. 489.

15. H. Alerding, *A History of the Catholic Church in the Diocese of Vincennes* (Indianapolis: Carlon and Hollenbeck, 1883), p. 337.

16. Joseph Bernard Code, *Dictionary of the American Hierarchy* (New York: Longmans, Green and Co., 1940), p. 77.

17. A.C.R., II Americana PCM 1, Knoll to Savini, July 13, 1864.

18. Baptismal Registry of St. Joseph's Church, June 26, 1864. Regina Zeitvogel was born in Benetsville on June 9, 1864. Columban Zeitvogel and Clara were the parents. Barnabas Klehamer acted as sponsor.

19. *Ibid.,* June, 1864 through January, 1865. In early January, Fr. H. Panzer was named as pastor.

20. A.C.R., *loc. cit.*

21. Webb, *op. cit.,* p. 492.

22. A.C.W., Reichwein, *op. cit.,* f. 2r-2v.

23. A. LMV., Knoll to LMV, October 13, 1864. (LMV Leav. I 3/7).

24. *Ibid.*

25. A.C.W., Reichwein, *op. cit.,* p. 2v.

26. Wiley Britton, "Resume of Military Operations in Missouri and Arkansas, 1864-1865." *Battles and Leaders of the Civil War,* (New York: Thomas Yoseloff, Inc., 1966), IV: 374-377. Cf. Richard Hinton, *Rebel Invasion of Missouri and Kansas,* and the campaign of the army of the border against General Sterling Price in *October and November, 1864* (Chicago: Church and Goodman, 1865).

27. A. LMV., *loc. cit.*

28. Sister Mary Paul Fitzgerald. *John Baptist Meiege, S.J. Historical Records and Studies,* XXIV (1934), 359.

29. James A. McGonigle, "Rt. Rev. John B. Miege, S.J., First Catholic Bishop of Kansas," *Kansas State Historical Society Collection,* IX: 159.

30. Donald Shearer, O.F.M. Cap., *Pontificia Americana: Documentary History of the Catholic Church in the United States, 1784-1884.* (Washington: Catholic University of America Press, 1933), pp. 266-67.

31. A recent authoritative work on this topic is presented by William Frank Zornow, Kansas: *A History of the Jayhawk State* (Norman: University of Oklahoma Press, 1967), pp. 67-91.

32. J. Garin, *Notices Biographiques sur Mgr. J. B. Miege, Premier Vicarire Apostolique du Kansas et sur les Pretes de la Paroisse de Chevron (Savoie)* (Moutiers: Cane Soeurs, 1886), p. 108.

33. A. LMV., Heimann to LMV, January 5, 1869. (LMV Leav. I 1/6-6).

34. *Wahrheitsfreund,* December 11, 1866.

35. A.LMV., Fisch to LMV, February 26, 1861. (LMV Leav. I 2/6-8). Heimann to

LMV, January 5, 1859. (LMV Leav. I 1/5-6) has 77.

36. *Wahrheitsfreund,* September 8, 1859.

37. A. LMV., Heimann to LMV, January 5, 1859. (LMV Leav. I 1/5-6.)

38. *Ibid.,* Fisch to LMV, February 25, 1861. (LMV Leav. I 2/6-8).

39. *Souvenir Booklet of the Rededication of St, Joseph's Carmelite Church,* (June, 1964), p. 10.

40. A. LMV., Fisch to LMV, August 30, 1861. (LMV Leav. 1 2/12).

41. *The Illustrated Guide to Fort Leavenworth, Leavenworth and Vicinity* (Fort Leavenworth, Kansas: Rae Bresnahan, 1959), p. 16.

42. As cited in *Souvenir Booklet of the Rededication of St. Joseph's Carmelite Church, op. cit.,* pp. 11-12.

43. In his account of the affair to his brother Bishop Meige wrote that he "went to see the General of the fort, who immediately ordered the arrest of the officers, the evacuation of the church and the payment of all damages." He asserted that the regiment was composed of Forty-eighters, which explained their conduct. Garin, *op. cit.,* p. 132.

44. A. LMV., Fisch to LMV, June 23, 1860. (LMV Leav. I 2/1); *Idem.,* February 25, 1861. (LMV Leav. I 2/6-8).

45. *Kansas Annual Register,* 1864, pp. 92-92.

46. Peter Beckman, O.S.B., *The Catholic Church on the Kansas Frontier, 1850-1877* (Washington: Catholic University of Press, 1943), p. 70.

47. *Berichte der Leopoldinen-Stiftung,* XXXV (1865).

48. By December 1864, the pioneering life for Fr. Heimann should have seemed about over. He was pastor of the Cathedral parish in the most rapidly growing diocese in America, the cornerstone of whose magnificent cathedral church had just been laid. He was about fifty. Years of strenuous missionary activity were behind him. Surely one would think now as the time for Fr. Heimann to take advantage of the position he had earned: to enjoy his place of honor in the diocese and the close friendship of his bishop. He did nothing of the kind. He left his magnificent cathedral and went to the little frame church of the struggling German parish of St. Joseph. Heimann asked Knoll for admission to the Order on December 18, 1864. Three weeks later he was joined by Fr. Guenther, a young priest ordained by Bishop Miege the previous August. Bonaventure Gilmore, O. Carm., "Rev. Albert Heimann, O. Carm.," *The Sword,* VII (1943), 171-72.

49. For his biography, see Anthony G. Dressel, O. Carm., "Rev. Louis Kilian Guenther, O. Carm.," *The Sword,* V (1941), 163-55.

50. A.C.R., II Americana PCM 1, Knoll to Savini, December 6, 1864.

51. Baptismal Registry of St. Joseph's Church, June 1864 through January 1865.

52. Beckman, *op. cit.,* p. 71.

53. *Ibid.*, p. 8.

54. *Geschichte der St. Bonifazius Gemeinde, Scipio, Anderson County Kansas* (Lawrence, Kansas: Verlag der Germania Publishing Co., 1903), p. 2.

55. *Centennial, St. Boniface Church, 1858-1958, Scipio, Kansas,* pp. 4-6.

56. A. LMV., Heimann to LMV, January 5, 1859. (LMV Leav. I 1/5-6). The chapel was dedicated March 13, 1859 by Frs. Schacht and Ponziglione. *Catholic Telegraph* April 9, 1859 from *Freeman's Journal.*

57. *Centennial, St. Boniface Church, 1858-1958, Scipio, Kansas, op. cit.,* p. 8.

58. *Geschichte der St. Bonifazius Gemeinde, op. cit.,* p. 5.

59. Beckman, *loc. cit.*

60. A.C.R., II Americana PCM 1, Knoll to Savini, December 6, 1864.

61. LMV., Knoll to LMV, October 13, 1865. (LMV Leav. I 3/7).

62. *Ibid.*

63. *Ibid.* Because of the variability of the economy, it is hard to accurately estimate the value of this appeal in U.S. currency. Using several scales, one estimate suggests 1250 francs then translated into about US$300.

64. *Ibid.,* Heimann to LMV, January 5, 1859. (LMV Leav. I 1/6-6).

65. A.C.R. II Americana PCM 1, Knoll to Savini, September 26, 1866.

66. *Ibid., Regesta Savini,* f .79v.

67. A.C.R., II Americana PCM 1, Koehler to Savini, May 19, 1865.

68. *Ibid.,* October 15, 1865.

69. *Ibid.,* Knoll to Savini, September 26, 1865.

70. A. LMV., Knoll to LMV, October 13, 1865. (LMV Leav. I 8/7).

71. *Ibid.*

72. Gerald Shaughnessy, *Has the Immigrant Kept the Faith?* (New York: Macmillan Co., 1925), pp. 224-231. The complete text of Bishop England is given followed by a critical evaluation of the points raised by the Bishop's famous letter.

73. John Tracy Ellis, *American Catholicism* (Chicago: University of Chicago Press, 1956), p. 128.

74. Colman J. Barry, O.S.B., *The Catholic Church and German Americans* (Washington: Catholic University Press, 1963), p. 7.

75. Summary reasons are given by Shaughnessy, *op. cit.,* pp. 146-47.

76. A.C.R., II Americana PCM 1, Knoll to Savini, January 31, 1866. Reichwein states that Huber was in Europe for more than eighteen months. A.C.W., Reichwein, *op. cit.,* f. 3r. The letters addressed to Rome by Knoll contradict this testimony.

Endnotes

77. *Ibid.*

78. *The Illustrated Guide to Fort Leavenworth, op. cit.,* p. 17.

79. W. Weston, *Weston's Guide to the Kansas Pacific Railway* (Kansas City: Kansas City Bulletin Steam Printing, 1872), p. 128.

80. A.C.R., II Americana PCM 1, Knoll to Savini, October 8, 1866. Cf. A. LMV., Knoll to LMV, November 22, 1866. (LMV Leav. I 3/10).

81. Frs. Alexius and Evodius were destined by Fr. Savini for the mission in America. Evodius Bartsch never got to America. On April 16, 1867, he wrote to the prior general from his native town of Lemkendorf near Wartenburg, explaining that his health would not permit him to embark with Fr. Alexius. He later secularized and became assistant in the parish of Gruentegernbach bei Dorfen, Bavaria. Frs. Alexius of St. Joseph, to use his full name, served briefly in Cumberland and Kansas, but on November 26, 1868, petitioned for dispensation from his vows and permission to enter a Polish speaking congregation. Smet, "Americana in the Regesta Savini," pp. 319-20.

82. A. LMV., Koehler to LMV, October 31, 1865. (LMV Leav. I 3/6).

83. A.C.R., II Americana PCM 1, Koehler to Savini, December 18, 1866.

84. *Ibid.,* Knoll to Savini, January 31, 1866.

85. *Ibid.,* "Regesta Savini," f. 69v.

86. *Ibid.,* f. 75r.

87. *Ibid.,* II Americana PCM 1, Heimann to Meagher, April 1, 1869.

88. A.C.W., Pius Mayer, *Summaria Historia Provinciae SS. Cordis Mariae, O.C.C. in America.* This manuscript consists of nine unnumbered, unruled pages of fine parchmentlike paper, 25 x 20 cm. The year of writing is 1892. A copy of the manuscript is in the Carmelitana Collection, Whitefriars Hall, Washington, D.C.

89. A.C.R., II Americana PCM 1, Knoll to Savini, October 8, 1866.

90. *Ibid.,* Knoll to Savini, September 26, 1865.

91. Gilmore, *op. cit.,* p. 172. During his novitiate Fr. Albert assumed the parochial duties at Scipio for only the month of July 1865. Baptismal Records of St. Boniface's Parish, July 1865.

92. There are numerous commemorative booklets relating the history of these mission stations and the administration of the Carmelites. Cfr, Cecil Moore and Joy Fox, *Through the Years* (Greeley, Kansas: Kansas, Greeley Centennial Committee, 1957); *St. Patrick's, Emerald, Centennial Booklet; A History of Saint Patrick's Church, Emerald in Kansas.*

93. A.C.R., II Americana, PCM 1, Heimann to Meagher, April 1, 1869.

94. *Ibid.*

95. *Ibid.,* Knoll to Savini, June 22, 1866.

96. For a complete biography of the Redemptorist Provincial, see Michael J. Curley, *The Provincial Story* (Washington: Redemptorist Province Printing, 1963), pp. 158 ff.

97. *Ibid.*

98. *Ibid.*, October 3, 1866.

99. *Ibid.*

100. A.C.R., Mayer, *Historia Provinciae Americanae, op. cit.*, f. 7. Fr. Helmpraecht sold the monastery and all the lands to the rear of the church on Johnson and Fayette Streets, namely lots 147, 145, 150, 151 and also the small piece of ground which formed part of Plumb Alley.

101. Thomas J. Stanton, *A Century of Growth* (Baltimore: John Murphy Co., 1900), I: 43-48.

102. Michael J. Curley, C.S.S.R., *Venerable John Neumann* (Washington: Catholic University of America Press, 1962), p. 41.

103. Curley, *Provincial Story, op. cit.*, p. 118.

104. Stanton, *op. cit.*, pp. 49-63.

105. Joseph Wuest, *Annales Congregationis S.S. Redemptoris Provinciae Americanae* (Ilchester, Md.: Privately printed, 1888-1924), IV, 2, pp. 433-35.

106. Curley, *Provincial Story, op. cit.*, p. 144.

107. Wuest, *op. cit.*, V. 1.

108. John Byrne, C.S.S.R., *The Redemptorist Centenaries* (Philadelphia: Dolphin Press, 1932), p. 213.

109. Curley, *Provincial Story, op, cit.*, p. 110.

110. *Ibid.*, pp. 138-39.

111. *Ibid.*, pp. 167-68.

112. A.C.R., II Americana PCM 1, Knoll to Savini, October 3, 1866.

113. Brother Simon Edenhofer was one of the pioneers of the Order in America. He arrived in Leavenworth from Straubing in 1866 and soon afterward accompanied Fr. Cyril Knoll when he opened the house in Cumberland. A.C.R., II Americana PGM 1, Knoll to Savini, October 6, 1866. When in February of 1869 Frs. Peter Thomas Maher and Theodoric McDonald began the foundation in Marlboro, Brother Simon went with them. *Ibid.*, Knoll to Savini, February 12, 1869. He remained, however, only about a month before returning to Straubing. When Knoll went to Germany in 1872, he brought Brother Simon back to Cumberland. *Ibid.*, Knoll to Savini, July 11 and October 17, 1872. When Knoll founded the convent in Pittsburg in 1875, Brother Simon again accompanied him together with Frs. Elias Maier and Anselm Duell. *Ibid.*, Knoll to Savini, August 24, 1875. His relations were marked by a series of misunderstandings and reconciliations. On December 2, 1875, he was transferred to Straubing and Brother Dionysius Kumplinger came from Straubing to take his

place. *Ibid.,* "Regesta Savini, f, 68r.

114. A.C.R., II Americana PCM 1, Knoll to Savini, Ootober 3, 1866.

115. Several of the Redemptorists remained until the entire Carmelite community arrived. Frs. Ambrose and Wuest, the last to leave, stayed until Huber arrived on October 30. Wuest, *op. cit.,* V. 1, p. 129.

116. Beckman, *op. cit.,* p. 50, note 169. Knoll indicated that Vogg had been dismissed from the Benedictine Order and had joined the ranks of the secular clergy in St. Louis before he applied to the Carmelites for admission. When he entered the Carmelite Order, he brought with him $900 in gold and $100 in silver. Some of this money was used for the initial payment of the Cumberland monastery. A.C.R., II Americana PCM 1, Knoll to Savini, January 9, 1867.

117. Wuest, *loc cit.*

118. A.C.R., Mayer, *Historia Provinciae Americanae, loc. cit.* Redemptorists received $2000 in cash and promissory notes for June 1, 1872.

119. A.C.W., Reichwein, *op. cit.,* f. 3v.

120. *Fifty Years of S.S. Peter and Paul's Church* (Cumberland: Cumberland Freie Press Print, 1898), p. 63.

121. A. LMV., Knoll to LMV, November 22, 1866. (LMV Leav. I 3/10).

122. A.A.B., 34-P-4, Knoll to Spalding, November 1, 1866. Knoll attempted to present his plans to the Archbishop in person but Spalding was occupied with the Second Plenary Council of Baltimore which had begun on the second Sunday of October, 1866.

123. A.C.R., Mayer, *Historia Provinciae Americanae, loc. cit.*

124. Clear information on Carmelite assistance at the various missions for these years is found in the annual editions of *Sadlier's Catholic Directory.* In 1867, the *Directory* lists: "Alleghany County, Cumberland, Sts. Peter and Paul (German). The Carmelite Fathers." (p. 55). "Oakland, St. Peter's. Attended once a month from Cumberland by the Carmelite Fathers. Fifteen Mile Creek. Attended by the Carmelites of Cumberland. Westernport, St. Peter's. Attended twice a month by the Carmelites." (p. 56). "School at S. S. Peter and Paul's. Pupils, 220." (p. 61).

125. *St. Peter in Chains,* Westernport, Maryland (Piedmont, W. VA.: Herald Printing House, 1923), f. 3r.

126. *One Hundred Years, 1852-1952: St. Peter's Parish, Oakland, Maryland,* pp. 8r-8v.

127. Stanton, *op. cit.,* I: 153.

128. *Ibid.,* I: 204-07.

129. A. LMV., Knoll to LMV, November 22, 1866. (LMV Leav. I 3/10). What had made the Redemptorists so welcome at Cumberland was their routine of services. They had increased the number of Sunday Masses. On Sunday afternoons Solemn Vespers and Benediction were held. The devotions of the Confraternity of the Sa-

cred Heart of Mary were held the first Sunday evening of every month. The Holy Rosary was recited and Benediction given every Saturday evening and on the vigils of feasts. St. Stephen's day was always celebrated as a feastday with a High Mass and sermon. On St. John's Day High Mass was sung at an early hour and wine was blessed. On Candle-Mass Day candles were blessed followed by a solemn procession and a Solemn High Mass. During the last three days of Holy Week divine services were conducted at seven in the morning and at seven in the evening. The Resurrection was celebrated with great solemnity; a procession took place either with the Blessed Sacrament or with a crucifix. On Ascension the children received first Holy Communion. May devotions and Forty-Hours devotions were celebrated, as was the feast of the consecration of the church and the feast of Saints Peter and Paul. On the feast of the Finding and Elevation of the Holy Cross, a relic of the holy cross was presented to be kissed by the faithful. During the octave of All Souls, the Way of the Cross, five *Our Fathers*, the Litany of All Saints and all the prayers connected with it were said. In addition to the foregoing, the Confraternity of the Sacred Heart of Mary and the Living Rosary existed from the very beginning of the Congregation. The members exchanged their rosary cards every month at the monastery door. Great attention was given to the Confraternity of Scapulars and the Confraternity of the Holy Family, as well as the Confraternity of the Poor Souls. *Fifty Years of S.S. Peter and Paul's Church, op. cit.,* pp. 54-57.

130. A.C.R., II American PCM 1, Knoll to Savini, October 5, 1866.

131. An examination of baptismal and matrimonial records of the Maryland missions reveals that the last baptism performed by Huber was on December 5, 1867. Knoll himself told Archbishop Spalding that Huber left the missions on December 19, 1867. A.A.B., 34-P-4, Knoll to Spalding, March 10, 1868.

132. A.C.R., II Americana PCM 1, Knoll to Savini, August 7, 1867.

133. A.C.R., "Regesta Savini," f. 65v indicates that a letter of obedience was issued on May 6, 1867 to these two fathers assigning them to Cumberland. They arrived September 19, 1867. Knoll had paid for their trip. A. LMV., Knoll to LMV, August 7, 1867 (LMV Leav. X 3/18).

134. Hugh Fitzpatrick, O. Carm., "Carmel in Knocktopher," *Zelo,* IX (1957), 9f.

135. A. LMV., Knoll to LVM, January 29, 1868. (LMV Leav. I 3/19).

136. A.A.B., 34-P-6, Knoll to Spalding, March 10, 1868. The tone of this letter indicates that Spalding suspected that more of the Carmelite community had been engaged in "practicing medicine."

137. A.C.R., Knoll to Savini, January 9, 1867.

138. A.C.R., Mayer, *Historia Provinciae Americanae, loc. cit.*

139. *Ibid.*

140. Smet, "Americana in the Regesta Savini," p. 320, note 11.

141. A.C.R., Mayer, *Historia Provinciae Americanae, loc. cit.*

142. *Ibid.,* II Americana PCM 1, Huber to Savini, June 10, 1868.

143. *Ibid.,* Knoll to Savini, January 8, 1868.

144. *Ibid.,* Knoll to Savini, July 15, 1868.

145. Ibid., "Regesta Savini," f. 80r.

146. A.C.W., Smits, "Notes," *op. cit.,* lv.

147. A.C.R., Mayer, *Historia Provinciae Americanae, loc. cit.*

148. *Ibid.,* II Americana PCM 1, Knoll to Savini, July 15, 1868.

149. *Fifty Years of S.S. Peter and Paul's Church, op. cit.,* p. 62.

150. A.C.W., Smits, "Notes," *loc. cit.*

151. "Father Cyril Knoll, O. Carm.," *The Sword,* II: 463. The criterion for acceptance into the seminary was certainly not too demanding. The ease with which one could enter the seminary is reflected in the account Kreidt gives of his acceptance. "On Epiphany Day I went to New York to see the Christmas crib in the Franciscan church on 30th St. I assisted at Vespers. After the *Magnificat* a religious in a white cloak over a brown habit ascented the pulpit. He preached on the Star of the Magi. Among other things he said, pointing toward me: Young man! There is the star in your sky calling you to your Lord. Do not turn away your eyes. Look upward and follow.' After the sermon I asked my neighbor in the pew who that was preaching. He said it was a Carmelite Father ... He (Huber) told me to go to Cumberland. 'But my dear Father,' I remonstrated, 'you do not even know my name.' 'Never mind,' was his response. 'I am sure you are of a good Catholic family and go to Vespers on a holyday. That's enough. Follow your star.' I wrote a letter to the Carmelite Superior at Cumberland and showed him all the reasons why I should not be accepted. His answer came shortly: 'My dear Boy, come and fetch what you possess in books and clothes. Yours in Christ, Fr. Cyril Knoll, O.C.C.' I arrived there Feb. 2, 1870." "Father Anastasius J. Kreidt, O. Carm. Our Second Provincial, 1879-1903," *The Sword,* II (1938), 39-40. In May of 1870 Knoll preached at the same St. John the Baptist Church. At that time, the archbishop was willing to give the Carmelites the care of the church if an Irish pastor could be stationed there. Knoll was unable to meet this demand. A.C.R., II Americana PCM 1, Knoll to Savini, October 31, 1870. This account also reflects how Scripture was interpreted in that time. The Historical-Critical Method, so taken for granted today, was undeveloped then.

152. A.C.W., Smits, "Notes," *loc cit.*

153. A.C.R., Mayer, *Historia Provinciae Americanae, loc. cit.* This statement contradicts evidence that suggests Knoll actually asked the General to appoint Smits as prior. Cfr. A.C.R., II Americana PCM 1, Knoll to Savini, July 15, 1868.

154. A. LMV., Knoll to LMV, September 10, 1868. (LMV Leav. I 3/23).

155. A.C.R., II Americana PCM 1, McDonald to Savini, November 3, 1868.

156. *Ibid.,* Mayer, *Historia Provinciae Americanae, loc. cit.*

157. *Ibid.,* II Americana PCM 1, McDonald to Savini, November 3, 1868; *Ibid.,* Knoll to Savini, November 4, 1868; *Ibid.,* Meagher to Savini, November 5, 1868; *Ibid.,* Smits to Savini, November 5, 1868 ; *Ibid.,* Knoll to Savini, November 10, 1868.

158. Fr. Peter Thomas Meagher on August 14, 1868 had actually been appointed as local superior of the houses in Kansas, though he continued to reside at Cumberland. *Ibid.,* "Regesta Savini," f. 20v.

159. A.A.B., 34-P-7, Knoll to Spalding, December 16, 1868.

160. A.C.W., Smits, "Notes," *op. cit.,* 2r.

161. *Ibid.*

162. A report of Huber's trip to seek funds in New York is found in his correspondence. A.C.R., II Americana PCM 1, Huber to Savini, October 20, 1868.

163. A.C.R., II Americana PCM 1, Undated letter of Brother Berthold to Savini.

164. A.A.B., 36A-O-1, Meagher to Spalding, January 28, 1869.

165. A.C.R., II Americana PCM 1, Knoll to Savini, February 12, 1869.

Chapter Three: Separatist Movements

1. A. LMV., Heimann to LMV, November 4, 1868. (LMV Leav. I 3/24).

2. *Souvenir Booklet of the Rededication of St. Joseph's Carmelite Church, op. cit.,* p. 14.

3. A. LMV., Heimann to LMV, September 17, 1867. (LMV Leav. I 3/24).

4. A.C.R., II Americana PCM 1, Huber to Savini, October 20, 1868. Huber was actually recalled in Cumberland in January 1869. *Ibid.,* Guenther to Meagher, February 17, 1869. Huber returned to Kansas to collect funds for the houses there on March 17, 1869. *Ibid.,* Heimann to Meagher, April 1, 1869.

5. A.C.W., Reichwein, *op. cit.,* 3v.

6. *Ibid.*

7. A. LMV., Heimann to LMV, November 4, 1868. (LMV Leav. I 3/24).

8. A.C.W., Reichwein, *loc. cit.*

9. Beckman, *op. cit.,* p. 82.

10. A.LMV., Knoll to LMV, October 26, 1869 (LMV Leav. I 3/27).

11. *Supra,* ch. 3, n. 4.

12. A.C.R., II Americana PCM 1, Guenther to Meagher, February 17, 1869. Meagher forwarded the note to the Carmelite General in Rome.

13. *Ibid.,* Heimann to Meagher, April 1, 1869.

14. *Ibid.,* Heimann to Savini, December 1869.

15. *Ibid.,* Heimann to Meagher, February 17, 1869.

16. *Supra,* ch. 2, n. 158.

17. A.C.R., II Americana PCM 1, Meagher to Heimann, January 26, 1869; *Ibid.,* Guenther to Meagher, February 17, 1869 ; *Ibid.,* Meagher to Heimann, March 1, 1869; *Ibid.,* Heimann to Meagher April 1, 1869; *Ibid.,* Meagher to Heimann December 4, 1869; *Ibid.,* Heimann to Meagher, January 1870; *Ibid.,* Heimann to Savini, January 22, 1870; *Ibid.,* Savini to Heimann, May 23, 1870.

18. *Ibid.,* Meagher to Heimann, January 14, 1870.

19. *Ibid.,* Heimann to Savini, January 22, 1870.

20. *Ibid.,* Knoll to Savini, June 18, 1870.

21. *Ibid.,* Savini to Heimann, May 23, 1870.

22. *Ibid.,* Knoll to Savini, June 25, 1870. Knoll argued that the new jurisdictional arrangement would raise many problems. He could not determine the status of men from the house in Kansas who were residing at Cumberland. Since Huber collected alms for both Knoll and Heimann, his position raised even more questions.

23. *Historical Sketch of St. Joseph's Parish.* This is a typed essay. Author and date of writing are unknown. It is contained in the Carmelitana Collection, Whitefriars Hall, Washington, D.C. A descriptive announcement was carried by the press: "St. Joseph's new German Catholic Church will be solemnly dedicated to the service of Almighty God on Sunday next, the 18th instant. The Right Reverend Bishop Fink, Coadjutor Bishop, Leavenworth, will perform the ceremony of consecration, commencing at 7 o'clock a.m. Right Reverend Bishop Miege will sing a Pontifical Mass which will commence at 10 o'clock A.M. The Rev. Father Corbett will preach at the High Mass. The sermon, in German, will be in the afternoon. At 7:30 o'clock there will be solemn vespers, after which Rev. Father preached after Mass. The Holy Sacrament of Confirmation will be administered at 3 o'clock in the afternoon. At 7:30 o'clock there will be solemn vespers, after which Rev. Father Butler will preach and then *Te Deum* will be solemnly sung. About twenty of the reverend clergy are expected to be present." "Solemn Consecration," *The Leavenworth Times,* June 16, 1871.

24. Frank Krause, O. Carm., "History of St Joseph's Parish," *Sword,* III (1939), 477.

25. A.C.W., Reichwein, *op. cit.,* 3v-4r.

26. *Historical Sketch of St. Joseph's Parish, loc. cit.*

27. The date of their departure for Marlboro was February 12, 1869. A.C.R., II Americana PCM 1, Knoll to Savini, February 12, 1869.

28. "Father Theodore J. McDonald, O. Carm.," *Sword,* III (1939), 56.

29. A.C.R., II Americana PCM 1, Meagher to Heimann, January 14, 1870. A news item reveals some of the first apostolic endeavors of the new Carmelite community! "A correspondent has furnished the following programme of the religious services at St. Mary's Church this week. The ceremonies of Holy Week at St. Mary's Catholic Church in this village will be as follows: On Thursday the first Mass will be celebrated at 8 o'clock, the second Mass at 10.30 A.M. after which Rev. Theodore McDonald will deliver a sermon on the 'Institution and Excellence of the Holy Sac-

rament of the Eucharist.' After the last Mass the Holy Sacrament will be removed to an altar prepared for that purpose on the right side of the High Altar, Public vespers will not be sung in the evening. At 5 o'clock the prayers of the Stations of the Cross and other appropriate prayers will be offered.

On Good Friday the ceremonies will commence at 10 o'clock A.M. On this day no Mass is celebrated; the Church offers no sacrifice; the Holy Eucharist is not on this day consecrated, so that in the office performed instead of the Mass, the church contents herself with the bare representation of the Passion of Jesus Christ. To this end, she reads such lessons, tracts, etc., as contain predictions of his coming for our redemption, and types of his immolation on the cross afterwards the history of his passion, as related by St. John to show how the law and the prophets were veried by the Gospel.

On Holy Saturday at half-past nine, a.m. will commence the reception into the Church, and baptism of those persons who for some time past have been preparing to receive that Sacrament, under the care and instruction of the Rev. Father Maher. After the baptism and other ceremonies are finished the High Mass will commence which will terminate the offices and ceremonies of Holy Week." "Religious Notices," *Marlboro Gazette* and *Prince George's Advertiser,* March 24, 1869.

30. *History of St. Ignatius Roman Catholic Church, Oxon Hill, Maryland* (no. Publ., n.d.), 6r-6v. Fr. Meagher performed the first baptism at St. Ignatius' Church on February 21, 1869. *Baptismal Register of St. Ignatius' Church,* February 21, 1869.

31. A.A.B., 36A-N-15, McDonald to Spalding, June 30, 1871. McDonald also requested permission to convert a house for which the parish was collecting $16 per month rent into a school. Some of the people were planning to send their children to the Methodist school. The congregation had promised to support two Black sisters from Baltimore, if they could be obtained.

32. Peter Guilday (ed.), The National Pastorals of the American Hierarchy (Washington: National Catholic Welfare Council, 1923), pp, 220-21.

33. *Concilii Plenarii Baltimorenzis II, in Ecclesia Metropolitana Baltimorensi, ad Die VII ad Diem XXI. Octobris, A.D., MDCCCLXVI, Habiti, et a Sede Apostolica Recogniti, Acta et Decreta.* (Baltimore: John Murphy Company, 1868), p. 246.

34. *Ibid.*, p. 245,

35. Spalding to John McCloskey, October 9, 1865, in Vincent de Paul McMurray, S.S., *The Catholic Church during Reconstruction, 1865-1877* (Unpublished Master's thesis, Catholic University of America, 1950), p. 197.

36. Spalding, op. cit., p. 338.

37. Smet, "Americana in the Regesta Savini," Sword, *op. cit,* XVII (1954), 322, n. 16. Fr. Angelus Dwyer, formerly a candidate in the Dominican Order was brought by Fr. Peter Thomas Meagher from Ireland to Marlboro, Maryland and ordained by Archbishop Spalding. He began his novitiate in the Carmelite Order, July 16, 1869, and in due course was professed. He labored zealously in Marlboro for six years, but then in a quarrel with Meagher over money matters, he left the Order. *Infra,* ch. 4.

38. On January 6, 1869, Brocard Murphy was among the professed clerics sent

from Traspontina to Capenae.

A.C.R., "Regesta Savini," f. 66r. On August 16, 1870, he alone was sent to Marlboro. *Ibid.*, f. 67r. According to the Register of St. Thomas Seminary and Preston Park Seminary (Louisville, KY: Lyons Collection), he entered the seminary in February 1871 (p. 35), and was ordained to the priesthood on June 21, 1872.

39. A.C.R., "Regesta Savini," *op. cit.* The Archbishop lent the Carmelites $100 to pay his passage from Ireland. For his biography, see Anthony Dressel, O. Carm., "Rev. Joseph John Walsh, O. Carm.," *Sword* V (1941) 261-262.

40. A.C.R., "Regesta Savini," *op. cit.,* F. 67v. For his biography see Stephen J. McDonald, O. Carm., "Rev. Cyril John Feehan, O. Carm.," *Sword*, IV (1940) 213-219.

41. Effie Gwynn Bowie, *Across the Years in Prince George's County* (Richmond, VA: Garrett and Massie, Inc., 1947), p. 323. On January 5, 1874, Mrs. Graham, eldest daughter of William Gaston, illustrious Catholic congressman and jurist from North Carolina, also gave 2.5 acres for a cemetery. *Ibid.*, p. 324.

42. *Fifty Years of S.S. Peter and Paul's Church, op. cit.*, pp. 62-67.

43. *Ibid.* $5000 of the costs had been raised at a fair. A. LMV., Knoll to LMV, October 24, 1871. (LMV Leav. I 3/29).

44. Gohmann, *op. cit.*, p. 106.

45. A.C.R., II Americana PCM 1, Knoll to Savini, April 16, 1870.

46. *Fifty Years of S.S. Peter and Paul's Church, op. cit.* pp. 66-75.

47. *Ibid.*, pp. 73-75.

48. *Cumberland Daily News*, June 19, 1871.

49. *Ibid.*

50. A.C.R., Mayer, *Historia Provinciae Americanae, op. cit.*, f. 10.

51. *Ibid.*, II Americana PCM 1, October 30, 1870.

52. "Collectane," *Central Blatt and Social Justice*, XXII: 359.

53. A thorough examination of Catholic colonization experiments is given by James P. Shannon, *Catholic Colonization on the Western Frontier* (New Haven: Yale University Press, 1957).

54. Leo J. Walter, O. Carm., "History of St. John's Monastery," *Sword*, II (1939), 224-25. A copy of the manuscript history of New Baltimore by Mr. William Lucken, a settler in the Pennsylvania community, is now preserved in the Carmelitana Collection, Washington, D.C.

55. *Ibid.*

56. Edmond Prendergast, D.D., (ed.), *Diary and Visitation Record of the Rt. Rev. Francis Patrick Kenrick* (Lancaster: Wickersham Printing Co., 1916), p. 38.

57. Walter, *op. cit.*, Ill: 342.

58. *Ibid.*, II: 225.

59. *Ibid.*, II: 343.

60. Prendergast, *op. cit.*, pp. 209-10 (July 12, 1842).

61. Walter, *op. cit.*, II: 346.

62. James MacNees, "Canal Boats That Went Over Mountains," *Sunday Sun Magazine*, July 28, 1963.

63. Walter, *op. cit.*, II: 468.

64. A most comprehensive account of the history of this area with special emphasis was carried by the centennial editions of the *Paducah Sun Democrat*. Ten sections over a period of thirteen publishing days were presented to the public. A special staff had been assigned for many months to write the history. A general review of the history of the area was presented in the first centennial edition, July 22, 1956. Cfr., Bill Powell, "1856 Paducah: Firm Foundation For A Growing City," *Paducah Sun Democrat*, July 22, 1956, sec. C, pp. 2-3 ; Don Pepper, "Houses of God," *Ibid.*, p. 11; "Paducah Grew in Colorful Sections," *Ibid.*, pp. 12-13. The only parish not assigned to the Carmelites was St. John the Evangelist parish in McCracken County.

65. John T. Donovan, *The History of the Catholic Church in Paducah, Kentucky* (Paducah: Young Printing Company, 1934), pp. 18-21.

66. *Ibid.*, p. 30.

67. *Ibid.*, p. 32. Fr. Ive Schacht in 1857 left Nashville to offer his services to the bishop of Kansas. In 1859, he established St. Patrick's Church in Emerald, Kansas and St. Boniface's Church in Scipio, Kansas. In 1869 he went to Paducah. The fact that the Carmelites were heirs to those churches has misled some writers into thinking Fr. Schacht was a Carmelite. After his stay in Paducah, he went to St. Stephen's Church, Owensboro, Kentucky, where he died on April 10, 1874. *Ibid.*, p. 42.

68. Webb, *op. cit.*, p. 431.

69. A.C.R., II Americana PCM 1, Knoll to Savini, January 14, 1871.

70. His biographer assessed his abilities for the new duties at Paducah by describing Meagher as "a good speaker, an energetic and talented man, a splendid teacher and organizer, a man of winning, congenial ways and an excellent spiritual leader." Anthony Dressel, O. Carm., "Very Rev. Peter Thomas Meagher, O. Carm.," *Sword* VII (1943) 364-67.

71. Fr. Aloysius Rabata Kammer donned the habit in Cumberland under Cyril Knoll, June 8, 1867, at the age of twenty-six. A.C.R., II Americana PCM 1, Knoll to Savini, April 24, and June 15, 1868. After his novitiate he was sent, in November 1868, to Leavenworth, where he taught school while carrying on his studies. After his ordination by the Bishop of Leavenworth, *Ibid.*, Knoll to Savini, November 4, 1869, he remained briefly in Kansas, but soon moved to Cumberland, whence on January 1, 1871, he and Fr. Peter Thomas Maher left to found the house in Paducah. *Ibid.*, Meagher to Savini, February 12, 1871. After a brief stay he returned to Cumberland, *Ibid.*, Knoll to Savini, December 27, 1872, and when that house was given

up in 1876, he was placed in charge of New Baltimore. *Ibid.,* Knoll to Savini, August 24, 1875. The following year he was in Pittsburg. *Ibid.,* Knoll to Savini, December 12, 1876. After a trip abroad, he was unwilling to return to the jurisdiction of Knoll, and went with Fr. Smits in Englewood. *Ibid.,* Kammer to Savini, October 8, November 17, December 6, 1877. Not long after, he left the Order.

72. Born at Aachen, Germany (*Fifty Years of S.S. Peter and Paul's Church, op. cit.,* p. 66.) about 1829, Benno studied law at Heidelberg and then became an officer in the Prussian army. (*Glaubensbote,* July 10, 1871). He professed his simple vows in Cumberland on December 16, 1870 (A.C.R., H Americana PCM 1, Knoll to Savini, January 14, 1871).

73. "Father Anastasius J. Kreidt, O. Carm.," *Sword,* II (1938) 39-50.

74. Anthony C. Dressel, "Rev. Bernard G. Fink, O. Carm.," *Sword,* VII (1943) 181-85.

75. *Ibid.,* "Rev. Anselm Sebastian Duel, O. Carm.," *Sword,* VII (1943) 368-70.

76. *Ibid.,* "Rev. Brocard Lawrence Murphy, O. Carm., *Sword,* VII (1943) 266-68.

77. Webb, *op. cit.,* p. 367.

78. Fred G. Neuman, *The History of Paducah* (Paducah: Young Printing Co., 1920), p. 86.

79. Donovan, *op. cit.,* pp. 154-55.

80. *Ibid.,* pp. 44-46.

81. Dressel, "Very Rev. Peter Thomas Meagher," *op. cit,,* VII: 366.

82. *Ibid.,* "Rev. Anselm Sebastian Duel, O. Carm.," *op. cit.,* VII: 368.

83. *Gabensbote,* April 26, 1871.

84. Information on parochial activities is lacking to a great extent due to the fact that newspaper files were ruined in the flood of 1937.

85. The Register of St. Thomas Seminary and Preston Park Seminary, *loc. cit.*

86. Donovan, *loc. cit.*

87. A.C.R., Mayer, *Historia Provinciae Americanae, op. cit.,* f. 11.

88. *Ibid.,* II Americana PCM 1, Knoll to Savini, December 27, 1872.

89. *Ibid.,* Heimann to Savini, (June 1873)

90. Dressel, "Rev. Brocard Lawrence Murphy," *op. cit.,* VII: 267.

91. A.C.R., II Americana PCM 1, Feehan to Savini, April 30, 1873.

92. *Ibid.,* "Regesta Savini," *op. cit.,* f. 54v.

93. *Diamond Jubilee: St. Cecilia Church: An Historical Sketch in Word and Picture* (Louisville: Schuhmann Printing Co., 1948), p. 14.

94. Sister M. Hildegarde Yeager, C.S.C., *The Life of James Roosevelt Bayley* (Wash-

ington: Catholic University of America Press, 1947), p. 431.

95. *Ibid.,* p. 358.

96. *Ibid.,* n. 56.

97. A.C.R., Mayer, *Historia Provinciae Americanae, op. cit.,* f. 7.

98. A.A.B., 39A-A-6, Knoll to Spalding, June 6, 1871.

99. Leighton, *op. cit.,* pp. 65-66.

100. A.C.R., II Americana PCM 1, Meagher to Savini, August 28, 1873.

101. *Diamond Jubilee: St. Cecilia Church, op. cit.,* p. 13.

102. A.C.R., II Americana PCM 1, Meagher to Savini, *loc. cit.*

103. Webb, *op. cit.,* pp. 514-29.

104. A.C.R., "Regesta Savini," *op. cit.,* f. 75v.

105. Webb, *op. cit.,* p. 528.

106. *Catholic Advocate* (Louisville), September 4, 1873.

107. Diamond Jubilee: St. Cecilia Church, *op. cit.,* p. 15.

108. Meagher had suggested these reasons in earlier correspondence. A.C.R., II Americana PCM 1, Meagher to Savini, November 9, 1873. Cfr. *Ibid.,* Feehan to Savini, February 27, 1874.

109. *Ibid.,* Mayer, *Historia Provinciae Americanae, op. cit.,* f. 11.

110. Those who returned with Meagher were Sisters Rose Meagher, Gonzales Meagher, Lauretta Meagher, Constance Davis, Fathers Daniel O'Connell and Thomas J. Hayes.

111. *Diamond Jubilee:* St. Cecilia Church, *loc. cit.*

112. *Ibid.,* p. 14.

113. *Ibid.,* p. 35.

114. *Ibid.*

115. *Ibid.*

116. *Ibid.,* p. 14; "Father Theodore J. McDonald," *op. cit.,* III: 56.

117. Webb, *op. cit.,* p. 528.

118. A.C.R., "Regesta Savini," *op. cit.,* f. 76v.

119. *Ibid.,* f. 21r.

120. Anthony Dressel, O. Carm., "Rev. Albert Michael Murphy, O. Carm.," *Sword,* VII (1943) 269-72. The Register of St. Thomas Seminary and Preston Park Seminary, *op. cit.,* p. 37., indicates he entered the seminary on September 7, 1874, and was ordained to the priesthood on September 1, 1878, at Nazareth, Kentucky by Bishop McCloskey.

Chapter Four: Unifying Foundations

1. In a letter to the General, dated June 4, 1874, Fr. John Verheyen wrote that the lack of candidates to the Carmelite monastery at Cumberland made religious life impossible. He also noted that Knoll desired to be relieved as Commissary. A.C.R., II Americana PCM 1, Verheyen to Savini, June 4, 1874.

2. Leo J. Walter, O. Carm., "Holy Trinity Monastery, Pittsburgh, Penna.," *Sword* IX (1945) 41.

3. Walter, "The History of St. John's Monastery," *op. cit.*, IV: 44-45.

4. A.C.W., Reichwein, *op. cit.,* 6v.

5. *Fifty Years of SS. Peter and Paul's Church, op. cit,* p. 75.

6. A.C.W., Anastasius J. Kreidt, Diary, August 21, 1875. Kreidt kept his diary in various sorts of notebooks and memorandum pads. The entry in question is selected from a ledger book 22 x 16 cm. Kreidt entitled the book: "Journal commenced January the First, 1873 in Rome, Italy." An archivist has labeled the cover "Chronicle of Fr. Anastasius Kreidt, January 1, 1873-September 6, 1892." The diary has been poorly preserved; its entries are fading from view.

7. Angelitzus Eberl, *Geshichte der Bayriscen Kapuziner-Ordensprovinz* (Freiburg: Herders Verlagsverhandlung, 1902), p. 630.

8. Stanton, *op. cit.,* I. 69-70.

9. A.C.W., Reichwein, *loc. cit.*

10. Andrew A. Lambing, *A History of the Catholic Church in the Diocese of Pittsburgh and Allegheny.* (New York: Benziger Brothers, 1880), pp. 176-77.

11. A.C.W., Reichwein, *loc. cit.*

12. A.G.R., Mayer, *Historia Provinciae Americanae, op. cit.,* f. 12.

13. Lambing, *op. cit.,* p. 275.

14. Walter, "Holy Trinity Monastery," *op. cit.*, IX: 42, n. 2.

15. *Brochure Commorating the Diamond Jubilee of Holy Trinity Church, Pittsburgh, Pennsylvania,* p. 19. The history of the parish was written by Anthony G. Dressel, O. Carm.

16. Leland D. Baldwin, *Pittsburgh: The Story of a City* (Pittsburgh: University of Pittsburgh Press, 1938), p. 233.

17 *Brochure Commemorating the Diamond Jubilee of Holy Trinity Parish, loc. cit.*

18. Lambing, *op. cit.,* p. 274. The Carmelite Province gives a different account of these years indicating that the Benedictines had charge of the parish from 1865 to 1869 and were succeeded by the Capuchins. "Holy Trinity Parish," *Carmelite Review,* I (Sept., 1893) 37.

19. *Brochure Commemorating the Diamond Jubilee of Holy Trinity Parish, loc, cit.*

20. *Ibid.,* pp. 20-21.

21. *Ibid.*
22. Walter, "Holy Trinity Monastery," *op. cit.,* IX: 42.
23. *Ibid.*
24. A.C.R., II Americana PCM 1, Knoll to Savini, August 24, 1875.
25. *Ibid.,* Knoll to Savini, December 12, 1876.
26. *Ibid.,* Knoll to Savini, May 5, 1878.
27. *Brochure Commemorating the Diamond Jubilee of Holy Trinity Parish, loc. cit.*
28. Lambing, *op. cit.,* p. 175.
29. Walter, "Holy Trinity Monastery," *op. cit.;* IX: 42, n. 1.
30. A. LMV., Heimann to LMV, November 26, 1868. (LMV Leav. I 3/24).
31. A.C.W., Reichwein, *loo. cit.*
32. A.C.R., Mayer, *Historia Provinciae Americanae, op. cit.,* f. 7.
33. As recounted by Fr. Adrian Lickteig, O. Carm. to Fr. Franz Lickteig, O. Carm.
34. A.C.R., Mayer, "Historia Provinciae Americanae," *op. ait.,* f. 13.
35. A.C.W., Reichwein, *op. cit.,* f. 7-8.
36. *Centennial, St. Boniface Church, op. cit.,* pp. 10-11.
37. *Ibid.*
38. *Ibid.*
39. A.C.W., Reichwein, *op. cit.,* f. 7r.
40. Gilmore, *op. cit.,* VII: 175.
41. A.C.W., Reichwein, *loc. cit.*
42. This data was gathered by Rev. Franz Lickteig. At the time of this writing the author had access to the unpublished manuscript containing this data. Franz Lickteig, O. Carm., *The Scipio Brothers,* p. 7. A copy of this manuscript is available in the Carmelitana Collection, Washington, D.C.
43. A.C.W., Reichwein, *loc. cit.*
44. *Berichte der Leopoldinin-Stiftung,* XLV (1875) 76-77.
45. A.C.R., Mayer, *Historia Provinciae Americanae, op. cit.,* f. 13.
46. Gilmore, *op. cit.,* VII: 178.
47. A. LMV., Mayer to LMV, November 30, 1874. (LMV Leav. I 3/30b).
48. *Centennial, St. Boniface Church, op. cit.,* p. 12.
49. A.C.W., Reichwein, *op. cit.,* 7r-7v.
50. A.C.W., Reichwein, *op. cit.,* f. 9.

51. Lickteig, *op. ait.,* p. 25, n. 34.

52. A. LMV., Mayer to LMV, September 29, 1874. (LMV Leav. I 3/30a).

53. A.C.E,, II Americana P.C.M., 1, *loc. cit.*

54. *Ibid.*

55. A.C.W., Reichwein, *loc. cit.* In the Corporation Book of the Scipio Monastery there is a record of a corporation meeting on September 24, 1874 at which a mortgage on the Leavenworth property was made out to Owen Duffy for $13,580 at the customary rate of 12% interest. Gilmore, *op. cit.,* p. 176, n. 41.

56. *Centennial, St. Boniface Church, loc. cit.*

57. *Berichte der Leopoldinen-Striftung,* XLVI (1876) 81.

58. Beckman, *op. cit.,* p. 149. Currency was changing in Germany at this time; the mark was becoming the major unit. Conversion table suggest, however, that a gulden was worth about 65 cents in US currency.

59. A. LMV., Heimann to LMV, March 21, 1878 (LMV Leav. I 3/33).

60. Gilmore, *op. cit.,* VII: 176.

61. "Father Pius R. Mayer, O. Carm., Our First Provincial 1889-1897," *Sword* II (1938) 190.

62. Leo J. Walter, "The Carmel of St. Catherines, Ontario," *Sword,* I (October, 1937) 23-28.

63. A.A.T., Fink to Lynch, July 9, 1875.

64. *Ibid.,* Beerhorst to Lynch, August 4, 1875.

65. *Ibid.,* Beerhorst to Lynch, August 9, 1875.

66. *Ibid.,* Heimann to Lynch, August 16, 1875.

67. *Ibid.*

68. *Ibid.,* Heimann to Lynch, August 25, 1875.

69. A.C.R., II Americana PCM 1, Huber to Savini, September 13, 1875. At that time there was no city of Niagara Falls, Ontario. Clifton, Niagara Falls South, Lundy's Lane, and Falls View, later to be merged into the city, were hamlets struggling along the gorge of the Niagara River.

70. A.A.T., Heimann to Lynch, October 18, 1875.

71. A.C.N., Pius Mayer, O. Carm., *History of the Niagara Foundation.* The exact date of the arrival of the Carmelites is difficult to determine. The earliest entry in the parish records is that of marriage, dated October 24, 1875. The entry, however, bears no signature. A second marriage is recorded in the same hand for November 1, 1875, and this entry is signed by Ignatius Beerhorst, O. Carm.; it would seem therefore that the Carmelite Fathers arrived between October 18 and October 24. On October 20, Fr. Albert wrote to the Archbishop "trusting that Fr. Ignatius and Brother have arrived and that Fr. Leander will get there soon." A.A.T., Heimann to Lynch, October

20, 1875.

72. Archer Butler Hulbert, *The Niagara River* (New York: Putnam's Sons, 1908), pp. 173-75. This work cites in full Hennepin's account entitled "Nouvelle Decouverte (1607)."

73. *Ibid.*

74. *Archdiocese of Toronto and Archbishop Walsh, Jubilee Volume* (Toronto: G. Dixon, 1892) p. 331.

75. *Ibid.*

76. *Ibid.*

77. H. G. McKeown, *The Life and Labors of Most Rev. John Joseph Walsh, D.D.* (Toronto: James A. Sadlier, 1886), pp. 106-16. Bishop Lynch was a Vincentian.

78. *Ibid.*, pp. 74-76.

79. A.C.N., Blueprint Plan of the Lands of the Monastery of Mount Carmel in the Township of Stamford.

80. As cited by McKeown, *op. cit.*, pp. 214-22.

81. As quoted by Franz Lickteig, O. Carm., *The Shrine of Our Lady of Peace, Niagara Falls, Ontario and the Annual Pilgrimage in Honor of Our Lady of Mount Carmel*, pp. 12-13. This unpublished study is available in the Carmelitana Collection, Whitefriars Hall, Washington, D.C.

82. *Ibid.*, p. 32.

83. A.A.T., Beerhorst to Lynch, November 12, 1875.

84. McKeown, *loc. cit.*

85. A.A.T., Beerhorst to Lynch, July 26, 1876.

86. A.C.R., II Americana PCM 1, Mayer to Savini, November 18, 1876.

87. A.C.W., Philip Best, O. Carm., *Memoirs*. These private memoirs were written shortly before his death in 1925.

88. An account in the *Sword* differs from the information supplied here by Fr. Mayer in his manuscript history of the Niagara community: "... Father Knoll, greviously displeased because he neither received financial help nor even a report of their work sent Father Pius to visitate the house." "Father Pius Mayer," *loc. cit.*

89. Leo J. Walter, "Father Ignatius Beerhorst, O. Carm., *Sword*, XIV (1950) 26.

90. This was his second dismissal. A.C.R.., Mayer, "Historia Provinciae Americanae," *op. cit.*, f. 12.

91. A.A.T., Heimann to Lynch, December 19, 1876.

92. "Father Pius Mayer," *loc. cit.*

93. Leo J. Walter, O. Carm., "A History of the Niagara Carmel," *Sword* XIV (1950) 241. One of the students at this time was James Gilmour, afterwards manager of the

Hospice that was to be built by the Carmelites at Niagara Falls. He always boasted of his early associations with the Carmelites. On February 10, 1934, he wrote to Fr. Stephen McDonald, O. Carm., "It was Oct. 21st, 1877, when I first entered the study hall. The Prior: 'Fratres, this is Frater Hilarion.' That however was not my first visit to the monastery. I had had an introduction to the refectory in 1876 on a lovely June morning when the Archbishop took a bunch of the St. Michael Sanctuary boys for a trip.

94. A.C.R., II Americana PCM 1, Mayer to Savini, May 30, 1897. Fr. Mayer states that there were only 140 Catholic families scattered throughout the parishes.

95. "Father Pius Mayer," *op. cit.,* pp. 190-191.

96. A.A.T., Mayer to Lynch, July 3, 1880.

97. A. LMV., Heimann to LMV, August 15, 1877. (LMV Leav. I 3/33).

98. A.C.W., Reichwein, *op. cit,* f. 7r-7v.

99. A.C.E., II Americana PCM 1, Kammer to Savini, October 8, 1877.

100. A.C.W., Reichwein, *op. cit.* f. 5r-6v.

101. A.C.R., II Texas 1, Letter of Cyril Knoll for bishop Anastasius Peters, January 8, 1879.

102. The parochial assignment at Butler, Pennsylvania was surrendered to the bishop on October 5,1880. A.C.R., II Americana PCM 1, Knoll to Savini, October 27.

103. "The Late Father Albert Heimann, O.C.C.," *The Carmelite Review,* I (1893) 150.

104. A.C.W., Mayer, *Summaria Historia Provinciae SS. Cordis Mariae, O.C.C., op. cit.* f. 7.

105. A.A.B., 39A-A-6, Knoll to Spalding, June 6, 1871.

106. A.A.B., "Notitiae: Financial Statement," (St. Mary's, 1876), p. 2.

107. *Ibid.,* 41-G-10, O'Dwyer to Bayley, April 9, 1875.

108. A.C.R., II Americana PCM 1, Meagher to Savini, February 22, 1875.

109. *Ibid.,* "Regesta Savini," *op. cit.,* f. 21r.

110. *Ibid.,* II Americana PCM 1, March 17, 1876.

111. A.C.W., Kreidt, *Diary, op. cit.,* August 5, 1875.

112. *Ibid.,* August 21, 1875.

113. A.C.R., II Americana PCM 1, Meagher to Savini, March 17, 1876.

114. *Ibid.,* Meagher to Savini, July 26, 1876. The deed was given to "John E. Knoll" on February 19, 1874.   i

115. A.C.R,, II Americana PCM 1, Knoll to Savini, February 3, 1876.

116. *Ibid.,* Knoll to the Cardinal Protector, June 2, 1876.

117. *Ibid.,* Knoll to Savini, February 3, 1876; Knoll to Savini, April 21, 1876; Meagher to Savini, September 13, 1876.

118. *Ibid.,* Feehan to Savini, n. d.

119. *Ibid.,* "Regesta Savini," *op. cit.,* f. 68r.

120. Forrestal complained that he was suspended simply for questioning Meagher's policies. *Ibid.,* II Americana PCM 1, Forrestal to Savini, June 30, 1876.

121. *Ibid.,* Meagher to Savini, September 13, 1876.

122. A.C.W., Kreidt, *Diary, op. cit.,* October 14, 1876.

123. *Ibid.,* May 29, 1877.

124. A.C.R., II Americana PCM1, Meagher to Savini, April 9, 1877.

125. *Ibid.,* Feehan to Savini, February 9, 1878.

126. Donovan, *op. cit.* p.129.

127. *Paducah Daily News,* January 3, 1879.

128. Donovan, *op. cit.,* p. 46.

129. J. M. Keating, *The Yellow Fever Epidemic of 1878 in Memphis, Tenn.* (Memphis: Wrightson & Co., 1879), p. 94. A listing of those who died from the plague at Hickman is given on p. 261.

130. John Scanlon, "The Yellow Fever Epidemic of 1878 in the Diocese of Natchez," *Catholic Historical Review,* XL (1964) 29.

131. *Ibid.,* XL: 44.

132. Mother Mary Bernard McGiore, *The Story of the Sisters of Mercy* in *Mississippi, 1860-1930* (New York, 1931) p. 82.

133. Kreidt has made his simple profession on April 9, 1871. In the following year, he was sent by Meagher to study in Rome. With the turmoil that befell religious institutions following the revolution of Italy, Kreidt was forced to go to Holland to continue his studies. He had been ordained on November 19, 1876 by Bishop Paredis of Roermond, Holland. At the time of his ordination, the prior general sent him to the new Carmelite foundation of St. Leon in Montepellier. After two years in France, he came back to America. "Father Anasthius J. Kreidt," *op. cit.,* II: 39-46.

134. Dressel, "Very Rev. Peter Thomas Meagher, O. Carm.," *op. cit.,* VII: 366. Fr. Dressel places his death on August 8, 1880.

135. *Paducah Daily News,* August 3, 1880.

136. A.C.W., Kreidt, Dairy, op cit., August 15, 1880.

137. *Paducah Daily News,* August 9, 1880. The fourth session of the Provincial Chapter of 1890 proposed "that the remains of Fr. T. Meagher and Brocard Murphy be transferred from the state of Kentucky to some cemetery which is used to bury the members of the province." A.C.W., "Acta Capituli Porvincialis, 1890-1939 et Acta Definitorium." p. 7. At the following session, it was decided to transfer the remains

to St. Cecilia's cemetery in Englewood. *Ibid.,* p. 8.

138. A.C.R., II Americana PCM 1, Feehan to Savini, August 6, 1880.

139. *Ibid.,* Walsh to Savini, August 9, 1880.

140. *Ibid.,* Kreidt to Savini, August 23, 1880.

141. A.C.W., Kreidt, *Diary*, August 28, 1880.

142. *Paducah Daily News,* August 13, 1880.

143. A.C.R., "Regesta Savini," *op. cit,* f. 35r.

144. *Paducah Daily News,* August 25-December 25, 1880, *passim.*

145. A.C.R., "Regesta Savini," f. 21v.

146. "Father Anastasius J. Smits, O. Carm., Our Second Commissary General,1881-1886." *Sword* II (1938) 319-29.

147. *Ibid.,* p. 321.

148. A.C.W., Smits, "Notes," *op. cit.,* 2v.

149. "Father Anastasius J. Smits," *loc. cit.*

150. *Ibid.*

151. Stephen J. McDonald, O. Carm., "Carmel in the Northern Valley," *Sword,* VI (1942) 802.

152. Fr. Angelus Kempen was, with Fr. Albert Heimann and Louis Guenther, one of the first to enter the Order in America, though unlike these two, he did not persevere. A native of Prussia, he was born November 30, 1833, receiving the name William in Baptism. He was clothed in the habit at Leavenworth, August 20, 1865, being at the time already in his second year of theology. (A.C.R., II Americana PCM 1, Knoll to Savini, September 26, 1865). On his ordination by Bishop John B. Miege, S.J., August 24, 1866, he was immediately placed in charge of Scipio, for after Fr. Knoll opened the house in Cumberland, Frs. Angelus and Louis were left alone in Kansas *(Ibid.,* Knoll to Savini, October 5, 1866). He did not remain there long, and in December of 1867 he was in Cumberland whence he interviewed the archbishop in Baltimore, apparently with a view to secularization *(Ibid.,* Knoll to Savini, April 24, 1868), On April 24, 1868, he wrote to the General, requesting dispensation from simple vows, and giving as his reason poor health as a result of falling through the ice into a river while on a sick call in Kansas in January of 1867. The dispensation was granted, as appears from this entry in the register, but Kempen himself soon appeared in Rome, and apparently decided not to avail himself of it. This would seem to be the explanation of the word "sospesa" in the register. The dispensation, or a copy of it, dated July 18, 1868, is still in the archive. Kempen received permission to visit Germany on his way back to America and spent some time with his parents in Golkerath, Prussia, and at the spa of Aachen *(Ibid.,* Kempen to Savini, September 9, 1868). On his arrival in America, Fr. Anastasius Smits persuaded him to remain and help him in Fort Lee, instead of going on to Kansas. *(Ibid.,* Smits to Savini, October 1869). On December 16 of

that year, Kempen again applied for dispensation, this time with permanent results. (*Ibid.,* "Regesta Savini," *op. cit,* f. 66r).

153. *The Catholic Church in Englewood* (Englewood: St. Cecilia's Church, 1924), p. 18.

154. *Ibid.,* p. 17.

155. For the text of the Bull *Apostolici Ministerii,* see Shearer, *op. cit,* pp. 283 ff.

156. Yeager, *op. cit,* p. 99.

157. A detailed account of the development of various settlements and Catholic churches within New Jersey is given by Joseph M. Flynn, *The Catholic Church in New Jersey.* (Morristown: Publisher's Printing Co., 1894).

158. *The Catholic Church in Englewood, op. cit,* p. 5.

159. *Ibid.,* p. 11.

160. *Ibid.,* pp. 19-24, *passim.*

161. This instruction is reprinted in full by John Tracy Ellis (ed.), *Documents of American Catholic History* (Milwaukee: Bruce Publishing Co., 1962), pp. 401-404.

162. Documents pertaining to the school question from the three plenary councils are presented by Frank L. Christ and Gerard E. Sherry (eds.), *American Catholicism and the Intellectual Life* (New York: Appleton-Century-Crofts, Inc., 1961). A very brief but illuminating treatment of the school question in the light of plenary council's decrees is given by Bernard J. Kohlbrenner, "The Indomitable School," *The American Apostolate,* ed. Leo Ward, C.S.C., (Westminister: Neuman Press, 1962).

163. *The Catholic Church in Englewood, op. cit,* pp. 24-25.

164. McDonald, "Carmel in the Northern Valley, *op. cit,* VI (1942) 397-99.

165. *The Catholic Church in Englewood, op. cit,* p. 26.

166. A.C.W., Smits, "Notes," *op. cit.,* 2v-3r.

167. "Father Pius R. Mayer," *op. cit.,* II: 191-192.

168. *Brochure Commemorating the Golden Jubilee of Our Lady of Mt. Carmel Church* (n. p. 1923), pp. 22-23.

169. A.C.R., II Americana PCM 1, Knoll to Savini, October 27, 1880.

170. A.C.W., Reichwein, *op. cit.,* f. 8r.

171. *Ibid.,* 7v.

172. Fr. John Verheyen, of the convent of Boxmeer, served in our province during the years 1874-1875 and 1878-1883. During the first period he acted as master of novices and professor of theology in Cumberland but he had hardly entered on his duties, when Fr. Cyril Knoll sold the convent and moved to Pittsburgh. Fr. John returned to Holland, but at the request of Knoll, returned to become prior in Pittsburgh until 1883, when he once again sought his native land. Before the American phase of his career he wrote or translated a number of devotional books found in the library

of the Carmelite Institute in Holland. Smet, "Americanana in the Regesta Savini," *op. cit.,* XVII: 318, n. 6.

173. A.C.W., Reichwein, *loc. cit.*

174. A. LMV., Knoll to LMV, January 20, 1880. (LMV Leav. I 3/34).

175. A.C.R., II Americana PCM 1, Van Riel to Savini, March 2, 1881.

176. *Ibid.,* McDonald to Savini, May 3, 1881.

177. Sister Mary Agnes McCann, *Archbishop Purcell and the Archdiocese of Cincinnati* (Washington: Catholic University of America Press, 1918) pp. 101-04.

178. *Centennial, St. Boniface Church, op. cit.,* p. 12.

179. Anthony Dressel, O. Carm., "Brother Michael Purdy," *Sword,* VIII (1944) 28-27.

180. A.C.W., Reichwein, *op. cit.,* f. 10.

181. *Ibid.,* f. 8r.

182. A.C.R., "Regesta Savini," f. 22r.

183. A.C.W., Reichwein, *loc. cit.*

184. A.C.R., II Americana PCM 1, Peters *et al.* to Savini, December 24, 1881.

Chapter Five: Province and Prospect

1. A.C.R., Mayer, *Historia Provinciae Americanae, op. cit.,* f, 15.

2. A.C.W., Reichwein, *op cit.,* f. 8v.

3. *Ibid.*

4. A.C.R., Mayer, *Historia Provinciae Americanae, loc. cit.*

5. *Ibid.,* II Americana PCM 1, Smits to Savini, June 16, 1882.

6. A.C.W., Reichwein, *op. cit.,* f. 9r.

7. A.C.R., II Americana PCM 1, Smits to Savini, July 1, 1882.

8. A.C.W., Reichwein, *op. cit.* f. 9r.

9. *Ibid.*

10. Franz Lickteig, O. Carm., is gathering materials for an extensive study of the entire Commissariate. His study soon to be published should provide the reader with the first authoritative account of this fascinating segment of Carmelite history. At present, there is available a study of the years spent by this group in Louisiana. Cfr. Blaise D'Antoni, Bayou Pierre: *Land of Yesteryear* (1958. n.p.). Without precise citations, however, this work stands as a popular evaluation.

11. The first contingent of settlers led by the Adam Konz family settled at Grelton, Texas on August 15, 1882. "Carmelite Monastery, Marienfeld, Martin County, Texas, U.S.A.," *Sword* IX (1945) 138-41. Grelton was merely a section station on the Texas and Pacific Railway. At the request of the settlers the name of the community was changed to Marienfeld. Work began in 1884 on an adobe church and monastery. A.C.R., Boniface Peters, O. Carm., "De Commissariatu Texas et Louisiana," f. 4. This is a six-page manuscript history written in 1891 and sent at that time to the prior general, Luigi Galli.

12. The stature of nineteenth century Catholicism in Texas is measured by Carlos Castenada, *Our Catholic Heritage in Texas* (Austin: Von Boeckmann-Jones, Co., 1958), v. VII. Mission stations were begun by the Carmelites at Big Springs, Odessa, Midland, Pecos, Toyah. Two priests and a brother were stationed at Fort Davis. The mission field from there spread over five counties. It was an outpost in the Santiago Mountains, about two hundred miles southeast of Marienfeld. The mission area of three hundred miles was traversed by the priests who took turns making a six-week tour of the area, six times a year by buggy. Typical of most of the mission stations was Alamito inhabited by only eight Spanish speaking families. (A.C.R., II Texas 1. Status Commissariatus Texas, 1895).

13. The settlement initiated by the Carmelites first prospered. Grain planted by the Texas and Pacific Railway grew surprisingly well. The wheat even won honors at the World's Fair in New Orleans. John Griffen, "Carmelites on the Staked Plains of Texas," *Little Flower,* XL (May 1959) p. 7. However, even at the beginning of the Carmelite missionaries increased endeavors, the Texan weather hampered their activities. Periods of drought hit West Texas. The once green fields became areas of burnt stubble. From 1886 until 1888 sandstorms were frequent. The settlers with no food and no money began to abandon their farm lands. The German farm colony began to lose its Catholic identity as more protestants moved into Marienfeld. In 1888 a drought of eight months duration fell upon West Texas. Because of all this Fr. Anastasius Peters was prompted to look for another location in which to start a monastery which would supplement the Texas community. This he found in the diocese of Natchitoches, Louisiana. The Catholics who moved out of the Texas community blamed their losses on the Carmelites who had enticed them to settle there. New settlers changed the name of the community to Stanton. "Carmelite Monastery, Marienfeld," *loc. cit.* For a complete review of agricultural conditions, see Rupert Richardson, *Texas: The Lone Star State* (New York: Prentice Hall, 1943) pp. 383-99.

14. The parish of De Soto at Bayou Pierre was taken over by Fr. Berthold Ohlenforst, O. Carm., in April 1888. The Carmelites had been offered the opportunity to open a house at Springfield, Louisiana. Bayou Pierre was situated in northwestern Louisiana, about eight miles northeast of Mansfield in a wooded district which contained small farms, cotton plantations, and an occasional whiskey distillery. In the mission taken over by the Carmelites there were about 1,600 parishioners, mostly Creoles and Blacks, all poor, slow and easygoing. The parishioners were scattered in small settlements over a thirty mile area and thus, when the Carmelites arrived, they had to establish mission stations in the surrounding towns of De Point, Spanish Town, Prairie River, Mansfield, Kingston, Bayou Dolle, Grand Cane, and Oxford. When Anastasius Peters accepted an appointment from the United States government as postmaster, the name of the area was changed to "Carmel." A monthly mag-

azine was published. Lickteig, "Scipio Brothers," op. cit., p. 17.

Ten Carmelites by June of 1889 had settled down at Carmel. (A.C.R., DC Texas 1. Peter to Galli, June 24, 1889). Anastasius Peters came from Texas to be the superior. *(Ibid.,* January 4, 1890). The church lands at Carmel at the time of the Carmelites' arrival contained a small (60 x 25 ft.) wooden church, a log-cabin rectory (36 x 18 ft.), a small garden, a ten-acre pasture and 260 acres of woodland. *(Ibid.,* Peters to Savini, December 25, 1888). It was a fertile country with wild fruit trees growing in the woods and wild vineyards that could be put to use for Mass wine. Under Fr. Anastasius Peters as prior, the small group of students and brothers were put to work on a building project. By May 1890, a new monastery, a school, and a chapel in De Point had been erected. *(Ibid.,* Peters to Galli, May 8, 1890).

The monastery was a large (92 x 40 ft.) two-story building built of logs, rook, masonry, and mud. The walls were held together by long iron rods securely fastened between the logs under each floor. The construction was probably supervised by Joseph Young, a stonemason who also helped the Carmelites build the "Rock Chapel." (J. A. Slawson, "Carmel and the Rock Chapel," *Mansfield Enterprise,* May 13, 1937). This chapel, built to accommodate the Blacks in the mission, was a small stone structure which stood on a bluff overlooking Bayou Lou in the wooded hills behind the monastery and was built by brothers and students in 1891. An addition was also built to the monastery to give added room for the new students who had just come from Marienfeld, as Carmel was designated in 1891 as the house of studies and novitiate of the commissariat for nearly twenty clerics and sixty postulants (A.C.R., II Texas 1 Peters to Galli, July 25, 1891).

15. Reichwein lists numerous charges of ill repute against members of the community. Mayer was sent by the prior general to visitate the foundation in 1890. (A.C.R., "Regesta Ordinis 1881-1896," f. 6v.) Reichwein claims that Fr. Peters forced the community to present facts that could only allow Mayer to make a favorable report. (A.C.W., Reichwein, *op. cit.,* f. l0r.) Anastasius Peters was, in view of Mayer's report, made Commissary General of the southern houses on June 16, 1890. (A.C.R., "Regesta Ordinis, 1881-1896," *loc. cit.)*

16. *Ibid.,* f. 74Cv.

17. *Ibid.,* II Americana PCM 1, Smits to Savini, July 1, 1882.

18. A.C.R., Mayer, *Historia Provinciae Americanae, loc. cit.* Verheyen was replaced by Fr. Mayer and sent to Englewood. Smet, "Americana in the Regesta Savini," *op. cit.,* XVII: 318, n. 6.

19. *Ibid.,* II Americana PCM 1, "Walsh to Savini, February 14, 1883.

20. *Ibid.,* Smits to Savini, April 6, 1883.

21. A.C.R., Mayer, *Historia Provinciae Americanae, loc cit.*

22. Joachim Smet, "Rectus Corde: Very Rev. Leo J. Walter, O. Carm.," *Sword,* XVI (1953) 313, n. 4.

23. United States of America Patent Office; Patent no. 1787, November 26, 1878.

24. A.C.W., Label of *Aqua A Santa Maria Delia Scala.* Submitted by A. J. Lerche,

Attorney and Solicitor for United States Patent No. 1787.

25. A.C.R., II Americana PCM 1, Smits to Savini, December 10, 1883.

26. *Ibid.,* "Regesta Savini," *op. cit.,* f. 14r.

27. *Ibid.,* "Regesta Ordinis, 1881-1896," *op. cit.,* f. 6r. Pfarrer I. R. Selig, Riedlingen, "Das Lehensbild eines bedeutenden Karmeliten (zum Gedachtnis an den Ordensgeneral der beshuchten Karmeliten P. Pius Mayer," *Karmel-Stimmen,* XVIII (1951) 52,, states incorrectly that Mayer was appointed on August 13, 1886.

28. "Father Pius Mayer," *op. cit.,* pp. 188-96.

29. A.C.R., II Americana PCM1, Mayer to Savini, December 11, 1888.

30. *Ibid.,* Mayer to Savini, April 13, 1889.

31. A.C.W., "Acta Capituli Provincialis, 1890-1939, et Acta Definitorium," *op. cit,* p. 93.

32. A.C.R., II Americana PCM 1, Mayer to Savini, April 13, 1889.

33. *Ibid,,* "Regesta Ordinis, 1881-1896," *op.* cit., f. 14r.

34. A.C.W., "Acta Capituli Provincialis, 1890-1939, et Acta Definitorium," *op. cit.,* pp. 94-97.

35. A.C.R., Mayer, *Historia Provinciae Americanae, loco. cit.*

36. *Ibid.,* f. 16

37. *Ibid.*

38. *Ibid.,* II Americana PCM 1, April 13, 1889.

39. A.C.W., "Acta Capituli Provincialis, 1890-1939, et Acta Deflnitorium," *loc. cit.*

40. A.C.R., Mayer, *Historia Provinciae Americanae, loc. cit.*

41. Gabriel Wessels (ed.), *Acta Capitulorum Generalium,* II: 487-94.

42. *Ibid., Historia Chronoligica Priorum Generalium Ordinis B. M. Virginis de Monte Carmelo* (Rome: Collegii S. Alberti, 1929), pp. 369-70.

43. A.C.R., Mayer, *Historia Provinciae Americanae, loc. cit,*

44. Kenneth Moore, O. Carm., "Acts of the First Provincial Chapter, May 1-7, 1890" *Sword* XVIII (1955) 152-62.

45. A.C.R., Mayer, *Historia Provinciae Americanae, loc cit.*

46. "Father Anastasius J. Kreidt," *op. cit.,* II: 39-50.

47. A.C.W., Walsh to Kreidt, May 23, 1890.

48. His first report submitted to the Provincial Chapter of 1894 lists the following contributions: 1890, $153; 1891, $4464.97; 1892, $5687.39; 1893, $4095.63.

49. "Notes and Queries," *Carmelite Review,* I (April 1893) 60. Cfr. A.C.R., Mayer, *Historia Provinciae Americanae, op. cit.,* f. 17.

50. "Miscellaneous," *Carmelite Review,* I (December 1893) 197.

51. A.C.R., Mayer, *Historia Provinciae Americanae, op. cit.,* f. 18.

52. *Ibid.*

53. A.C.W., Andrew Cavanaugh, O. Carm., "Memoirs."

54. These lands comprised lots 1-7 on the eastern end of the section bounded by McLeod Road on the north, Stanley Street on the east and the railroad on the south. The remaining lots 8-11 of about ten acres each had been deeded to the Carmelites by the Archbishop on March 11, 1882.

55. A.C.W., Chancellor of the Archdiocese of Toronto to Kreidt, June 13, 1893.

56. *Ibid.,* Walsh to Mayer, July 4, 1893.

57. *Ibid.,* Smits to Mayer, June 3, 1893.

58. As cited by Walter, "History of Niagara Carmel," *op. cit.,* XIV: 324.

59. *Ibid.,* XIV: 324-25.

60. A.C.W., Satolli to Mayer, July 4, 1893.

61. As cited by Walter, "History of Niagara Carmel," op. *cit,* XIV: 326-27.

62. A.C.W., Mayer to Kreidt, July 17, 1893.

63. The letter of Archbishop Walsh, already quoted, refers to this promise. It seems he had a copy before him as he wrote.

64. This document explodes the legend that the Carmelites originally owned the land down to the banks of the Niagara River, but that they surrendered the strip which intervened between their present holdings and the river to the government for a park without financial consideration.

65. A.C.W., Deed given by Lynch for Niagara property, March 11, 1882.

66. As cited by Walter, "History of Niagara Carmel," *op. cit,* XIV: 330-31.

67. *Ibid.,* XIV: 331.

68. *Ibid.,* XIV: 331-32.

69. "The Apostolic Delegate Blesses Our Review," *Carmelite Review,* I (December 1893) 191.

70. "Monsignor Satolli," *Carmelite Review,* I (December 1893) 191.

71. A.C.W., Memorandum of J. H. Gilmour.

72. *Ibid.*

73. A.C.W., Deed given by Walsh for Niagara property, February 9, 1894.

74. *Carmelite Review,* I: 88-89.

75. *Ibid.,* I: 156-57.

76. *Ibid.,* I: 157.

77. "Father Anastasius Kreidt," *op. cit,* II: 46.

78. Raphael Fuhr, "The Order, the Scapular and the Hospice of Mt. Carmel," *Carmelite Review,* II (1894), 201-05. This article presents the sermon delivered at the laying of the cornerstone of the Hospice.

79. A.C.W., "Acta Capituli Provincialis, 1890-1939, et Acta Definitorium," *op. cit,* pp. 20-25.

80. A.C.R., Mayer, *Historia Provinciae Americanae, op. cit.,* f. 18.

81. A. J. Kreidt, "The Hospice of Mt. Carmel," *Carmelite Review,* VII (1899) 237.

82. *Ibid.*

83. "Father Anastasius Kreidt," *op. cit,* II: 46.

84. A.C.W., Kreidt, *Diary,* August 28, 1899.

85. As cited in the *Carmelite Review* (July 1893) 98.

86. Valentine Boyle, O. Carm., *Mary and the Saints of Carmel, op. cit,* p. 126. Cfr. Alberto Fontana, *Vita e Miracoli di S. Alberto* (Bagnacavallo: Societa Tipografica Editrice del Ricreatorio, 1927).

87. Lickteig, "Shrine of Our Lady of Peace, Niagara Falls, Ontario and the Annual Pilgrimage," *op. cit,* pp. 25-26.

88. *Ibid.,* p. 26.

89. *Carmelite Review,* IV-VII, *passim.*

90. *Ibid.,* VII: 272-73.

91. A.C.W., Kreidt, *Diary,* February 17, 1882.

92. *Ibid.,* March 31-April 12, 1903.

93. *Ibid.,* April 4, 1903.

94. Anthony Dressel, O. Carm., "The Very Rev. Ambrose F. Bruder, O. Carm.," *Sword,* VI (1942) 403.

95. Julian Slobig, O. Carm., "The Very Reverend Basil Kohler, O. Carm.," *Sword,* I (April 1937) 38.

96. Stephen J. McDonald, O. Carm., "Rev. Philip Alban Best, O. Carm.," *Sword,* IV (1940) 344.

97. A.C.W., Kreidt, *Diary,* March 29, 1882.

98. Pius Mayer, "A Series of Short Sermons," pp. 1-2. These typescript sermons are now available in the Carmelitana Collection, Whitefriars Hall, Washington, D.C.

99. A.C.W., Acta Capituli Provincialis, 1890-1939, et Acta Definitorium, *op. cit.,* p. 41.

100. *Ibid.,* "Rules and Regulations For Our Missionaries." Issued November 1903.

101. Anthony Dressel, O. Carm., "History of Saint Cyril's Chicago," *Sword,* III

(1939) 44-45.

102. McDonald, "Rev. Philip Best," *op. cit,* IV: 341-42.

103. Sister Mary Augustine Kwitchin, O.S.F., *James Alphonsus McMaster: A Study in American Thought* (Washington: Catholic University of America Press, 1949) XI.

104. "Salutatory," *Carmelite Review* I (1893) 8.

105. Apollinaris W. Baumgartner, *Catholic Journalism* (New York: Columbia University Press, 1931) pp. 37-46.

106. Louis W. Reilly, "The Weak Points of the Catholic Press," *American Ecclesiastical Review,* X (1894) 117-25.

107. Baumgartner, *op. cit,* p. 52.

108. "To Our Friends," *Carmelite Review,* XII (1903) 271-72.

109. *Ibid.*

110. Senator A. C. Clark, "Burning of a Theatre," *New Carmelite Review,* XII (1904) 156-58.

111. McDonald, "Rev. Philip Best," *op. cit.,* IV: 342.

112. A.C.W., "Notes to the Definitory Meeting of July 1907."

113. A.C.W., Mayer, *Historia Provinciae Americanae, op. cit.,* f. 15.

114. *Ibid.*

115. *Ibid.,* f. 18.

116. *Ibid.,* f. 16.

117. *Ibid.,* f. 17.

118. *Ibid.*

119. *Ibid.*

120. *Ibid.,* f. 16.

121. *Ibid.,* f. 18.

122. *Ibid.,* f. 17.

123. *Ibid.,* f. 18.

124. A.C.W., "Acta Capituli Provincialis, 1890-1939, et Acta Definitormm," *op. cit.,* p. 99.

Ministries and Residences
of the
Carmelites of the Most Pure Heart of Mary Province
(Text in bold print are present houses or ministries)

St. Joseph Parish – St. Joseph Hill (Sellersburg), Indiana (1864-1865)

St. Joseph Parish – Leavenworth, Kansas – 1864

St. Joseph Priory- Leavenworth, Kansas-1864

    Novitiate 1865-1866

St. Boniface Parish – Scipio (Garnett), Kansas – 1865

    St. Patrick Parish – Emerald, Kansas (ca 1866-1884)

    St. John the Baptist – Greeley, Kansas (1881-ca 1901)

    Guardian Angel Parish – Garnett, Kansas (ca 1866-ca

    St. Mary Parish - Mineral Point, Kansas (ca 1878-ca 1891)

    St. Joseph Parish - Mount Ida, Kansas (ca 1878 – ca 1897)

    St. Teresa Parish - Westphalia, Kansas (ca 1881- ca 1897)

    Sacred Heart Parish – Colony, Kansas (ca 1877-1897)

    Mission Churches in Allen County, Kansas – Humboldt, Carlyl, Elizabeth Town, Geneva, Iola, Neosho Rapids, Ida (1865-1876)

    Mission Churches in Coffey County, Kansas – Burlington, Ottumwa, Waverly (ca 1870- ca 1878)

    Mission Churches in Woodson County, Kansas – Neosho Falls, Owl Creek, Trustland (irregularly ca. 1878-ca. 1890)

Mount Carmel/St. Boniface Priory-Scipio, Kansas-1865

    Novitiate 1866-1881 and 1890-ca 1900, House of Studies 1867-1876

    St. John the Evangelist Parish – Lawrence, Kansas (ca 1878-1890)

    Mission Churches in Douglas County, Kansas – Eudora, Baldwin City (ca. 1878-1890)

Sts. Peter and Paul Parish – Cumberland, Maryland (1866-1875)

St. Peter the Apostle Parish - Oakland, Maryland (1866-1868)

St. Peter in Chains Parish– Westernport, Maryland (1866-1868)

    St. Gabriel Mission Church– Barton, Maryland (1866-1868)

St. Mary Parish – Lonaconing, Maryland (1868-1870)

St. Cecilia Parish – Englewood, New Jersey – 1869

St. Ignatius Church – Oxon Hill, Maryland (1869-1875)

St. Mary of the Assumption-Upper Marlboro, Maryland (1869-1875)

    Holy Rosary Mission Church – Rosaryville, Maryland (1869-1875)]

St. John the Baptist Parish – New Baltimore, Pennsylvania (1870-1989)

St. John the Baptist Monastery-New Baltimore, Pennsylvania (1870-1989)

    Novitiate 1870-1871 and 1889-1901 and 1906-1909 and 1936-1968, House of Studies 1886-ca 1903 and 1909-1910

St. Francis de Sales Parish – Paducah, Kentucky (1870-1881)

St. Francis de Sales Priory – Paducah, Kentucky (1870-1881)

    Novitiate 1870-1880, House of Studies 1871-1880

St. Jerome Parish – Fancy Farm, Kentucky (1870-1881)

St. Bridget Parish – Hickman, Kentucky (1870-1881)

St. Patrick Parish--Fulton, Kentucky (1870-1881)

St. Cecilia Parish – Louisville, Kentucky (1873-1875)

St. Peter Parish – Butler, Pennsylvania (1873-1880)

St. Wendelin Parish – Carbon Center, Pennsylvania (1873-1880)

St. Mary Parish – Beaver Falls, Pennsylvania (1875-1883)

Mount Carmel Monastery – Niagara Falls, Ontario – 1875

    Our Lady of Peace Monastery-Falls View (Niagara Falls), Ontario (1875-1914)

    Novitiate 1875-1890, House of Studies 1876-1882 and 1909-1910

    Hospice of Mount Carmel-Niagara Falls, Ontario (1899-1914)

    Mount Carmel Monastery – Niagara Falls, Ontario – 1914

    Novitiate 1921-1936 and 1968-1972 and 1976-1977, Undergraduate College 1919-1968, Preparatory Seminary 1921-1966

Our Lady of Peace Parish – Niagara Falls, Ontario – 1875

St. Patrick Parish – Niagara Falls, Ontario – 1875

Mt. Carmel Cemetery – Paducah, Kentucky (1875-1881)

Holy Trinity Parish – Pittsburgh, Pennsylvania (1875-1958)

Holy Trinity Monastery-Pittsburgh, Pennsylvania (1875-1958)

    Novitiate 1878-1881 and 1904-1906

St. Mary Parish – Beaver Falls, Pennsylvania (1876-1886)

St. Cecilia Priory – Englewood, New Jersey – 1877

Novitiate 1913-1920

Our Lady of Mount Carmel Parish – Tenafly, New Jersey – 1878

St. Joseph Parish – New Germany (Snyder), Ontario (1880-1946)

Mount Carmel Cemetery – Tenafly, New Jersey (1880-2013)

St. Vincent de Paul Parish – Niagara-on-the-Lake, Ontario (1881-1884; 1987-1904)

Most Pure Heart of Mary Monastery– Marienfeld (Stanton), Texas (1882-1901)

Novitiate 1882-1889 and House of Studies 1882-1889

St. Joseph Parish-Marienfeld (Stanton), Texas (1883-1901)

St. Thomas Parish -Big Spring, Texas (1887-1901)

St. Mary Parish – Colorado City, Texas (1885-1901)

St. Catherine Parish – Pecos, Texas (1886-1901)

St. Emily Parish – Toyah, Texas (1886-1901)

St. Ann Parish – Midland, Texas (1885-1901)

Mission Chapel – Odessa, Texas (1888-1900)

Mission Chapel – Barstow, Texas (1888-1900)

St. Joseph Mission –Iatan, Texas (1886-1900)

Mission Chapel - Van Horn, Texas (1888-ca 1895)

Mission Chapel – Malaga, Texas (1888-ca 1897)

Mission Chapel – Red Bluff, Texas (1889-ca 1898)

Mission Chapel – Loving, Texas (1888-ca 1898)

Mission Chapel- Roswell, Texas (ca 1888-ca 1897)

Mission Chapel – Weed, Texas (ca 1890-ca 1897)

Toyah Creek Settlement Mission Stations: La Meta (1886-ca 1897), Santa Isabel (1886-ca. 1897), Brogado (1886-1897), Ojo (1886-1897), Victoria (1886-1897), Lindio (1886-1897)

Sacred Heart Mission – Saragosa, Texas (1886-1897)

St. Joseph Monastery – Carmel, Louisiana (1888-1897)

Novitiate 1889-1896 and House of Studies 1889-1895

Sts. Peter and Paul Parish-Carmel, Louisiana (1888-1897)

Rock Chapel Missions for African-Americans in DeSoto Parish, LA: Bayou Pierre, Rambin, Bayou Gloster, Bayou Walter (all from 1892-1897)

Mission Stations in DeSoto Parish, LA – Bayou Dole, Oxford, Mansfield, Bay ou Gloster, Cote d'Afrique, De Point, Gravelpoint, Clarence, Stonewall, Gloster, Rosalina, Bayou Bourbeaux (most from 1890 or 1892 to 1897)

St. Joseph Parish – Fort Davis, Texas (1892-1897)

    Our Lady of Peace Mission – Alpine, Texas (1892-1897)

    St. Mary Mission – Marathon, Texas (1893-1897)

    St. Mary Mission – Marfa, Texas (1892-1897)

    Mission Station – Valentine, Texas (1893-1897)

    Mission Station –Hermosa, Texas (1893-1897)

    St. Teresa Mission – Presidio, Texas (1892-1897)

    Mission Station – Baracho Rancho, Texas (1894-1897)

    Mission Station – Boquillas, Texas (1894-1897)

    Mission Station – San Vicente, Texas (1893-1897)

    Mission Station – San Esteban, Texas (1893-1897)

    Mission Station – Alamito, Texas (1893-1897)

    Mission Station – Casa Piedras, Texas (1894-1897)

    Mission Station – Alamito Ranch, Texas (1893-1897)

    Mission Station – Pulvo, Texas (1893-1897)

    Mission Station – Lajitas, Texas (1894-1897)

    Mission Station – Chisos, Texas (1893-1897)

    Mission Station – Terlingua, Texas (1893-1897)

    Mission Station – Terlingua Abaja (1893-1897)

    Mission Station – Study Butte, Texas (1893-1897)

    Mission Station – Faver Ranch, Texas (1893-1897)

    Sacred Heart Mission – Shafter, Texas (1893-1897)

    Our Lady of Perpetual Help Mission – Candelaria, Texas (1893-1897)

    Mission Station – Castalon, Texas (1894-1897)

    Mission Station – San Jose, Texas (1894-1897)

    Sacred Heart Mission – Ruidosa, Texas (1893-1897)

    Mission Station – Ranch de la Cruz, Texas (1893-1897)

    Mission Station – Ranch de la Cruz, Texas (1893-1897)

St. Joseph Parish--Fort Stockton, Texas (1892-1895)

St. Edward Parish – Eddy (Carlsbad), New Mexico (1892-1897)

Appendices

St. Barbara Parish – Thurber, Texas (1895-1896)

Choctaw Indian Mission (Dutch Province) – Tucker, Mississippi (-1903)

St. Cyril College – Chicago, Illinois (1900-1924)

Mount Carmel High School – Chicago, Illinois – 1900

St. Cyril Priory – Chicago, Illinois – 1900

> Novitiate 1902-1905, House of Studies 1902-1909 and 1911-1919, Theologate 1933-1938

St. Agatha Parish – New Athens, Illinois (1901-1904)

Native American Mission – Antlers, Indian Territory (Oklahoma) (1903-1904)

St. Cyril Parish – Chicago, Illinois (1904-ca 1969)

St. Columba Parish – Hegewisch, Illinois (1904-1935)

St. Clara Parish – Chicago, Illinois (1908-1969)

St. Anastasia Parish – Teaneck, New Jersey – 1909

St. Ann Parish – Niagara Falls, Ontario (1910-1946)

St. Joseph Parish – Bogota, New Jersey (1920-2013)

Society of the Little Flower – Chicago, Illinois (1923-1983); moved to Darien, Illinois – 1983

Immaculate Conception Parish – Norwood, New Jersey (1923-1994)

St. Therese of Lisieux Parish – Cresskill, New Jersey – 1924

Sacred Heart Parish – Chippawa, Ontario (1924-1954); (1990-2001)

St. Therese Priory (Whitefriars Hall) – Washington, DC – 1926

St. John Parish – Leonia, New Jersey (1926-2006)

Our Lady of Mount Carmel American Mission – Nablus, Palestine (1928-1948)

St. Elias Priory – Joliet, Illinois – 1933

Joliet Catholic High School – Joliet, Illinois (1933-1990)

St. Bernard Parish – Joliet, Illinois (1933-1970)

St. Raphael Parish – Los Angeles, California – 1934

St. Mary Carmelite Parish – Joliet, Illinois (1935-1991)

Camp Carmel – New Carlisle, Indiana (ca 1936)

St. Mary Parish – Closter, New Jersey (1937-1994)

St. Stephen Hungarian Chapel and Mission – Joliet, Illinois (1937-ca 1949)

Parroquia de Nuestra Senora del Carmen – Joliet, Illinois – 1939

Our Lady of the Scapular Mission (1940s-1951)

St. Therese of Lisieux Parish – Richmond (Garnett), Kansas – 1941

Carmelite Junior Seminary – Hamilton, Massachusetts (1945-1970)

Carmelite Brothers' Novitiate – Akron, Ohio (1947-1966)

Convento del Carmen – Miraflores, Lima, Perú – 1949

Parroquia Santo Cura de Ars – Santiago, Chile (1949-ca 1973)

St. Joseph Parish – Demarest, New Jersey (1950-2006)

Our Lady of Mount Carmel Parish – Houston, Texas (1952-2007)

Salpointe Catholic High School – Tucson, Arizona – 1953

Sacred Heart Parish – Tucson, Arizona (1953-2011)

Our Lady of Mount Carmel Parish – Warwick (Newport News), Virginia (1953-1990)

St. Joseph Priory (Provincial House) – Chicago, Illinois (1954-1964)

Carmel Retreat – Mahwah, New Jersey (1955-2011)

St. Joan of Arc Parish – Yorktown, Virginia (1955-1981)

[St. Francis] DeSales High School – Louisville, Kentucky (1956-1983)

[St. Francis] DeSales Priory – Louisville, Kentucky (1956-2004)

St. Andrew Corsini Parish – Ottawa, Ontario (1956-1958)

Mount Carmel High School – Houston, Texas (1956-1986)

Our Lady of Mt. Carmel Parish – Louisville, Kentucky (1956-2006)

Our Lady of Mount Carmel Priory – Tucson, Arizona – 1957

St. Leo Parish – Pittsburgh, Pennsylvania (1958-1992)

    Our Lady of Perpetual Help Mission (1958-1992)

Parroquia San Miguel – Santiago, Chile (1958-1971)

St. Simon Stock Priory – Darien, Illinois – 1959

    Provincial House 2013-Present

Crespi Carmelite High School – Encino, California – 1959

Our Lady of Mount Carmel Priory – Encino, California – 1959

St. Therese Chapel – Peabody, Massachusetts – 1959

Prelature of Sicuani – Sicuani, Perú (1959-2013)

Mount Carmel High School – Los Angeles, California ([1933] 1959-1976)

Mount Carmel Priory – Los Angeles, California ([1934] 1959-1997)

Carmel High School – Mundelein, Illinois – 1961

St. Jane Frances de Chantal Parish – North Hollywood, California – 1963

St. Joseph Priory (Provincial House) – Barrington, Illinois (1964-1993)

Our Lady of Mount Carmel House of Studies – San Diego, California (1965-1970)

Carmel Hall College Formation Program – Milwaukee, Wisconsin (1968-1978)

St. Clara-St. Cyril Parish – Chicago, Illinois (1969-?

St. Gelasius Parish – Chicago, Illinois (? – 2002)

St. Albert of Trapani Parish – Houston, Texas (1970-1999)

St. Therese Chapel – Paramus, New Jersey – 1970

Our Lady of the Scapular Priory – Peabody, Massachusetts – 1970

Our Lady of Mount Carmel Parish – Darien, Illinois - 1970

St. Gertrude Parish – Stockton, California (1971-1999)

Kino Institute – Phoenix, Arizona (1972-2004)

St. Agnes Parish – Phoenix, Arizona – 1972

Carmel West House of Studies – Los Angeles, California (1975-1990)

Convento del Senora del Carmen – Jose Galvez, Peru – 1976

St. Bernadette Soubirous Parish – Houston, Texas (1977-2008)

Carmelite House – Phoenix, Arizona – 1978

St. John of the Cross Parish – Mississauga, California (1978-2013)

Carmelite Carefree Village – Darien, Illinois (1979-2013)

Our Lady of Mount Carmel Parish – Fairfield, California – 1979

Carmel Hall House of Studies – Chicago, Illinois (1979-1987)

St. Raphael Parish – Glendale, Arizona (1980-2004)

Immaculate Conception Parish – Leavenworth, Kansas – 1981

Casa San Elias Formation House – Lima, Peru – 1983

St. Matthew Parish – Glendale Heights, Illinois (1986-2013)

Carmel in Venice – Venice, Florida (1987-2011)

St. Raphael Parish – Englewood, Florida – 1988

Carmelite Residence - Cieneguila, Peru - 1989

Joliet Catholic Academy – Joliet, Illinois – 1990

Casa Santa Teresita Formation House – Houston, Texas (1990-2007)

St. Paul the Apostle Parish – Gurnee, Illinois – 1991

St. John Vianney Parish – Barrie, Ontario (1992-1999)

St. Joseph Priory – Chicago, Illinois (1994 - 2003)

Parroquia de Transfiguración – Torreon, Mexico – 1995

St. Francis of Assisi Parish – Grove City, Florida (1996-2014)

Casa de Retiros "Villa Carmelitas" – Lurin, Peru – 1998

    Noviciado Carmelita – Lurin, Peru – 2006

Carmel at Mission Valley – Nokomis, Florida – 1999

Our Lady of Mount Carmel Parish – Osprey, Florida – 2000

Casa del Carmen Formation House – Mexico City, Mexico – 2000

St. Thomas the Apostle – Chicago, Illinois – 2002

St. Therese of Lisieux Priory – Phoenix, Arizona – 2003

St. Cyril of Alexandria Parish – Tucson, Arizona – 2006

Carith Carmelite Pre-Novitiate House – Chicago, Illinois – 2007

Centro Xiberta Formation House - Ciudad Delgado, El Salvador - 2008

Carmel of Sant' Angelo – Chicago, Illinois – 2008

Our Lady of Perpetual Help Retreat and Spiritual Center – Venice, Florida (2008-2014)

St. Teresa of Avila Parish – San Francisco, California – 2010

Carmelite Community at St. Thomas – Tucson, Arizona - 2013

Titus Brandsma Priory – Darien, Illinois – 2014

+   +   +

Residences of the Provincial and/or Offices

1889 – 1924: at Holy Trinity Priory, Pittsburgh, Pennsylvania (although Pius Maria Mayer, 1st Provincial, resided there and at St. John the Baptist Monastery in New Baltimore, Pennsylvania, off and on between 1891 and 1895)

1924 – 1954: at St. Clara Priory, Chicago, Illinois

1954 – 1964: at St. Joseph Priory, Chicago, Illinois

1964 – 1994: at St. Joseph Priory, Barrington, Illinois

1994 – 1996: at St. Joseph Priory, Chicago, IL/Office in Darien, Illniois

1996 – 2011: Residence (Winterberry) and Office in Darien, Illinois

2011 – 2013: at St. Cyril Priory in Chicago and Office in Darien, Illinois

2013 – Present: Residence (White House) and Office in Darien, Illinois

Provincial Leadership

Commmissary Generals

Cyril Knoll	1864 - 1881
Anastasius Smits	1881 - 1886
Pius Mayer	1886 - 1889

Priors Provincial

Pius Mayer	1890 - 1897
Anastasius Kreidt	1897 - 1903
Ambrose Bruder	1903 - 1909
Dionysius Best	1909 - 1914
Basil Kahler	1914 - 1924
Lawrence Diether	1924 - 1936
Matthew O'Neill	1936 - 1948
Leo Walter	1948 - 1951
Raphael Kieffer	1951-1960
Brendan Gilmore	1960 - 1966
Malachy Smith	1966 - 1972
Paul Hoban	1972 - 1978
John Malley	1978 - 1983
Murray Phelan	1983 - 1990
Quinn Conners	1990 - 1996
Leo McCarthy	1996 - 2002
John Russell	2002 - 2005
John Welch	2005 - 2011
Carl Markelz	2011 - 2013
William J. Harry	2013 -

About the Author

As a member of St. Clara's Carmelite Parish and as a student at Mount Carmel High School, both in Chicago, IL., Myron Judy, O. Carm. learned about the Carmelite Province of the Most Pure Heart of Mary(PCM) and its members firsthand. Attracted to the charisms of many devoted Carmelites, he began studies in Carmelite seminaries, leading to his ordination in 1963. Throughout his priestly life, he has been involved in a number of social justice and sacramental ministries.

In 1964, to celebrate and pay tribute to the early founders of the Province on the 100th anniversary of their initial foundations in North America, he wrote a thesis, *Carmel Came*, as part of his work at the University of Notre Dame toward a Master of Arts degree. Asked to represent this thesis at a gathering of the PCM Province on the occasion of the 150th anniversary, he decided to revise and update his research for publication in book format, as *Carmel in North America: The Early Founders and Foundations of the Province of the Most Pure Heart of Mary (1864-1900)*.

After a short teaching ministry at the University of Dayton and Mt. Carmel College, Ontario, Fr. Myron became involved in Student Personnel Administration at several universities including the Jesuit University of Detroit, where he was the Dean of Students. Following his years in educational ministries, he became very engaged in Catholic Health Care Administration for more than two decades. He currently provides chaplaincy services in the Mercy Health System, Philadelphia. At the time of this publication, Fr. Judy is also a Member of the PCM Provincial Council and the Director of Health Care for the PCM Province.

Fr. Judy has a license in theology (STL) from Catholic University, a MA from the University of Notre Dame, a M.Ed. from the University of Illinois and a MSW from the University of Pennsylvania. While this is his first book length offering, he has published other articles relating to American history, American Catholic Church history, education and health care.

+ + +

Recommended Carmelite Websites

For more information about the Carmelites today,
our spirituality and our ministries worldwide, visit:

carmelites.net

ocarm.org

carmelites.info

For a listing of Carmelite provinces worldwide, visit:

carmelites.info/provinces

For a listing of Monasteries of Carmelite nuns, visit:

carmelites.info/nuns

For a listing of Carmelite Hermitages, please visit:

carmelites.info/hermits

For a listing of sites about Lay Carmelites:

carmelites.info/lay carmel

For a listing of Affiliated Congregations and Institutes:

carmelites.info/congregations

For more information about our work
with the United Nations, visit:

carmelitengo.org

For more information about other publications
available from the Carmelites, visit:

carmelites.info/publications

Index

(Check listings under both ministry name and location)

A

Abensberg, Carmelite house suppressed 5, 6, 12
Abensberg, Germany, City of 12
Akron, Ohio, Carmelite Brothers' Novitiate 222
Alamito Ranch, Texas, Mission Station 220
Alburg, Germany 17
Allen County, Kansas - Mission Churches 217
Alpine, Texas, Our Lady of Peace Mission 220
Altendoerfer, Gerard, Carmelite 104
Amberges, Rev. 13
Anderson County, Kansas, mission of Scipio 39, 44
Angermueller, Rev. Joseph 7
Antlers, Indian Territory (Oklahoma), Native American Mission 221
Apologia xi
Aqua Santa Maria della Scala, see *Karmeliten Geist* 144
Archives, Carmelite ix, provision for 150
Ariel, ship of the Cunary Line 23
Aussterbekloster, central monastery during secularization 5

B

Bayley, James Roosevelt, bishop of Newark, New Jersey 54
Baldwin City, Kansas, Mission Church 217
Ballard County, Kentucky, ministry responsibility of Carmelites 85
Baltimore, First Plenary Council of, *see* First Plenary Council of Baltimore
Baltimore, Second Plenary Council of, *see* Second Plenary Council of Baltimore
Baltimore, Third Plenary Council of, *see* Third Plenary Council of Baltimore
Bamberg, Germany 5
Baracho Rancho, Texas, Mission Station 220
Barnas, John Alber 21
Barrie, Ontario 103, St. John Vianney Parish 103, 224
Barrington, Illinois, St. Joseph Priory (Provincial House) 223
Barstow, Texas, Mission Chapel 219
Barton, Maryland, description of, mission of Cummberland 49, St. Gabriel Mission Church 217
Baszez, Evodius, Carmelite 44
Bauer, Brocard, Carmelite 7, 11
Baurele, Bernhard, Carmelite x
Bausch, Norbert 41, sent to New Baltimore, Pennsylvania, 83, left the Order 146
Bavaria, King of Knoll's letter to 13

Bayerlein, Rev. Sylvester 6

Bayley, Bishop visit to Upper Marlboro, Maryland 88, 95, appointed to Baltimore, relation with Carmelites in Marlboro 110, suggest Carmelites join secular clergy 110, Knoll appeals to 111, advised Smits to secularize 116, charged with forming new diocese of Newark 117, names Englewood church "St. Cecilia's" 118

Bayou Bourbeaux, Louisiana, Mission Station 220

Bayou Dole, Louisiana, Mission Station 220

Bayou Gloster, Louisiana, African American Mission 219

Bayou Gloster, Louisiana, Mission Station 220

Bayou Pierre, Louisiana, African-American Mission 219

Bayou Walter, Louisiana, African American Mission 219

Beaver Falls, Pennsylvania, Knoll accepts ministry for 173, St. Mary Parish 218

Bedford Gazette, article detailing plan for university at New Baltimore, Pennsylvania 84

Beerhorst, Ignatius, Carmelite 100, 102, receives faculties in Toronto Archdiocese 103, missions of Flos, Medonte, and Vigo 103, 104, sent back to Kansas 107, allegedly receives promise from Bishop Lynch 159

Benedictines (Metten) 7, Charter of American 25, responsible for Holy Trinity parish, Pittsburgh, Pennsylvania 97

Bergen County, New Jersey, given to Carmelites by Bishop Bayley 54

Bergenfield, New Jersey, becomes separate parish 120

Berthold, Brother, Carmelite arrival at Cumberland 52, 53, 55

Berthold of Calabria 26

Best, Dionysius, Carmelite, work on mission band 168-169, Prior Provincial 225

Best, Philip, Carmelite, description of laying of cornerstone at Niagara for new monastery 107, 129, member of 2nd provincial chapter 135, characteristics of 168, editor of *Carmelite Review* 170

Big Spring, Texas, St. Thomas Parish 219

Blackburn, Dr. Luke, actions during Yellow Fever epidemic of 1878 112

Bloody August Monday, anti-Catholic riots in Louisville 34

Bogota, New Jersey, St. Joseph Parish 221

Boquillas, Texas, Mission Station 220

Bosworth, anti-Catholic preacher 164

Boxmeer, Netherlands, 1, 5

Brace, Charles Loring, record of visit to Pesth, Hungary 21

Brandstaetter, Ambrose, Carmelite, in Scipio, Kansas, community 67, member of 3rd provincial chapter 137

Brennan, Avertannus, Carmelite, 129 in Our Lady of Peace, Niagara Falls, Ontario, community 129, member of 2nd provincial chapter 135, and mission band 168

Brewery, Straubing monastery 7

Brocard, Fr., Carmelite, death of 121

Brogado, Texas, Mission of St. Joseph's Parish, Marienfeld, Texas 219

Brothers, provisions regarding in First Provincial Chapter 150

Index 233

Browne, Gabriel, Carmelite, member of 3rd provincial chapter 137
Bruder, Ambrose, Carmelite, member of 2nd provincial chapter and elected to definitory 135, elected provincial procurator 136, member of 3rd provincial chapter 137, elected definitor and appointed provincial procurator 138, develops rule and regulations for mission band members 169, Prior Provincial 225
Buggert, Donald, Carmelite xi
Burlington, Kansas, Mission Church 101, 217
Burnside, Ambrose, general, United States Army, 33
Butler, Pennsylvania, residence for Cyril Knoll 91, 96, parish given back 109, St. Peter Parish 218

C

Calloway County, Kentucky, ministry responsibility of Carmelites 85
Camp Carmel, New Carlisle, Indiana 221
Candelaria, Texas, Mission Station 220
Capuchin Order, served at Fort Lee, New Jersey for a time 117
Carbon Center, Pennsylvania, St. Wendelin Parish 218
Cardinal Primate of Hungry 16, visits to Pesth, Hungary, 17
Cardinal Protector of the Order, received appeal from Knoll 111
Carith Carmelite Pre-Novitiate House, Chicago, Illinois 224
Carlisle County, Kentucky, ministry responsibility of Carmelites 85
Carlsbad, New Mexico *see* Eddy, New Mexico
Carlyl, Kansas, Mission Church 217
Carmel at Mission Valley, Nokomis, Florida 224
Carmel Hall College Formation Program, Milwaukee, Wisconsin 223
Carmel Hall House of Studies, Chicago, Illinois 223
Carmel High School, Mundelein, Illinois 223
Carmel in Venice, Venice, Florida 223
Carmelite Brothers' Novitiate, Akron, Ohio 222
Carmelite Carefree Village, Darien, Illinois 223
Carmelite Community at St. Thomas, Tucson, Arizona 224
Carmelite House, Phoenix, Arizona 223
Carmelite Junior Seminary, Hamilton, Massachusetts 222
Carmelite Order, donors of land in Louisville affiliation to 89
Carmelite Order, John Lynch, archbishop of Toronto affiliated with 108
Carmelite Order, Bishop McCloskey affiliated to 91
Carmelite Order, origins of 26
Carmelite Review reorganized as the magazine of the province 136, German language edition instituted 138, as fundraising device for Niagara hospice 151, receives praise from Apostolic Delegate 163, 170-173, editorial policy 171, statistics for 170-171
Carmelite Spirits see *Karmeliten Geist*
Carmelites and Catholic education 118-119

Carmel, Louisiana, turned over to local diocese 137, St. Joseph Monastery 219, Sts. Peter and Paul Parish 219
Carmel of Sant' Angelo, Chicago, Illinois 224
Carmel Retreat, Mahwah, New Jersey 222
Carmel West House of Studies, Los Angeles, California 223
Carrieville [Northvale], New Jersey, mission of Fort Lee 116, removed as mission at Smit's request but later returned to care of Carmelites 116
Casa del Carmen Formation House, Mexico City, Mexico 224
Casa de Retiros "Villa Carmelitas," Lurin, Peru 224
Casa Piedras, Texas, Mission Station 220
Casa San Elias Formation House, Lima, Peru 223
Casa Santa Teresita Formation House, Houston, Texas 223
Castalon, Texas, Mission Station 220
Catalda, Joseph, Carmelite, prior general 6
Catholic Advocate, comments on Carmelites 89
Catholic Church in Englewood, The newspaper 119
Catholic education and Carmelites 118-119
Catholic press, weak points of, article on 171
Catholic University, Washington, DC x
Cavanaugh, Andrew, Carmelite, recalling of conflict with Archbishop of Toronto 152
Chamber of the Interior, Germany 9
Chapter, First PCM Provincial (1890), 133, summary of decisions made at 133-134, proposals of the first PCM provincial, 149-151
Chapter, Second PCM Provincial (1894), 135, summary of decisions made at 135-136
Chapter, Third PCM Provincial (1896), 137, summary of decisions made at 137-138
Charbonnel, bishop of Toronto retires 104
Chicago, Carmelite attempt to establish in 1868 53
Chicago, Illinois, Carith Carmelite Pre-Novitiate House 224
Chicago, Illinois, Carmel Hall House of Studies 223
Chicago, Illinois, Carmel of Sant' Angelo 224
Chicago, Illinois, Mount Carmel High School 221
Chicago, Illinois, Society of the Little Flower 221
Chicago, Illinois, St. Clara Parish 221
Chicago, Illinois, St. Clara-St. Cyril Parish 223
Chicago, Illinois, St. Cyril College 221
Chicago, Illinois, St. Cyril Parish 221
Chicago, Illinois, St. Cyril Priory 221
Chicago, Illinois, St. Gelasius Parish 223
Chicago, Illinois, St. Joseph Priory 224
Chicago, Illinois, St. Joseph Priory (Provincial House) 222
Chicago, Illinois, St. Thomas the Apostle 224
Chickasaws, sold "Jackson Purchase" land 85

Index

Chief Paduke, Chickasaw Indian chief, sold "Jackson Purchase" land 85
Chippawa, Ontario, 104, Sacred Heart Parish 221
Chisos, Texas, Mission Station 220
Choctaw Indian Mission (Dutch Carmelite Province), Tucker, Mississippi 221
Christian Brothers of De La Salle 102
Cincinnati, Archdiocese of, financial scandal 121
Ciudad Delgado, El Salvador Centro Xiberta - Casa de Formación 224
Civil War in USA, and Niagara Frontier 105
Clarence, Louisiana, Mission Station 220
Clark, State Senator, article on Iroquois theatre fire 172
Clifton House, hotel on Niagara frontier, Ontario ix
Clifton, Ontario, parish, accepted by Carmelites 104, new church built 173
Clondalkin, Ireland 102
Closter, New Jersey, under care of Carmelites 117, becomes a separate parish 120, St. Mary Parish 221
Cloud County, Kansas, mission of Scipio 44
Cody, Fr. 119
Coffey County, Kansas, mission of Scipio 39, 44, Mission Churches 217
Colony, Kansas, Sacred Heart Parish 217
Colorado City, Texas, St. Mary Parish 219
Columbus, Kentucky Carmelites assume the ministry for 85, 1871 Confirmation statistics 86, stats of the mission at Thomas Meagher's death 114
Commissariat of the South (Texas Commissariat), suppression of 143
Community life on Kansas frontier 45, resolutions concerning during organizational meeting in 1889 147
Congress of Vienna 4
Conners, Quinn, Carmelite, Prior Provincial 225
Convento del Carmen, Lima, Perú 222
Convento del Senora del Carmen, Jose Galvez, Perú 223
Corrigan, Bishop Michael, advises Smits to secularize 116
Cote d'Afrique, Louisiana, Mission Station 220
Covington, Kentucky, Diocese of, 34
Coyte's barn, site of first Mass in Tenafly 120
Crespi Carmelite High School, Encino, California 222
Cresskill, New Jersey, St. Therese of Lisieux Parish 221
Cumberland Daily News, description of celebration for anniversary of Pius IX 81
Cumberland, Maryland 45, Knoll's planned move to 45, served by the Redemptorists 46, monastery 46, during Civil War 47, reasons for selling to Carmelites 47, reasons for moving to 48, Knoll's consideration of leaving 50, reality of 52, novices 52, loss of mission stations 52, picture of Carmelite monastery and church 69, 71, improvements to 79-80, devotions at 80, removal of mission stations 82, reasons for leaving 82-83, 93, reasons for withdrawl and sale of 95-96, reaction to sale of 110-111, property discovered to be in Knoll's name 111, Sts. Peter and Paul Parish 217
Cunard vessel, carries Carmelites and Ursulines to USA 27

Curley, Michael J. viii

D

Daily, Peter Thomas, Carmelite 100
Darien, Illinois, Carmelite Carefree Village 223, Our Lady of Mount Carmel Parish 223, Society of the Little Flower 221, Titus Brandsma Priory 224
Dease, Mother Mary Teresa Elle, Loretto Sisters, 106
De Coen, Fr., SJ, account of US troops in St. Joseph's church 37
Demarest, New Jersey, became a separate parish 120, St. Joseph Parish 222
De Nigrorum Salute Procuranda (Ensuring the Welfare of the Negro), decree from Second Plenary Council in 1866 78
De Paula, Franzishus, Carmelite 4
De Point, Louisiana, Mission Station 220
DeSales High School, Louisville, Kentucky 222
DeSales Priory, Louisville, Kentucky 222
DeSoto Parish, Louisiana 219
Diether, Lawrence, Carmelite, Prior Provincial 225
Dingelfing, Germany 9
Dinkelsbuhl, Germany, Carmelite house suppressed 5
Discalced Carmelite, sponsors of Irish Carmelite Brothers 102
Domenec, Michael, bishop of Pittsburgh 96
Douglas County, Kansas, Mission Churches 217
Driessen, Hilarion, Carmelite apostatized 51
Drummondsville, Ontario, mission accepted by Carmelites 104
Duell, Anselm, Carmelite, arrives in Paducah, Kentucky 85, ordination of 86
Duffy, Owen, benefactor, 101
Duggan, James, bishop of Chicago 53, withdraws offer of house in Chicago 53
Dunn, Rev. William J., preaches at laying of cornerstone of St. Cecilia's, Louisville 89
Durbin, Fr. Elisha, circuit rider 85, Kentucky church builder 86, 115
Dutch Province of Carmelites requests for Knoll, 15, Chocataw Indian Mission 221
Dwyer, Angelus, Carmelite 79, leaves Upper Marlboro, Maryland for Paducah, Kentucky 110, leaves Order 111, joins secular clergy 121

E

Eberhardt, Rev., Redemptorist 49
Eddy (Carlsbad), New Mexico, St. Edward Parish 221
Edenhoefer, Simon, Carmelite 15, to Pesth, Hungary 16, 41, 44, 47, attempt to return to Straubing 53, 77
Eiremann, Mr., offered free living quarters to Anastasius Smits 117
Elder, William Henry, bishop of Natchez, Mississippi during epidemic of 1878 113
Elian ideal in Carmelite Order 26
Elijah, on Mount Carmel 26

Index 237

Elizabeth Town, Kansas, Mission Church 217
Ellis, Rev. John Tracy x
Emancipation Proclamation, The, its impact on Church life 77
Emerald, Kansas, mission of Scipio 44, St. Patrick's Parish 101, 217
Encino, California, Crespi Carmelite High School 222
Encino, California, Our Lady of Mount Carmel Priory 222
Engleton, Thomas, Rev. viii
Englewood, Florida, St. Raphael Parish 223
Englewood, New Jersey, given to Carmelites by Bishop Bayley 54, Kentucky missions joined to 115, mission of Fort Lee 116, life in 117, stats in, 1890 148, land purchased for new church 173, 217
Englewood, New Jersey, St. Cecilia Priory 219
Ensuring the Welfare of the Negro, see *De Nigrorum Salute Procuranda* 78
Eudora, Kansas, Mission Church 39, 101, 217
Eureka, Kansas 39

F

Fairfield, California, Our Lady of Mount Carmel Parish 223
Faley Reservation, site of first church in Tenafly 120
Falls View (Niagara Falls), Ontario, parish accepted by Carmelites, 104, Our Lady of Peace Monastery 218 *see also* Our Lady of Peace, Niagara Falls, Ontario
Fancy Farm, Kentucky, St. Jerome Parish Carmelites assume parochial duties for 85, 1871 Confirmation statistic 86, served by Sisters of the Third Order of St. Francis of the Immaculate Conception of the Blessed Virgin Mary 90, stats of parish after Meagher's death 114, 218
Faver Ranch, Texas, Mission Station 220
Feehan, Cyril, Carmelite 79, associate pastor of parish in Louisville 88, subdeacon at first mass celebrated in new St. Cecilia's, Louisville 90, becomes pastor of St. Cecilia's parish, Louisville 91, at Hickman, Kentucky 112, re-opens Paducah academy 112, activities of 114, appointed prior of Paducah, Kentucky *ad nutum* 114, transfers to Niagara Falls 120, in Our Lady of Peace, Niagara Falls, Ontario, community 129, member of 1st provincial chapter 133, work on mission band 169
Feehan, Fr. Richard, brother of Cyril, 115
Fink, Bernard, Carmelite 52, arrives in Paducah, Kentucky 85, 98, member of 1st provincial chapter 133
Fink, Louis, bishop of Leavenworth, Kansas 76, 102, comments on the Carmelites 102-103
First Plenary Council of Baltimore on Catholic education 118
Fisch, Fr. William 37
Flaget, Benedict, bishop of Louisville 34
Flos, Ontario, mission, Beerhorst responsible for 103
Formation, resolutions concerning at organizational meeting in 1889 148
Forrestal, Fr., Carmelite, problems at Paducah, Kentucky 111, death of 121

Fort Davis, Texas, St. Joseph Parish turned over to diocese 137, 220
Fort Lee, New Jersey 54, removed from care of Carmelites 117
Fort Stockton, Texas, St. Joseph Parish 220
Franklin County, Kansas, mission of Scipio 39, 44
Franz Joseph, Hapsburg king 18
Freeman's Journal 171
Freiburg, University of 4
French Revolution 3, 5
Fritz, Louis, Carmelite 7, actions as prior 9-11, 13, 15-18, 24, 45
Fuhrwerk, Andreas, Carmelite, moved to Texas 142
Fulton County, Kentucky, St. Patrick Parish responsibility of ministry assumed by Carmelites 85, 218

G

Galicia, Province of 6
Galli, Aloysius Maria, prior general, sends visitator to Marienfeld, Texas 148, 165
Gallo-Belgium, Carmelite Province of 5
Garesche, SJ, preaches at ceremony to lay cornerstone for new church in Leavenworth, Kansas 74
Garnett, Kansas *see* Richmond, Kansas 222
General Chapter of 1838 5
General Chapter of 1856 6, 12
General Chapter of 1889 6, 148
Geneva, Kansas, Mission Church 217
German Carmelites, object to Anastasius Smits as Commissary 123
German immigration to America 42
Gibbons, James, Cardinal vicar apostolic of North Carolina, performs confirmation at Cumberland, Maryland 81, 151
Gilmore, Brendan, Carmelite Prior Provincial x, 225
Gilmore, Rev. Bonaventure viii
Glendale, Arizona, St. Raphael Parish 223
Glendale Heights, Illinois, St. Matthew Parish 223
Gloster, Louisiana, Mission Station 220
Goodwin, Rev. Aeneas, editor of *Carmelite Review* 171, dismissed as editor 172
Goor, Baptist, Carmelite, member of Scipio, Kansas, community 67
Gordon, Rev. Edward, at Falls View, Ontario parish 104
Gozowsky, Joseph, OCD, first pastor at New Baltimore, Pennsylvania 84
Graham, Eliza G., donation to Carmelites at Upper Marlboro, Maryland 79, 88
Gravelpoint, Louisiana, Mission Station 220
Graves County, Kentucky, ministry responsibility assumed by Carmelites 85
Greeley, Kansas, St. John the Baptist Church mission of Scipio 44, 101, 217
Greineder, Marina, Sister, Ursuline sister 27
Grennan, Fr., Carmelite, sent from Ireland to Niagara 108
Grief, John, home used for religious services 85
Grove City, Florida, St. Francis of Assisi Parish 224

Guardian Angel Parish, Garnett, Kansas 217
Guenther, Louis (Kilian), Carmelite, student at Latrobe, Pennsylvania 29, joining the Carmelites 38-39, profession 44, novitiate experience 45, leaves for Cumberland 47, anxious to return to Kansas 50, returns to Kansas 53, given charge of Kansas parish 74, 75, pastor in Leavenworth 99, sent as visitator to New Baltimore and Pittsburgh 121, member of 1st provincial chapter 133, member of 2nd provincial chapter, 135, member of 3rd provincial chapter 137, returns to Scipio as superior 142
Gurnee, Illinois, St. Paul the Apostle Parish 224

H

Hamilton, Diocese of, offer to Carmelites 148
Hamilton, Massachusetts, Carmelite Junior Seminary 222
Handl, Thomas, Carmelite, sent to Poxau, Germany 15
Harris, V. Rev. Dean 164, lead pilgrimage to Niagara 167
Harry, William J, Carmelite, Prior Provincial 225
Hegewisch, Illinois, St. Columba Parish 221
Heilbronn, Germany, Carmelite house supressed 5
Heilmeyer, Victor, Carmelite, member of Scipio, Kansas community 67
Heimann, Albert (Joseph), Carmelite, joined Carmelites 38, comments on collecting money in America 41, profession and assignment at Leavenworth 44, on community life on Kansas frontier 45, 63, 73, plan to remove Kansas from Knoll's control 74, plans for Carmelites in Leavenworth and views of Knoll's leadership 75, named superior of Kansas Carmelites and directly resposible to prior general 76, efforts to build formation house and plans for Scipio 98, move to Scipio 99, correspondence with archbishop of Toronto 103, sends Pius Mayer to Niagara 107, reassessment of Kansas dreams 108, visit to Knoll in Butler, Pennsylvania 108, leaves Kansas for Niagara 109, as novice master and acting prior in Niagara Falls 109, member of 1st provincial chapter and appointed definitor 133, appointed second definitor 149, allegedly received promise from Bishop Lynch 159, death of 173
Heitzer, Peter, Carmelite 6-7, portrait of 59
Helmpraecht, Rev., provincial of Redemptorists 45, reasons for selling Cumberland 47, 52
Hennepin, Fr. chaplain to early explorers of Niagara peninsula 104, celebrates first Mass above the Niagara River 104
Hermosa, Texas, Mission Station 220
Heyden, Rev. Thomas, officiated at dedication of New Baltimore church 84
Hickman County, Kentucky, ministry responsibility of Carmelites 85
Hickman, Kentucky, St. Bridget Parish Carmelites assume parochial duties for 85, 1871 Confirmation statistic 86, statistics for Yellow Fever epidemic of 1878 112, stats of at the time of Meagher's death 114, 218
Hinde, Canisius Peter, Carmelite x
History of the Catholic Church in the Niagara Peninsula (book) by Dean Harris 164

Hoban, Paul, Carmelite, Prior Provincial 225
Hoffmann, Anselm, Carmelite 13, 15, to Pesth 16
Hogl, Bernard, on character of Xavier Huber 27
Holy Cross, Kansas, mission of Scipio 101
Holy Roman Empire 4
Holy Rosary Mission Church, Rosaryville, Maryland 218
Holy Trinity Church, Pittsburgh, Pennsylvania, offered to Carmelites 96, description of 96-97, laying of cornerstone and dedication 97, Knoll erects monastery 98, refuses to contribute to new monastery in Scipio 121, concerns over paying for Scipio house 122, financial status in 1890 150, new church an school built 173, 218
Holy Trinity Monastery, Pittsburgh, Pennsylvania site of 1st provincial chapter 133, 218, 224
Homestead Act of 1862 43
Horarium, Straubing 8
Hospice of Mount Carmel, Niagara Falls, Ontario ix-x, photo of 131, approval by archbishop and fundraising 151-152, cash for construction of used on buying land 163, first year 165, 218, *see also* Mount Carmel Monastery, Niagara Falls, Ontario
Houston, Texas, Casa Santa Teresita Formation House 223
Houston, Texas, Mount Carmel High School 222
Houston, Texas, Our Lady of Mount Carmel Parish 222
Houston, Texas, St. Albert of Trapani Parish 223
Houston, Texas, St. Bernadette Soubirous Parish 223
Huber, Xavier, Carmelite i-iii, 7, ordination of 8, to Poxau, Germany 15, to Pesth 16, chaplain in Sossau, Germany 23, biographical information 26, character of and decision to go to America 27, charge against Huber 27, 31, in Louisville, Kentucky 34, pastoral work at St. Joseph's, Sellersburg, Indiana 35, back in Indiana 38, to Europe to obtain funds 41, collection of alms for Leavenworth, Kansas 47, anxious to return to Kansas 50, dependence upon for alms 50, banished to Kansas 51, report to prior general about Knoll 51, angers archbishop of New York 54, picture of St. Joseph parish in Sellersburg, Indiana 63, directed to Cumberland, Maryland, and restored to fundraising role 74, visit to archbishop of Toronto, Ontario 103
Hughes, John, archbishop of New York and comments on the scapular 164
Humboldt, Kansas, Mission Church 101, 217

I

Iatan, Texas, St. Joseph Mission 219
Ida, Kansas, Mission Church 217
Immaculate Conception Parish, Leavenworth, Kansas 223
Immaculate Conception Parish, Norwood, New Jersey 221
Imperial Diet 4
Ingersoll, Robert, visit to Niagara Falls and comments againt the Church 163-164

Iola, Kansas, Mission Church 217
Ireland, John, archbishop of St. Paul, Minnesota 83
Ireland, Carmelite Province of 5, 6
Irish Carmelite Brothers in Clondalkin 102, sponsored by the Discalced Carmelites in Ireland 102
Iroquois theatre fire, article in *New Carmelite Review* 172
Italy, State of Order in 1832 in 5

J

Jackson, Andrew, general, United States Army, purchased land in Western Kentucky from Indians 85
Jackson Purchase, Kentucky, Carmelites given ministry responsibility for 85
Jansen, Benno, Carmelite, arrives in Paducah, Kentucky 85, death of 86, death in Kentucky 121
Janssens, Francis archbishop of New Orleans 151
Jesuits, founders of the Osage Catholic mission 39
John of the Cross, Carmelite saint 26
Johnson County, Kansas mission of Scipio 39
Joliet Catholic Academy, Joliet, Illinois 223
Joliet Catholic High School, Joliet, Illinois 221
Joliet, Illinois, Joliet Catholic Academy 223
Joliet, Illinois, Joliet Catholic High School 221
Joliet, Illinois, Parroquia de Nuestra Senora del Carmen 222
Joliet, Illinois, St. Bernard Parish 221
Joliet, Illinois, St. Elias Priory 221
Joliet, Illinois, St. Mary Carmelite Parish 221
Joliet, Illinois, St. Stephen Hungarian Chapel and Mission 221
Josepha, Mother, Ursuline sister 23
Joyce, Fr., celebrates first mass in new St. Cecilia's church in Louisville 90
Judy, Myron, Carmelite v, 227
Juhel, Rev. Victor, expands St. Edward's church building, Falls View, Ontario 104
Juliana, virgin 15

K

Kahler, Basil, Carmelite, mission band work 168, characteristics of 168, Prior Provincial 225
Kammer, Aloysius, Carmelite, associate pastor in Paducah, Kentucky 85-87
Kansas, put under Smits' responsibility 122
Karmeliten Geist, provincial chapter agrees to produce 138, project of and patent for 144, directions for using 145, 147
Kauffmann, Rev. Joseph, pastor of Holy Trinity parish, Pittsburgh, Pennsylvania 97
Keber, Anton, Carmelite, moves to Texas 142
Keening, Rev. Leander, preaches dedication of St. Cecilia's church, Louisville 91

Kehoe, Cyril, Carmelite, member of Our Lady of Peace, Niagara Falls, Ontario, community 129, member of 2nd provincial chapter and elected to definitory 135, member of 3rd provincial chapter 137, works on mission band 169

Keller, Rev. B. 34

Kempen, Angelus, Carmelite, 41, ordination of 44, stationed at Scipio, Kansas 45, move to secularization 51, joins Anastasius Smits at Englewood, New Jersey 117, receives dispensation from vows 117, joined secular clergy 121

Kenrick, Francis, bishop of Philadelphia, describes New Baltimore, Pennsylvania 84

Kentucky Commissariat, reason for failure 90, foundations 93, situation of following Meagher's death 114, reasons for ceasing 115

Kentucky, statistics of Carmelites in 120

Kerschner, Elias, Carmelite, to Poxau, Germany 15

Kieffer, Raphael, Carmelite, Prior Provincial 225

Kingston, Ontario, Diocese of, as high school, novitiate and scholasticate 148

Kino Institute, Phoenix, Arizona 223

Kirchenreuth, Germany, birthplace of Xavier Huber 27

Kirschner, Elias, Carmelite 13

Knocktopher, Ireland, Carmelite College of the Immaculate Conception 51, 91

Knoll, Cyril (John) i-iii, vii-viii, 1, 3-4, 8-9, re-entry into Carmel 9, appointed vicar prior of Straubing 10, as prior 11, appeal to Cardinal Primate of Hungary 12, letter to King of Bavaria 13, 14-15, on Poxau, Germany 15, feeling about Straubing 16, reaction to Pesth 16, 17, 20-21, initiates plan for American foundations 23, 24-25, first impressions of New York 28, 31, in Louisville 34, decision to leave Louisville 35, on arriving at Miege's residence 35, on St. Joseph's parish 35, first impression of Leavenworth 38, appeal of Order on frontier 40, Leavenworth construction plans 40, attempts to foster interior life 40, view on American Catholicism 41, leaves for Cumberland 47, Xavier Huber complaints about his purchase of Cumberland, Maryland 51, idea of ideal candidates 51, 52, problems with candidates accepted by 53, view on Leavenworth, Kansas 74, removed from responsibility for Kansas 76, rumors of his resignation as commissary 76, improvements to Cumberland 79, devotions at Cumberland, Maryland 80, improvements at Cumberland 80, request for Ursuline nuns at Cumberland, Maryland 80, difficulties at Cumberland, Maryland 82, reasons for leaving Cumberland, Maryland 83, 87, relationship with prior general 87, views on Meagher 87, Kentucky and Marlboro officially removed from Knoll's responsibility 91, reflections to prior general on Carmel in America 95, offered Holy Trinity parish and arrival at 96, comments on himself as formator 98, visit of Albert Heimann in 1879 108, Anastasius Scipio placed under in 1879 109, suggests Smits as head of Commissariate of Kentucky, New Jersey, and Niagara Falls 120, financial irregularities of 121, named to definitory of province 133, appointed first definitor of province 149, death of 173, Commissary Provincial 225

Koehler, Peter, Carmelite 15, disciplining of Huber 27

Koenig, Leander, Carmelite second rector at Scipio, Kansas 100, 102, 104, dismissed from the Order 107

Konz, John, Scipio, Kansas, farmer interested in Texas settlement 142

Krebs, Francis, Carmelite, work on mission band 169

Kreidt, Anastasius, Carmelite, arrives in Paducah, Kentucky 85, recalling bishop of Louisville's refusal to make guarantees to the Carmelites about status at St. Cecilia's parish 110, recalling prior general's reaction to sale of Cumberland 111-112, arrival in Paducah 113, relationship with Peter Thomas Meagher 113, written memorial to Meagher at his death 113, follow-up letter to prior general about appointing a superior 114, sent to Hickman, Kentucky, by Feehan 114, writes prior general after death of Meagher 114, moves to Englewood, New Jersey 120, member of 1st provincial chapter and selected assistant provincial 133, appointed provincial chronicler 134, member of 2nd provincial chapter 135, directed to take loan to complete hospice 136, member of 3rd provincial chapter and made presiding officer of chapter 137, elected provincial 138, appointed assistant provincial 149, fundraising for Niagara Falls hospice 151, prior of Niagara, Falls, Ontario 151, efforts of sisters towards fundraising for Niagara Falls hospice 152, employs Protestant solicitor in conflict with archbishop of Toronto, Ontario 153, accepts offer of land at Niagara Falls, Ontario 163, ministry of, against anti-Catholics 163-164, comments about 164, collection for Niagara Falls hospice 164, elected provincial 165, and the travelling mission band 168, named to head the mission band 169, develops ministry of written communications 170, Prior Provincial 225

Kuhls, Fr. Anton 37

Kulturkampf 4, 96

L

Ladies of Loretto (Loretto Sisters), establish convent in Niagara Falls, Ontario 106

Lager, Angelus, Carmelite, at 2nd provincial chapter

Laigneil, Rev. Aloysius, named rector of Scipio, Kansas, college 100, leaves Scipio, Kansas 100

Lajitas, Texas, Mission Station 220

La Meta, Texas, Toyah Creek Settlement Mission 219

La Salle, French explorer 104

Latin language, required knowledge of 150

Lauzau, Berthold, member of Our Lady of Peace, Niagara Falls, Ontario, community 129, member of 3rd provincial chapter 137, work on mission band 169

Lavialle, Peter J., 3rd bishop of Louisville, Kentucky 35

Lawrence, Kansas, St. John the Evangelist Church 39, 217

Leavenworth, status of Catholic church in 37, description of 37, Knoll's consideration of leaving 50, 73, placed under Knoll in 1879 109, monastery and land to be sold 136, stats in, 1890 148, Immaculate Conception Parish

223
Leipold, Wendelina, Ursuline sister 27
Leipzig, Germany 3-4
Lenarkiewicz, Alexis, Carmelite sent to USA 44
Leonia, New Jersey, St. John Parish 221
Leopolinen Stiftung 101
Leo XIII, attempts to increase devotion to Our Lady of Mount Carmel 165
Lickteig, Mr. and Mrs. A. x
Lickteig, Franz, Carmelite x
Lima, Perú, Casa San Elias Formation House 223
Lima, Perú, Convento del Carmen 222
Lindio, Texas, Mission Station 219
Link, Felix, Carmelite 100
Lobina, Joseph, prior general 6, 10
Lofehl, Laurent, contractor 19
Lonaconing, Maryland, mission of Cumberland, St. Mary Parish 49, 217
Longinqua Oceani, encyclical of Leo XIII 171
Loreto, Pennsylvania 83
Loretto, Sisters of, founders of Osage Catholic mission 39
Los Angeles, California, Carmel West House of Studies 223
Los Angeles, California, Mount Carmel High School 222
Los Angeles, California, Mount Carmel Priory 223
Los Angeles, California, St. Raphael Parish 221
Louisville, Kentucky iii, arrival of Ursuline sisters at 23, 24, 28, 31, in 1864 33, during Civil War 33, diocese of, state of in 1864 34, in 1848, Catholic community of 34, 71, diocese of 83, Carmelites given responsibility for Western Kentucky 85, diocese of, Carmelite return to 85, description of in 1873 88, 91
Louisville, Kentucky, DeSales High School 222
Louisville, Kentucky, DeSales Priory 222
Louisville, Kentucky, Our Lady of Mt. Carmel Parish 222
Louisville, Kentucky, St. Cecilia Parish 218
Loving, Texas, Mission Chapel 219
Lower German Province 4
Ludwig I, king 7, portrait 59
Ludwig Missionsverein 27, aid to St. Joseph's parish in Leavenworth 37, 40-41, 44, 47, 48, requested to help build new church in Leavenworth 74, 101, requested to pay dept on St. Joseph's church, Leavenworth 121
Lurin, Perú, Casa de Retiros "Villa Carmelitas" 224
Lurin, Perú, Noviciado Carmelita 224
Lynch, John, archbishop of Toronto, ideas of Niagara frontier 102, plans for Niagara frontier 105, issues pastoral letter welcoming Carmelites to diocese 106, view of Carmelites ministry in Niagara frontier 106, conflict with Carmelites over ownership of land in Niagara Falls, Ontario 152-163

Index 245

M

Madonna Church, Fort Lee, New Jersey 116
Maher, Fr., attempt to found Chicago house in 1868 53, 55
Mahwah, New Jersey, Carmel Retreat 222
Maier, Joseph, Carmelite 11, 15, qualifications for prior 16, 17, work with 3rd Order of St. Francis 17-18, 24, 45
Malaga, Texas, Mission Chapel 219
Malley, John, Carmelite, Prior Provincial 225
Mallia, Angelus, Carmelite 108
Mansfield, Louisiana, Mission Station 220
Marathon, Texas, St. Mary Mission 220
Marfa, Texas, St. Mary Mission 220
Marian devotion and Carmelite Order 26
Marienfeld (Stanton), Texas, Most Pure Heart of Mary Monastery 3rd provincial chapter decision on 137, 219
Marienfeld (Stanton), Texas, St. Joseph Parish 3rd provincial chapter decision on 137, 219
Markelz, Carl, Carmelite, Prior Provincial 225
Marlboro, Maryland 95, statistics of Carmelites in 120 *see also* Upper Marlboro, Maryland 83
Marshall County, Kentucky, ministry responsibility of Carmelites 85
Marshall County, Kansas, mission of Scipio 44
Mary Boniface, Ursuline sister, sent to Cumberland, Maryland 80
Mary Magdalene de' Pazzi, Carmelite saint 26
Mary Margaret, Ursuline sister, sent to Cumberland, Maryland 80
Mary Xavier, Ursuline sister, sent to Cumberland, Maryland 80
Maurer, Augustine, Carmelite, member of Scipio, Kansas, community 67
Maximilian IV, king 4, 7
Mayer, Aloysius, Carmelite appointment to St. Boniface, Kansas 39
Mayer, Pius, Carmelite, gives reason for leaving Pesth 22, reflections on Cumberland, Maryland 51, vicar to Heimann at Niagara Falls, Ontario 73, 101, visitation of Niagara Falls, Ontario 107, appointed vicar-prior of Niagara Falls, Ontario 107, preaching and parish missions 108, 109, pictured at New Baltimore, Pennsylvania 127, member of 1st provincial chapter and appointed prior provincial 133, member of 2nd provincial chapter and elected provincial 135, member of 3rd provincial chapter 137, elected delegate to general chapter and definitor of province to general chapter 138, named general commissary in 1886 146, goals for Commissariat 146, description of 146, relation with Archbishop of Toronto, Ontario 147, named Titular Provincial of Saxony 147, organizational meeting in 1887 147, meeting of superiors in 1889 147, at General Chapter of 1890 148, named prior provincial 149, conflict with Archbishop Lynch over ownership of land in Niagara Falls, Ontario 152-163, work on the mission band 167-168, 224, Commissary Provincial 225, Prior Provincial 225
Mayer, Rev. Rudolph, *see* Mayer, Pius

Mayfield, Kentucky Carmelites assume the parochial duties for 85
McAvoy, Rev. Thomas viii, x
McCarthy, Leo, Carmelite, Prior Provincial 225
McCloskey, Cardinal, refuses Carmelite presence in New York 54,
McCloskey, William, bishop of Louisville, conditions for Carmelites 87, gives Carmelites parish in Louisville 88, recipient of land for new parish 89, lays cornerstone for St. Cecilia's parish, Louisville 89, leaves with Meagher for Ireland 90, affiliated to the Order 91, declines to assure Carmelites of permanent stay at St. Cecilia's, Louisville 110
McCracken County, Kentucky, responsibility for given to Carmelites 85
McDonald, John, Carmelite at Englewood, New Jersey 120
McDonald, Stephen J., appointed editor of *New Carmelite Review* 172
McDonald, Theodore, Carmelite, ii, 51, 53-55, part of Heimann's plan for Leavenwoth 75, 77, pastor of St. Cecilia Parish in Louisville, Kentucky 88, name on cornerstone of St. Cecilia's parish 89, assisting deacon at first mass celebrated in St. Cecilia's, Louisville 90, moves to Fancy Farm, Kentucky 91, on Catholic school at Tenafly, NJ 119, supports charges against Knoll 121, member of 2nd provincial chapter and elected delegate to general chapter 135, member of 3rd provincial chapter 137, elected as definitor 138, work on mission band 168
McGonigle, James, on Bishop Miege 36
McHale, Fr., led pilgrimage to Niagara Falls, Ontario 167
McMahon, Patrick, vicar general of diocese of Pittsburgh, lays cornerstone for Holy Trinity parish 97
McMaster, James A. 171
Meagher, Meagher, Peter Thomas, Carmelite 51, 53, acceptance of Upper Marlboro, Maryland 54, part of Heimann's plan for Leavenworth 75, named local superior of Kansas Carmelites 75, rumors of Knoll's resignation as commissary 76, comments on leaving Cumberland for Upper Marlboro, Maryland 77, superior in Paducah, Kentucky 85, 86-88, awarded Doctor of Divinity degree 87, acting pastor of Cumberland, Maryland 87, attacked by Yellow Fever 87, 1874 trip to Europe 89, appointed commissary general for Kentucky 91, report to prior general on St. Cecilia's, Louisville 110, discovers financial irregularities 111, effects of Yellow Fever attack 112-113, relationship with Anastasius Kreidt 113, death of 113, memorial editiorial on 113, 121
Medonte, Ontario, mission Beerhorst is responsible for 103
Merry del Val, Cardinal visits hospice in Niagara Falls, Ontario 165
Merthys Tydvill, South Wales 52
Messmer, Rev. Sebastian Genhard, advised Anastasius Smits to secularize 116
Methodists, impact on missions at Upper Marlboro, Maryland 77
Metzler, Vincent, Carmelite, work on mission band 169
Mexico City, Mexico, Casa del Carmen Formation House 224
Miami County, Kansas, mission of Scipio 44
Midland, Texas, St. Ann Parish 219

Index 247

Miege, John Baptist, vicar apostolic, Bishop of Leavenworth 29, 35, description of 36, reaction to possible move of Carmelites 44, affiliated to Order 44, pleads with Knoll 50, 52, lays cornerstone of church in Leavenworth 74, informed of Knoll's resignation as commissary at Vatican I 76

Mill Hill Fathers, 79, assume responsibility for Marlboro, Maryland, missions 110

Mills, Frank J., "station" in home that was ministered from Fort Lee, New Jersey 116

Milwaukee, Wisconsin, Carmel Hall College Formation Program 223

Mineral Point, Kansas, St. Mary Parish 217

Miraflores, Lima, Perú, *see* Lima, Perú 222

Mission Band, iii, members participating 167-168, principle means of support for province in 1903 169, rules and regulations 169

Mission Chapel, Barstow, Texas 219

Mission Chapel, Loving, Texas 219

Mission Chapel, Malaga, Texas 219

Mission Chapel, Odessa, Texas 219

Mission Chapel, Red Bluff, Texas 219

Mission Chapel, Roswell, Texas 219

Mission Chapel, Van Horn, Texas 219

Mission Chapel, Weed, Texas 219

Mission Station, Alamito Ranch, Texas 220

Mission Station, Alamito, Texas 220

Mission Station, Baracho Rancho, Texas 220

Mission Station, Boquillas, Texas 220

Mission Station, Casa Piedras, Texas 220

Mission Station, Castalon, Texas 220

Mission Station, Chisos, Texas 220

Mission Station, Faver Ranch, Texas 220

Mission Station, Hermosa, Texas 220

Mission Station, Lajitas, Texas 220

Mission Station, Pulvo, Texas 220

Mission Station, Ranch de la Cruz, Texas 220

Mission Station, San Esteban, Texas 220

Mission Station, San Jose, Texas 220

Mission Station, San Vicente, Texas 220

Mission Station, Study Butte, Texas 220

Mission Station, Terlingua Abaja 220

Mission Station, Terlingua, Texas 220

Mission Station, Valentine, Texas 220

Mississauga, California, St. John of the Cross Parish 223

Moerland, left the Order 146

Moore, Rev. Kenneth, Carmelite x

Morgan, John 33

Most Pure Heart of Mary Monastery, Marienfeld (Stanton), Texas 3rd provincial chapter decision on 137, 219

Most Pure Heart of Mary, province of, vii, viii, first provincial chapter 133-134, second provincial chapter 135-136, third provincial chapter 137-138, status of at 3rd provincial chapter 137, established 148-149, first provincial chapter held 149, proposals of first PCM provincial chapter, 149-151, provincial chapter of 1896, held at hospice 165, statistics of 173,
Mount Carmel, Palestine 26
Mount Carmel Cemetery, Paducah, Kentucky 112, 218
Mount Carmel Cemetery, Tenafly, New Jersey 219
Mount Carmel College, Chicago, Illinois 173
Mount Carmel High School, Chicago, Illinois 221
Mount Carmel High School, Houston, Texas 222
Mount Carmel High School, Los Angeles, California 222
Mt. Carmel Monastery, Niagara Falls, Ontario 73, 93, Carmelite's preferred location in archdiocese of Toronto 104, original monastery 108, ecclesiastical barn, overflow building for sleeping 108, Kentucky missions joined to 115, too small in 1878 147, used as novitiate 147, stats in, 1890 148, novitiate transferred from to New Baltimore 150, conflict with Archbishop of Toronto 152-163; pilgrimages to 167, 218
Mount Carmel Priory, Los Angeles, California 223
Mount Carmel/St. Boniface Priory-Scipio, Kansas picture of 67, 217
Mount Ida, Kansas, St. Joseph Parish 217
Mount St. Joseph, Clondalkin, Ireland 102
Muller, Rev. Michael, Redemptorist 46
Mundelein, Illinois, Carmel High School 223
Munster, University of 4
Murphy, Albert, Carmelite 91, pastor at Fancy Farm, Kentucky 112, writes prior general after death of Meagher 114, transfers to Niagara Falls, Ontario 120, member of 1st provincial chapter 133
Murphy, Brocard, Carmelite 79, arrives in Paducah, Kentucky 85, ordained 86, death of 87, remains transferred to Mount Carmel Cemetery, Paducah, Kentucky 112

N

Nablus, Palestine, Our Lady of Mount Carmel American Mission 221
Napoleon 3, 4
Native American Mission, Antlers, Indian Territory (Oklahoma) 221
Nayhurst, Rev. John, 34
Nemaha County, Kansas, mission of Scipio 44
Neosho Falls, Kansas, Mission Church 217
Neosho Rapids, Kansas, Mission Church 217
Neubau, Germany, mission served by Cyril Knoll 9
Neumann, John C.S.S.R, saint, book about ix
Neustadt an der Saale, Germany, Carmelite house suppressed 5

Index 249

Newark, New Jersey, diocese of, status of in 1850s 117
New Athens, Illinois, St. Agatha Parish 221
New Baltimore, Pennsylvania description of 83-84
New Baltimore, Pennsylvania, St. John the Baptist Monastery 96, 98, novitiate transferred by provincial chapter 134, students moved to 147, stats in, 1890 148, need to enlarge as house of studies 148, expansion of 150, novitiate transferred to 150, new addition to house completed 173, 218, 224
New Baltimore, Pennsylvania, St. John the Baptist Parish new brick rectory in 1873 95, Anastasius Peter pastor of 109, new church built 173, 218
New Carlisle, Indiana, Camp Carmel 221
New Carmelite Review, Chicago publication of *Carmelite Review* 171, editorial vision for 172, subscribers reaction 172, problems with 173
New Germany (Snyder), Ontario, St. Joseph Parish 219
Newman, John Cardinal xi
Newport News, Virginia, Our Lady of Mount Carmel Parish 222
Niagara Falls, Ontario, Mt. Carmel Monastery/Our Lady of Peace Monastery 73, 93, Carmelite's preferred location in archdiocese of Toronto 104, original monastery 108, ecclesiastical barn, overflow building for sleeping 108, Kentucky missions joined to 115, photograph of original building 129, photograph of Carmelite community in 1883 129, community novitiate changed from by provincial chapter 134, too small in 1878 147, used as novitiate 147, stats in, 1890 148, novitiate transferred from to New Baltimore 150, conflict with Archbishop of Toronto 152; pilgrimages to Niagara 167, 218
Niagara Falls, Ontario, Our Lady of Peace Parish/Shrine name change 105, photograph of in 1937 131, 218
Niagara Falls, Ontario, St. Ann Parish 221
Niagara Falls, Ontario, St. Patrick Parish 218
Niagara-on-the-Lake, Ontario, St. Vincent de Paul Parish 219
Nokomis, Florida, Carmel at Mission Valley 224
North Hollywood, California, St. Jane Frances de Chantal Parish 223
Northvale, New Jersey, becomes separate parish 120
Norwood, New Jersey, becomes separate parish 120, Immaculate Conception Parish 221
Nothaas, chaplain at Sossau 12
Notre Dame University viii, x
Noviciado Carmelita, Lurin, Perú 224
Nuestra Senora del Carmen, Joliet, Illinois 222

O

Oakland, Maryland, mission of Cumberland 49, St. Peter the Apostle Parish 217
Obermuller, Joseph, testimony about Xavier (Joseph) Huber 27
O'Brien, Romaeus, Carmelite x
O'Connor, Michael, bishop, dedicated Holy Trinity church, Pittsburgh, Pennsylvania 97

O'Connor, Denis, archishop of Toronto, blesses hospice at Niagara Falls, Ontario 165, heads pilgrimage to Niagara Falls, Ontario 167
O'Connor, Richard A, bishop, preaches at dedication of hospice at Niagara Falls, Ontario 165
Odessa, Texas, Mission Chapel 219
Ojo, Texas, Mission of Marienfeld 219
Olathe, Kansas, mission of Scipio 44
O'Malley, Dominic, Carmelite 114, member of 1st provincial chapter and named to definitory 133, member of 2nd provincial chapter 135, member of 3rd provincial chapter 137, selected as assistant provincial 138
O'Neill, Matthew, Carmelite, Prior Provincial 225
O'Reilly, Rev. 49
Osage, Kansas, Catholic mission 39
Osprey, Florida, Our Lady of Mount Carmel Parish 224
Ottawa, Kansas, mission of Scipio, Kansas 44, 101
Ottawa, Ontario, St. Andrew Corsini Parish 222
Ottumwa, Kansas, Mission Church 217
Our Catholic Heritage in Texas ix
Our Lady of Mount Carmel American Mission, Nablus, Palestine 221
Our Lady of Mount Carmel, devotion to iii
Our Lady of Mount Carmel House of Studies, San Diego, California 223
Our Lady of Mount Carmel Parish, Darien, Illinois 223
Our Lady of Mount Carmel Parish, Fairfield, California 223
Our Lady of Mount Carmel Parish, Houston, Texas 222
Our Lady of Mount Carmel Parish, Osprey, Florida 224
Our Lady of Mount Carmel Parish, Tenafly, sisters assigned to Catholic school of 119, 219, parish boundaries 120
Our Lady of Mount Carmel Parish, Warwick (Newport News), Virginia 222
Our Lady of Mount Carmel Priory, Encino, California 222
Our Lady of Mount Carmel Priory, Tucson, Arizona 222
Our Lady of Mt. Carmel Parish, Louisville, Kentucky 222
Our Lady of Peace Parish/Shrine, Niagara Falls, Ontario, story of the shrine 104-105, name change 105, photograph of original building 129, photograph of Carmelite community in 1883 129, photograph of church in 1937 131, annual pilgrimage 165, granted indulgence 166, pilgrimage described 167, 218
Our Lady of Peace Mission, Alpine, Texas 220
Our Lady of Peace Monastery, Falls View, Ontario 218 *see also* Mount Carmel Monastery
Our Lady of Perpetual Help Mission, Candelaria, Texas 220
Our Lady of Perpetual Help Mission, Pittsburgh, Pennsylvania 222
Our Lady of Perpetual Help Retreat and Spiritual Center, Venice, Florida 224
Our Lady of the Scapular Mission, 222
Our Lady of the Scapular Priory, Peabody, Massachusetts 223
Our Lady of Victories or of Peace, Niagara Falls, Ontario, name change 105

Index

Owl Creek, Kansas, Mission Church 101, 217
Oxford, Louisiana, Mission Station 220
Oxon Hill, Maryland, mission from Upper Marlboro, Maryland 77, St. Ignatius Church 218

P

Paducah, Kentucky, St. Francis DeSales Catholic church in 85-86, Carmelite school for boys 86-87, 1871 confirmation statistic 86, 91, 95
Paducah Daily News, memorial editiorial on Peter Thomas Meagher, O. Carm. 113
Paducah, Kentucky, Mt. Carmel Cemetery 218
Paducah, Kentucky, St. Francis de Sales Parish 218
Paducah, Kentucky, St. Francis de Sales Priory 218
Paducah, Kentucky, description of 85
Panzer, Herman, priest, pastor of St. Joseph Church, St. Joseph's Hill, Indiana 38
Paramus, New Jersey, St. Therese Chapel 223
Passionist Fathers, served at Fort Lee, New Jersey for a time 117
Peabody, Massachusetts, Our Lady of the Scapular Priory 223
Peabody, Massachusetts, St. Therese Chapel 222
Pecos, Texas, St. Catherine Parish 219
Pennsylvania, put under Anastasius Smits responsibility 122
Perryville, Battle of 33
Pesth (Pest), Hungary foundation at 15-17, first years at 18-20, and effects of nationalism 21-22, letter from City authorities expelling Carmelites 22, 24
Peters, Anastasius, Carmelite, assignments of 109, appointed prior of Scipio, Kansas 121, begins church in Scipio in 1881 122, objections to Smits as Commissary 122, actions during Smits visit to Scipio 142, removed as superior of Scipio 142, plans for Texas foundation 142, moved to Texas 142
Peters, Boniface, Carmelite, appointed master of novices 121
Phelan, Richard, Archbishop of Pittsburgh 151
Phelan, Murray, Carmelite, Prior Provincial 225
Phoenix, Arizona, Carmelite House 223
Phoenix, Arizona, Kino Institute 223
Phoenix, Arizona, St. Agnes Parish 223
Phoenix, Arizona, St. Therese of Lisieux Priory 224
Pilgrimages to Niagara Falls, Ontario 167
Piscataway, mission of Upper Marlboro, Maryland 77
Pittsburgh, Pennsylvania, Holy Trinity Monastery, 93, 218
Pittsburgh, Pennsylvania, Holy Trinity Parish 218
Pittsburgh, Pennsylvania, Our Lady of Perpetual Help Mission 222
Pittsburgh, Pennsylvania, St. Leo Parish 222
Pittsburgh, 93, stats in, 1890 148
Pius IX, pope, i, iv, 10, 36 anniversary celebration at Cumberland, Maryland 81, declares Our Lady of Peace a pilgrimage site 105
Poels, Rev. J.P. 116

Poland, Carmelite Province of 5
Poppel, Valentine, Carmelite 7
Portugal 5
Pottawatomie settlement, Scipio, Kansas 39
Poxau, Germany 15, 24
Prairie City, Kansas 101
Praying for the dead, practice instituted at Cumberland, Maryland 80
Prelature of Sicuani, Sicuani, Perú 222
Presidio, Texas, Mission Station 220
Preston Park Seminary, Kentucky 91
Primbs, Eliseus, Carmelite 7
Prince George County, Maryland, Carmelite mission from Upper Marlboro, mission to Blacks 54, 77
Prior general, gives permission to make foundations in America 25, reaction to sale of Cumberland 96, reaction to sale of Cumberland, Maryland 111
Prior provincial residences, Province of the Most Pure Heart of Mary 224
Priori, Jerome, procurator general of Order 11, 1853 visitation of Straubing 11, prior general 20
Propaganda of the Faith, Congregation of, on Catholic education 118
Proposals, of the first PCM provincial chapter 133-134, 149-151, of the second PCM provincial chapter 135-136, of the third PCM provincial chapter 137-138
Province of Most Pure Heart of Mary (PCM), *see* Most Pure Heart of Mary Province
Provincial of Scotland, Knoll named 12
Pulvo, Texas, Mission Station 220
Purcell, Archbishop of Cincinnati, involvement in financial scandal 121-122
Purcell, Fr. Edward, of Archdiocese of Cincinnati, involvement in financial scandal 121-122
Purdy, Michael, Carmelite, works in Scipio, Kansas standstone quarry 122

Q

Queenston, Ontario 104
Quigley, William, Carmelite, agent for *Carmelite Review* 171

R

Rambin, Louisiana, African American Mission 219
Ranch de la Cruz, Texas, Mission Station 220
Ravensburg, Germany, Carmelite house suppressed 5
Red Bluff, Texas, Mission Chapel 219
Reddy, Fr., Carmelite, sent from Ireland to Niagara 108, writes prior general after death of Meagher 114, goes to Niagara Falls, Ontario 120
Refugium peccatorum, Scipio, Kansas as a 101
Regensburg, Diocese of 1, 7, 8

Index 253

Reibensdorf, Germany 12
Reichsdesputationshauptschluss 4
Reichwein, Jerome, Carmelite, 35, description of movement to Texas from Scipio, Kansas 142-143, work on mission band 169
Reilly, Louis W. 171
Reinhart, Henry, Carmelite 98
Reitmeier, Mother Salesia, Ursuline sister 23, photograph of 61
Republic County, Kansas mission of Scipio, Kansas 44
Residences of PCM prior provincials 224
Resurrection cemetery chapel, Hungary, staffed by Carmelites 16
Richmond (Garnett), Kansas, 101, Guardian Angels Parish 217, St. Therese of Lisieux Parish 222
Rider, Dominic Peter, Carmelite 98
Rock Chapel, Louisiana, Missions for African-Americans 219
Roman Province of Carmelites in 1832, state of 5
Rosalina, Louisiana, Mission Station 220
Rosaryville, mission from Upper Marlboro, Maryland 77, Holy Rosary Mission Church 218
Rossweg, Rev. Jacob, term as pastor of Holy Trinity parish, Pittsburgh, Pennsylvania 97
Roswell, Texas, Mission Chapel 219
Rottenburg am Necker, Germany, Carmelite house suppressed 5
Ruidosa, Texas, Mission Station 220
Rule of St. Albert and mitigation 26
Rundschau vom Berge (*The News Magazine from the Mountain*) 170
Russell, John, Carmelite, Prior Provincial 225
Ryan, Stephen, CM, Bishop of Buffalo, New York 102
Ryan, Paul, Carmelite, at 2nd provincial chapter 135, at 3rd provincial chapter 137, work on mission band 169
Ryan, Rev. Francis, Toronto archbishop's representative to Niagara pilgrimage 167

S

Sacred Heart Mission, Ruidosa, Texas 220
Sacred Heart Mission, Saragosa, Texas 219
Sacred Heart Mission, Shafter, Texas 220
Sacred Heart Parish at Hickman, Kentucky 86
Sacred Heart Parish, Chippawa, Ontario 221
Sacred Heart Parish, Colony, Kansas 217
Sacred Heart Parish, Tucson, Arizona 222
St. Agatha Parish, New Athens, Illinois 221
St. Agnes Parish, Phoenix, Arizona 223
St. Albert of Trapani Parish, Houston, Texas 223
St. Albert's Blessed Water 166
St. Anastasia Parish, Teaneck, New Jersey 221

St. Andrew Corsini Parish, Ottawa, Ontario 222
St. Ann Parish, Midland, Texas 219
St. Ann Parish, Niagara Falls, Ontario 221
St. Barbara Parish, Thurber, Texas 221
St. Bernadette Soubirous Parish, Houston, Texas 223
St. Bernard Parish, Joliet, Illinois 221
St. Boniface Parish, Scipio, Kansas 39, description of new church 100, school constructed 173, construction of new church in 1881 122, 217
St. Boniface/Mount Carmel Priory, Scipio, Kansas photography of and community 65, 67, 73, as possible formation house 98, Albert Heimann's plans for 99, laying of cornerstone for college building 100, description of life at 99-101, description of new monastery 100, failure of Mt. Carmel college 100, as *refugium peccatorum* 101, placed under Knoll in 1879 109, cornerstone laid at 122, visit of Smits 142, reopened as novitiate in 1888 147, stats of in, 1890 148, 217
St. Boniface Settlement *see* Scipio, Kansas
St. Bridget Parish, Hickman, Kentucky 218
St. Catherine Parish, Pecos, Texas 219
St. Catherines, Ontario 102
St. Cecilia Parish, Englewood, New Jersey photograph of original church 69, vote to erect school 119, 118, 217
St. Cecilia Parish, Louisville, Kentucky description of church 90, first mass celebrated 90, school described 90, costs of church reported to prior general 110, 218
St. Cecilia Priory, Englewood, New Jersey life at 117, 219
St. Clara Parish, Chicago, Illinois 221
St. Clara Priory, Chicago, Illinois 224
St. Clara-St. Cyril Parish, Chicago, Illinois 223
St. Columba Parish, Hegewisch, Illinois 221
St. Cyril College, Chicago, Illinois 221
St. Cyril of Alexandria Parish, Tucson, Arizona 224
St. Cyril Parish, Chicago, Illinois 221
St. Cyril Priory, Chicago, Illinois 221, Provincial House 224
St. Edward Parish, Eddy (Carlsbad), New Mexico 221
St. Edward's Church, Falls View, Ontario *see* Our Lady of Peace Shrine
St. Elias Priory, Joliet, Illinois 221
St. Emily Parish, Toyah, Texas 219
St. Francis de Sales Parish, Paducah, Kentucky 85, changes to in 1872 86, sketch of church 125, photograph of interior of church 218
St. Francis de Sales Priory, Paducah, Kentucky 218
St. Francis of Assisi Parish, Grove City, Florida 224
St. Gabriel Mission Church, Barton, Maryland 217
St. Gelasius Parish, Chicago, Illinois 223
St. Gertrude Parish, Stockton, California 223
St. Ignatius Church, Oxon Hill, mission of Upper Marlboro, Maryland 77, Mary-

Index 255

land 218
St. Jane Frances de Chantal Parish, North Hollywood, California 223
St. Jerome Parish, Fancy Farm, Kentucky 86, 218
St. Joan of Arc Parish, Yorktown, Virginia 222
St. John Neumann, Redemptorist, visit to Cumberland, Maryland 46
St. John of the Cross Parish, Mississauga, California 223
St. John Parish, Leonia, New Jersey 221
St. John's, Kentucky 85
St. John the Baptist Parish, Greeley, Kansas 217
St. John the Baptist Monastery, New Baltimore, Pennsylvania description of 83-84, new brick rectory in 1873 95, 96, 98, Anastasius Peter pastor of 109, photograph of original church and monastery 127, photograph of community 127, photograph of 2nd provincial chapter 135, students moved to 147, stats in, 1890 148, need to enlarge as house of studies 148, expansion of 150, novitiate transferred to 150, new church built 173, new addition to house completed 173, 218, 224
St. John the Baptist Parish, New Baltimore, Pennsylvania 218
St. John the Evangelist Parish, Lawrence, Kansas 217
St. John Vianney Parish, Barrie, Ontario 224
St. Joseph as patron of a happy death, novena devotion at Cumberland, Maryland 80
St. Joseph Mission, Iatan, Texas 219
St. Joseph Monastery, Carmel, Louisiana 219
St. Joseph Parish, Bogota, New Jersey 221
St. Joseph Parish, Demarest, New Jersey 222
St. Joseph Parish, St. Joseph's Hill, Indiana, first foundation of Carmelites in USA 34, 38, photograph of in 1864 63
St. Joseph Parish, Fort Davis, Texas 220
St. Joseph Parish, Fort Stockton, Texas 220
St. Joseph Parish, Leavenworth, Kansas, description of 37, transferred to Carmelites 38-39, photograph of church and school 63, built by Albert Heimann 73, stats for new church 74, cost of new church 76, as possible formation house 98 school built 173, 217
St. Joseph Parish, Marienfeld (Stanton), Texas 219
St. Joseph Parish, Mayfield, Kentucky 86
St. Joseph Parish, Mount Ida, Kansas 217
St. Joseph Parish, New Germany (Snyder), Ontario 219
St. Joseph Parish, Sellersburgh, Indiana 217
St. Joseph Priory, Barrington, Illinois prior provincial residence 223, 224
St. Joseph Priory, Chicago, Illinois prior provincial residence 222, 224
St. Leo Parish, Pittsburgh, Pennsylvania 222
St. Martin Parish, Louisville, Kentucky 23, 34, Knoll assisting at 35
St. Mary Carmelite Parish, Joliet, Illinois 221
St. Mary Mission, Marathon, Texas 220
St. Mary Mission, Marfa, Texas 220

St. Mary of the Assumption, Upper Marlboro, Maryland 218
St. Mary Parish, Beaver Falls, Pennsylvania 218
St. Mary Parish, Cloister, New Jersey 221
St. Mary Parish, Colorado City, Texas 219
St. Mary Parish, Lonaconing, Maryland 217
St. Mary Parish, Mineral Point, Kansas 217
St. Mary's Academy, Paducah, Kentucky, Carmelites as chaplains 85
St. Mary's Church, Alleghany, Pennsylvania 96
St. Mary's Church in Beaver Falls, Pennsylvania, mission of Holy Trinity parish, Pittsburgh, Pennsylvania 98
St. Mary's Church, Marlboro Maryland, mission of Upper Marlboro, Maryland 77
St. Matthew Parish, Glendale Heights, Illinois 223
St. Nicholas School, Christian Brothers of De La Salles and 102
St. Nicholas Separate School, Irish Carmelite Brothers and 102
St. Patrick Parish, Emerald, Kansas 217
St. Patrick Parish, Fulton, Kentucky 218
St. Patrick Parish, Niagara Falls, Ontario 218
St. Paul's Orphan Asylum, Pittsburgh, Pennsylvania 98
St. Paul the Apostle Parish, Gurnee, Illinois 224
St. Peter and Paul Parish, Cumberland, Maryland 79
St. Peter and Paul's Church, East Liberty, Pennsylvania 96
St. Peter in Chains Parish, Westernport, Maryland 217
St. Peter Parish, Butler, Pennsylvania Knoll assumes responsibility for in 1873 95, 217
St. Peter the Apostle Parish, Oakland, Maryland 217
St. Philomena Parish, Pittsburgh, Pennsylvania 96-97
St. Raphael Parish, Englewood, Florida 223
St. Raphael Parish, Glendale, Arizona 223
St. Raphael Parish, Los Angeles, California 221
St. Simon Stock Priory, Darien, Illinois 222
St. Stephan, Smithland, Kentucky 86
St. Stephen Hungarian Chapel and Mission, Joliet, Illinois 221
St. Teresa Mission, Presidio, Texas 220
St. Teresa of Avila Parish, San Francisco, California 224
St. Teresa Parish, Westphalia, Kansas 217
St. Therese Chapel, Paramus, New Jersey 223
St. Therese Chapel, Peabody, Massachusetts 222
St. Therese of Lisieux Parish, Cresskill, New Jersey 221
St. Therese of Lisieux Parish, Richmond (Garnett), Kansas 222
St. Therese of Lisieux Priory, Phoenix, Arizona 224
St. Therese Priory (Whitefriars Hall), Washington, DC 221
St. Thomas Parish, Big Spring, Texas 219
St. Thomas the Apostle, Chicago, Illinois 224
St. Vincent de Paul Parish, Niagara-on-the-Lake, Ontario 219
St. Vincent's Benedictine Abbey (Pennsylvania) 28

Index 257

St. Wendelin Parish, Carbon Center, Pennsylvania 218
Sts. Peter and Paul Parish, Carmel, Louisiana 219
Sts. Peter and Paul Parish, Cumberland, Maryland 48, Knoll's desciption of 49, 217
Saint-Palais, Jacques-Maurice de, bishop of Vincennes, Indiana 35
Salpointe Catholic High School, Tucson, Arizona 222
San Diego, California, Our Lady of Mount Carmel House of Studies 223
San Esteban, Texas, Mission Station 220
San Francisco, California, St. Teresa of Avila Parish 224
San Jose, Texas, Mission Station 220
San Miguel, Parroquia de, Santiago, Chile 222
San Vicente, Texas, Mission Station 220
Santa Isabel, Toyah Creek Settlement Mission 219
Santiago, Chile, Parroquia de San Miguel 222
Santiago, Chile, Parroquia de Santo Cura de Ars 222
Santo Cura de Ars, Parroquia de, Santiago, Chile 222
Saragosa, Texas, Sacred Heart Mission 219
Satolli, Msgr. Francesco, apostolic delegate in DC, involvement in conflict with archbishop of Toronto 154-158, visit to hospice in Niagara Falls 163
Savini, Angelus, carmelite prior general i-ii, at Congregation of Bishops and Regulars 28, 38, petitioned to send Carmelites to USA 50, joins Kentucky missions to other established houses 115, requested by Knoll to unite USA houses under Anastasius Smits 122, report from Smits about commissariat in 1882 143, summary of term as prior general 149
Saxony, Titular Provincial of, Mayer named as 147
Scapular confraternity, in organizational meeting in 1889 148
Scapular devotion 26, in organizational meeting in 1889 148
Scapular of Our Lady of Mt. Carmel, devotion at Cumberland, Maryland 80
Schacht, Rev. Ivo, pastor of Paducah, Kentucky 39, 85
Scheffler, Rev., Redemptorist 97
Schellenberg, Germany 3
Scholl, Dominic, Carmelite 98
Schonhofer, Mother Pia, Ursuline sister 23
Schorner, Mother Aloysia, Ursuline sister 27
Schuermann, Anthony, OFM Cap 96
Scipio, Kansas 73, as possible formation house 98, Albert Heimann's plans for 99, laying of cornerstone for Mt. Carmel college building 100, description of life at 99-101, description of new church and monastery 100, failure of Mt. Carmel college 100, as *refugium peccatorum* 101, placed under Knoll in 1879 109, construction of new church in 1881 122, cornerstone laid at 122, monastery and land to be sold 136, visit of Smits 142, reopened as novitiate in 1888 147, stats in, 1890 148
Scotland, Titular Provincial of, Cyril Knoll named as 12, Anastasius Smits named as 146, 147
Second Plenary Council of Baltimore (1866) ii, reaction to Emancipation Proc-

lamation 77, *De Nigrorum Salute Procuranda (Ensuring the Welfare of the Negro)*, decree from Second Plenary Council in 1866 78, on Catholic education 118
Seelos, Rev. Francis Xavier, Redemptorist 46
Seitowski, Joseph, primate of Hungary 12, positive response from 15
Seitz, OSB, Rev. Casimir 37
Shafter, Texas, Mission Station 220
Sherman, William Tecumseh, general, United States Army 33
Sicuani, Perú, Prelature of Sicuani 222
Sisters of Charity of Convent Station, teachers at St. Cecilia's, New Jersey 119
Sisters of Charity of Leavenworth, responsibility for St. Joseph's school, Leavenworth, Kansas 76
Sisters of Charity of Nazareth, Kentucky 85, postulants from Ireland come with Meagher 90
Sisters of Divine Providence, responsible for Holy Trinity school, Pittsburgh, Pennsylvania 98
Sisters of St. Joseph 102
Sisters of the Third Order of St. Francis of the Immaculate Conception of the Blessed Virgin Mary, in charge of St. Cecilia's school, Louisville 90
Slattery, Rev. 49
Slevin, Thomas, Louisville developer suggest Carmelites be approach to organize new parish 89
Smet, Joachim, Carmelite historian, viii, x
Smithland, Kentucky, Carmelites assume the ministry duties for 85
Smith, Malachy, Carmelite, x, Prior Provincial 225
Smits, Anastasius, Carmelite, ii, arrival at Cumberland 52-53, attempt to found Chicago house in 1868 53, attempts foundation in New Jersey 54, appointed prior and novice master 53, 55, description of 115, head of English speaking houses 115, assignments of 116, transfers residence from Fort Lee to Englewood, New Jersey 116, condition of parish in early years as pastor 118, on generosity of parishioners towards building 118, popularity with parishioners 119, on Catholic education 119, vote to erect school at St. Cecilia's, Englewood 119, appointed head of Commissariat of Kentucky, New Jersey, and Niagara Falls 120, as member of Our Lady of Peace, Niagara Falls, Ontario, community 129, member of 2nd provincial chapter, elected to definitory, elected delegate to general chapter 135, member of 3rd provincial chapter 137, elected definitor and elected delegate to general chapter 138, thoughts on his assignment as Commissary 141, visit of to Scipio 142, attempt to restore order 143, as commissary 144, report to prior general of state of commissariat in 1882 144, and *Karmeliten Geist* 144, goals for Carmelite life 145, named Titular Provincial of Scotland 146-147, interference in relationship between Pius Mayer and Archbishop of Toronto 147, involvement in conflict with Archbishop of Toronto 156, work on mission band 167-169, Commissary Provincial 225
Society of the Little Flower 221

Index

Sossau, Germany 12-18, 24
Spalding, Martin J, bishop of Louisville appointed archishop of Baltimore 34, 54, on ministry to the ex-slaves 78, promise on Upper Marlboro, Maryland 88
Spalding, Rev. Benedict J. 34
Stanton, Texas, *see* Marienfeld 219
Steinberger, Mary (Sr. Georgianna), Ursuline sister 27
Stockton, California, St. Gertrude Parish 223
Stonewall, Louisiana, Mission Station 220
Stralsund, Germany 6
Straubing vii, 1, 5, 6, 7, 8, 15, 16, 17, Ursuline nuns from Straubing in Louisville 24, 25, entrance of Huber to 27, photographs of monastery and church 57, 59, home of Anastasius Peters 109, 173
Streber, Rev. Leander, OFM, 23, plea for priests 24, 34
Study Butte, Texas, Mission Station 220
Sword (Journal) viii

T

Tamchina, Rev. J., pastor at Holy Trinity 97, causes conflict at Holy Trinity parish 97
Teaneck, New Jersey, St. Anastasia Parish 221
Temperance Society of St. Cecilia parish, New Jersey 118
Tenafly, New Jersey, Mount Carmel Cemetery 219
Tenafly, New Jersey, Our Lady of Mount Carmel Parish Kentucky missions joined to 115, removed at Smits request but later returned to responsibility of Carmelites 116 mission of Fort Lee 116, 219
Tenhaap, Bonaventure, Carmelite, member of Scipio, Kansas, community
Teresa of Avila, Carmelite saint 26
Terlingua Abaja, Texas, Mission Station 220
Terlingua, Texas, Mission Station 220
Texas and Pacific Railway, offer of land from 142
Texas, Carmelite ministry to German families in 142
Texas Commissariat, life in 143
The American Ecclesiastical Review, article on Catholic publications 171
Therese of Lisiuex, Carmelite saint, spirituality of iii
Third Plenary Council of Baltimore ii, on Catholic education 119, and promotion of Catholic publications 171
Thurber, Texas, St. Barbara Parish 221
Titus Brandsma Priory, Darien, Illinois 224
Toronto, Archbishop of, and relation to Pius Mayer 147, conflict with over Niagara land 152-163
Torreon, Mexico, Parroquia de la Transfiguración 224
Toties Quoties, papal letter granting indulgence 165
Toyah Creek Settlement Mission Stations: La Meta 219
Toyah, Texas, St. Emily Parish 219

Traidner, Angelus, Carmelite 21
Transfiguración, Parroquia de, Torreon, Mexico 224
Troy, Leander, Carmelite, x
Trustland, Kansas, Mission Church 101, 217
Tucker, Mississippi, Choctaw Indian Mission (Dutch Province) 221
Tucson, Arizona, Carmelite Community at St. Thomas 224
Tucson, Arizona, Our Lady of Mount Carmel Priory 222
Tucson, Arizona, Sacred Heart Parish 222
Tucson, Arizona, Salpointe Catholic High School 222
Tucson, Arizona, St. Cyril of Alexandria Parish 224
Tuigg, John, bishop of Pittsburgh, Pennsylvania 109
Twain, Mark, American writer i

U

Underground Railroad and Niagara Frontier 105
Upper German Carmelite Province 4, 5
Upper Marlboro, Maryland 54, 71, missions 77, reaction to mandate to minister to ex-slaves 78, findings of visit of Bishop Bayley 88, state of at Carmelites departure 110, St. Mary of the Assumption Church 218
Urbanszeck, Rev. Anthony, Redemptorist 46
Ursula, Sister of Charity of Nazareth, remains transferred to Mt. Carmel cemetery, Paducah, Kentucky 112
Ursuline Sisters ii, in Straubing 8-9, mission to Kentucky 23, invite Knoll to Louisville 24, 31, sketch of convent and school in Straubing 61, invited to Cumberland, Maryland 80, 91

V

Valentine, Texas, Mission Station 220
Van de Braak, Rev. 46
Van der Erf, Gregory, Carmelite, entrusted with formula for *Karmeliten Geist* 144
Van der Heuval, Leo, Carmelite, member of 1st provincial chapter and named member of definitory 133, member of 2nd provincial chapter 135
Van der Staay, Ferdinand, Carmelite, member of 3rd provincial chapter 137
Van Horn, Texas, Mission Chapel 219
Van Riel, Elias, discovers irregularities of Knoll 121, left the Order 146
Van Snepsen, Augustine, Carmelite, entrusted with formula for *Karmeliten Geist* 144, agent for *Carmelite Review* 171
Venice, Florida, Carmel in Venice 223
Venice, Florida, Our Lady of Perpetual Help Retreat and Spiritual Center 224
Verhayen, John, Carmelite, prior of Pittsburgh, Pennsylvania 121, refuses to give Smits surplus funds 144
Vicksburg, Mississippi, statistics of Yellow Fever epidemic of 1878 112
Victoria, Texas 219
Vigo, Ontario, mission, Beerhorst responsible for 103

Index 261

Vogg, Philip, Carmelite 47, 49, 51
Vogler Company and *Karmeliten Geist* 147
von Frauenhofen, Baron Karl 15
von Mongelas, Count anti-Catholic minister of Maximilian IV 7
von Riedel, Valentin, bishop of Regensburg 7, involvement at Straubing 10
von Schwabel, Franz Xavier, bishop of Regensburg 7
von Senestry, Ignatius, bishop of Regensburg 23

W

Wadesboro, Kentucky 85
Wagner, Albert, Carmelite, moves to Texas 142
Waldhausen on the Ens possible purchase of private home as new monastery 23
Walsh, death of 121
Walsh, John, archbishop of Toronto 151, lays cornerstone on hospice 165
Walsh, John Francis, Carmelite, suffering from Yellow Fever 87, at Fancy Farm, Kentucky 112, responsible for Columbus, Kentucky 112, actions during Yellow Fever epidemic of 1878 112, death of due to effects of Yellow Fever 112, writes prior general after death of Meagher 114, follow-up letter to prior general explaining true situation in Kentucky 114, transferred to Scipio, Kansas 120
Walsh, Joseph John, Carmelite, member of Scipio, Kansas, community 67, 79, 86, leaves Upper Marlboro, Maryland for Paducah, Kentucky 110, suspended then reinstated at New Baltimore, PA 111, transferred 121
Walter, Leo, Carmelite, Prior Provincial 225
Wartner, Berthold, Carmelite 7
Washington County, Kansas, mission of Scipio 44
Waverly, Kansas, Mission Church 217
Weed, Texas, Mission Chapel 219
Weiss, Albert, Carmelite 7, 9
Welch, John, Carmelite, Prior Provincial 225
Wenninger, Mary (Sr. Antonia), Ursuline sisters 27
Wenninger, SJ, encourages new church at Leavenworth, Kansas 73, preaches at laying of cornerstone to new church 74
Werling, Norman, Carmelite viii, x
Werner, Anselm, Carmelite, work on mission band 169
Western Kentucky 71
Westernport, Maryland, St. Peter in Chains Parish, mission of Cumberland 49, 217
Westphalia, Kansas, St. Teresa Parish, mission of Scipio 44, 101, 217
Wheeling, diocese of 83
Whitefriars Hall, Washington, DC *see* St. Therese Priory 221
White House, Darien, Illinois 224
Whitely, Fr., Carmelite, sent from Ireland to Niagara 108
Wickliffe, Kentucky 85
Wiedemann, Otto, Carmelite member of Our Lady of Peace, Niagara Falls,

Ontario, community 129, member of 1st provincial chapter 133, member of 2nd provincial chapter and elected to definitory 135, member of 3rd provincial chapter 137, elected definitor and *custus* of province, selected novice master 138,
Wieselhuber, Gerhard, Carmelite 13, 15
Wimmer, Boniface, Benedictine founder in USA 25, archabbot of Benedictines 28
Windsor House, hotel on Niagara frontier, Ontario ix
Withinger, Edmund, Carmelite 7
Wolf, Francis, OFM Cap 96
Woodson County, Kansas, Mission Churches 217
Wurzburg, Germany, Carmelite house suppressed 5
Wurzburg, University of 4

X

Xaveria, Mother, Ursuline sister 13
Xavier, Mother, Convent Station and Catholic education 119
Xiberta, Centro, El Salvador casa de formación 224

Y

Yorktown, Virginia, St. Joan of Arc Parish 222

Z

Zeitvogel, Regina, Knoll's first baptism at St. Joseph's 35
Zink, Wendelin, Carmelite 6-7
Zwingler, Maximillian, Ursuline sister 23

www.ingramcontent.com/pod-product-compliance
Lightning Source LLC
Chambersburg PA
CBHW020834160426
43192CB00007B/638